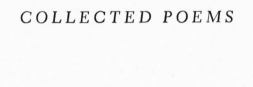

COLLECTED POEMS

MARK VAN DOREN

COLLECTED POEMS

NEW YORK

HENRY HOLT AND COMPANY

PREFACE

Except for certain changes and omissions, and except for the twenty-one new poems in the section called America's Mythology, this collection reproduces the contents of six volumes written since 1922 and published since 1924. None of the volumes is reprinted in its entirety, a total of forty-five poems having been suppressed, and changes having been made in a considerable number of those that remain. In two cases the alterations have been radical: We Come Too Late, from "Now the Sky and Other Poems," has been greatly shortened, and the third part of "Jonathan Gentry" has been not only shortened but in places rewritten. The other revisions are best characterized by saying that I shall be content if they pass without notice; they are many, but even those which were difficult to make are in most instances minor.

I am indebted to Thomas Seltzer for permission to reprint portions of "Spring Thunder and Other Poems" and "7 P.M. and Other Poems," and to Albert and Charles Boni for a like favor in the case of "Now the Sky and Other Poems" and "Jonathan Gentry."

M. V. D.

New York
1938

CONTENTS

SPRING THUNDER AND OTHER POEMS—1924

7 P.M. AND OTHER POEMS—1926

I

II

III

NOW THE SKY AND OTHER POEMS—1928

I

II

ix

JONATHAN GENTRY—1931

I

IV

V

SPRING THUNDER AND OTHER POEMS

1924

To
Dorothy

SPRING THUNDER

Listen. The wind is still,
And far away in the night—
See! The uplands fill
With a running light.

Open the doors. It is warm;
And where the sky was clear—
Look! The head of a storm
That marches here!

Come under the trembling hedge—
Fast, although you fumble.
There! Did you hear the edge
Of winter crumble?

TRAVELLING STORM

The sky above us here is open again.
The sun comes hotter, and the shingles steam.
The trees are done with dripping, and the hens
Bustle among bright pools to pick and drink.
But east and south are black with the speeding storm.
That thunder, low and far, remembering nothing,
Gathers a new world under it and growls,
Worries, strikes, and is gone. Children at windows
Cry at the rain, it pours so heavily down,
Drifting across the yard till the sheds are grey.
A county farther on, the wind is all:
A swift dark wind that turns the maples pale,
Ruffles the hay, and spreads the swallows' wings.
Horses, suddenly restless, are unhitched,
And men, with glances upward, hurry in;
Their overalls blow full and cool; they shout;
Soon they will lie in barns and laugh at the lightning.
Another county yet, and the sky is still;
The air is fainting; women sit with fans
And wonder when a rain will come that way.

3

FORMER BARN LOT

Once there was a fence here,
    And the grass came and tried,
Leaning from the pasture,
    To get inside.

But colt feet trampled it,
    Turning it brown;
Until the farmer moved
    And the fence fell down.

Then any bird saw,
    Under the wire,
Grass nibbling inward
    Like green fire.

PIGEON

This bird is used to sitting on bright ledges
And looking into darkness. Through the square
High window in the barn the mow is black
To one here by the fence. But there he sits
And treads the sun-warm sill, turning his breast
Toward all the musty corners deep within.
They flash no colors on him, though the sky
Is playing bronze and green upon his back.
Gravely he disappears, and spiders now
Must hurry from the rafter where his beak
Searches the seed. The afternoon is slow
Till he returns, complacent on the ledge,
And spreads a breast of copper. But the sun
Is nothing to a pigeon. On the ground
A grain of corn is yellower than gold.
He circles down and takes it, leisurely.

RIVER SNOW

The flakes are a little thinner where I look,
For I can see a circle of grey shore,
And greyer water, motionless beyond.
But the other shore is gone, and right and left
Earth and sky desert me. Still I stand
And look at the dark circle that is there,
As if I were a man blinded with whiteness,
And one grey spot remained. The flakes descend,
Softly, without a sound that I can tell;
When out of the further white a gull appears,
Crosses the hollow place, and goes again.
There was no flap of wing; no feather fell.
But now I hear him crying, far away,
And think he may be wanting to return.
The flakes descend. And shall I see the bird?
Not one path is open through the snow.

IMMORTAL

The last thin acre of stalks that stood
    Was never the end of the wheat.
Always something fled to the wood,
    As if the field had feet.

In front of the sickle something rose:
    Mouse, or weasel, or hare;
We struck and struck, but our worst blows
    Dangled in the air.

Nothing could touch the little soul
    Of the grain. It ran to cover,
And nobody knew in what warm hole
    It slept till the winter was over,

And early seeds lay cold in the ground.
    Then, but nobody saw,
It burrowed back with a sun-white sound,
    And awoke the thaw.

5

HISTORY

I crossed the swinging bridge, and there
  The little town I came to see
Was ashes. In the April air
  Ruined rafters poked at me.

I ran, imploring why and when,
  But though I searched on every side
The little town was bare of men;
  The very voice of it had died.

Only past a pile of stone
  Was any sound. I crept, afraid.
There upon the grass alone
  Nell, the shepherd bitch, was laid

And seven puppies pulled at her
  That never saw the little town,
Or the angry wagoner
  Who whipped his horses up and down.

BARRICADE

Come to the other hole, and fit your tin,
And start your spike;
And if you hear the rat within,
Strike!

Rats can gnaw, but suddenly a nail
Can eat an inch.
Let him see our teeth, and quail,
And flinch.

Now he scampers—pound more loudly yet
To kill my fear.
The feet are what I must forget.
Hear?

MIDWIFE CAT

Beyond the fence she hesitates,
  And drops a paw, and tries the dust.
It is a clearing, but she waits
  No longer minute than she must.

Though a dozen foes may dart
  From out the grass, she crouches by;
Then runs to where the silos start
  To heave their shadows far and high.

Here she folds herself and sleeps;
  But in a moment she has put
The dream aside; and now she creeps
  Across the open, foot by foot,

Till at the threshold of a shed
  She smells the water and the corn
Where a sow is on her bed
  And little pigs are being born.

Silently she leaps, and walks
  All night upon a narrow rafter;
Whence at intervals she talks
  Wise to them she watches after.

DRIVER LOST

Roads are flowing everywhere
  In the night, beneath the moon.
But one of them the homing mare
  Is certain of; and soon

The barn will be in plainest sight,
  Grey beyond the grove.
To her the misty way is bright,
  As if another drove.

She points an ear at every turn
  Before a hoof arrives.
What hand is here from which to learn?
  Who is it sits and drives?

7

CROW

A hundred autumns he has wheeled
Above this solitary field.
Here he circled after corn
Before the oldest man was born.
When the oldest man is dead
He will be unsurfeited.
See him crouch upon a limb
With his banquet under him.
Hear the echo of his caw
Give the skirting forest law.
Down he drops, and struts among
The rows of supper, tassel-hung.
Not a grain is left behind
That his polished beak can find.
He is full; he rises slow
To watch the evening come and go.
From the barren branch, his rest,
All is open to the west;
And the light along his wing
Is a sleek and oily thing.
Past an island floats the gaze
Of this ancientest of days.
Green and orange and purple dye
Is reflected in his eye.
There is an elm tree in the wood
Where his dwelling place has stood
All the hundred of his years.
There he sails and disappears.

TO A CHILD WITH EYES

Footprints now on bread or cake
Merely are what a mouse can make.
You cannot open any door
And find a brownie on the floor,
Or on the window where he went,
A fork, a spoon, a finger-dent.
Farmers climbing from the mow
Surprise no imp beneath a cow,

Milking madly. Breakfast bells
Are never tinkled from dry wells.
The commonwealth is gone that shut
Its felons in a hazelnut.
Forests are no longer full
Of fairy women who can pull
A leaf around them, and can dance
Upon the very breath of plants.
River rocks are bare of men
Who wring their beards and dive again.
Is there nothing left to see?
There is the squirrel. There is the bee.
There is the chipmunk on the wall,
And the first yellow every fall.
There is the hummingbird, the crow.
There is the lantern on the snow.
There is the new-appearing corn.
There is the colt a minute born.
Run and see, and say how many.
There are more if there is any.

AFTERNOON ALONE

She leaves the kitten at her cream
And runs to watch. But all the glass
Is covered over with a steam
That hides the people who would pass.

Sad awhile, she draws a thumb
Across the pane and through the slit
Sees a purple face has come
To stare at her. Afraid of it,

All her hand she takes to wipe
The streak away; but now the tramp
Stands entirely with his pipe,
And his clothes are foul and damp.

So she flies and shuts the door
And is by the stove again,
Where the kitten lets her pour
Milk enough for nine or ten.

NOBLESSE

The stubble is an upstart thing,
    A summer's growth, that as we walk
Turns—the envious underling—
    And stabs us with its stalk.

Weeds, arriving everywhere,
    Are insolent as soon as come.
They shout upon the morning air
    Until the flowers are dumb.

But in this corner, past the gate,
    Safe from where the horses turned,
I used to lie till it was late;
    And here it was I learned

How blue-grass is the gentlest born
    Of all the gentle things that stand,
Holding, without a spear or thorn,
    Hereditary land.

FALL

Winter and Spring and Summer are this or that:
A white old man, a girl, a drowsing tree.
The Fall is a covered bridge that crosses the river
Down from my father's house. The foam and the rocks
Grow suddenly to a grey there, as the sky
Returns one day to roof the valley in.
The bridge's darkened mouth, so cool all summer,
Gathers descending leaves; already warm there,
The shadows settle to sleep, and a yellow cart,
Flickering through the leaf-shower down the highway,
Comes on with noiseless wheels and disappears.

FALLEN BARN

The sun came white upon these shingles once,
And a few rotted edges let it in.
But the hay held it, as it held the rain
That dripped on other days and slowly dried.
No sky ever could pierce to where the stalls
Gathered familiar gloom. Their corners filled
Each year with heavier cobwebs, and the dust
Mingled with many odors never dead.
But yesterday the farmer hitched four teams
In turn to all the uprights; and they fell.
The sun has followed through, and soon the rain
Will soak the oldest timbers into sod.
Here in the weeds a manger plank was thrown.
You see it, bitten thin. The horse is gone
That found it every evening with his nose
And smoothed it, long ago. Nothing remains
Of what it was that made these beams a barn.

WATER WHEEL TO MEND

There have been times I thought these paddles moved
To music, not to water. Should that hush,
And cataracts descend here with no song,
The axle would not answer with its groan;
The great spokes that swung in solemn circle
Would ponderously wait upon new tunes.
But water still is noisy in the sluice,
And the splashed wheel is motionless. The stream
Foams out below with even a louder voice,
Calling upon the mighty arms to go.
They cannot go; the axle, old and deaf,
Is unaware this Spring of water sounding.

MOUNTAIN HOUSE: DECEMBER

Anyone on the road below
  Can see it now; the boughs are bare
That hung about it months ago,
  Beautiful, and thick as hair.

It is a white and silent face
  That some will talk of, driving by.
None will turn to reach a place
  So cold and high.

No summer walkers up that way,
  Arriving half in shadow, stand
And wait upon the sign to stay
  From a slow hand.

The house's hands are folded in,
  For warmth; but all the warmth is fled:
It climbed the stairs, and stricken thin
  Died one evening on your bed.

WATERFALL SOUND

In the middle of the wood it starts,
Then over the wall and the meadow
And into our ears all day. But it departs,
Sometimes, like a shadow.

There is an instant when it grows
Too weak to climb a solid fence,
And creeps to find a crack. But the wind blows,
Scattering it hence

In whimpering fragments like the leaves
That every autumn drives before.
Then rain again in the hills, and the brook receives
It home with a roar.

ALTERATION

I did not ask to have the shed
   Pulled down, although it leaned so sickly.
But, now the proper word is said,
   Let it come quickly.

Bring rope and pulley, axe and bar,
   And while you hammer I will pry.
Shingles can be sent as far
   As feathers fly.

Naked beams can tumble faster
   Than cobwebs in a sudden gust;
Floors can stand on end; and plaster
   Soon is dust.

I did not think this valley view
   Deserved that any roof should fall.
But, now the word is said by you,
   I want it all.

PREMONITION

It was September, and the weeds were mowed
For the last time along the narrow road.
Sunlight speckled down, as leaves would fall,
Shortly, upon the gravel; and by the wall
Chipmunks quietly ran that soon would sound
More loudly on the green and yellow ground.
A woodchuck crossed beyond me as I went,
So slowly that he seemed indifferent;
As if he slept already out of sight,
Deep in a burrow, with the meadows white.
I soberly advanced, and all the way
Was proof that nothing now could ever stay
Of the soft summer. Even when I stood
At last upon the border of the wood,
And the bright Hollow lay a mile below,
The light dazzled, and I thought of snow.

13

GRASS

Poppies are burning; daisies dip their faces;
The gentle ageratum at my side
Offers a pale blue cheek to the afternoon.
Something has brought the swallows whence they hid;
They tumble up and dizzy the warm day,
Speeding against the calm or dropping straight:
Dropping to cut and float. Along the walk
A black hose runs, and ends in a tall spray;
Catbirds hop to the bath, and flirt and shine.
I look, but do not see these things; or care
When a brown, erring rabbit bounces in,
Fears the immaculate garden, and is gone.
Further across the way there quietly feed
A few round sheep in a shade. And out of sight
Momently there is a pattering among branches,
And ripened apples thud upon the ground.
I look and look, but do not see these things.
My mind is lost in the river of bright green
That, smoothly out from between those highest elms,
Issues under the sun. It does not pause,
But dreaming spreads and flows. So I am taken
Beyond all flutter of birds, all cry of flowers,
All nibble and leap and fall, to lie in grass.

WIND IN THE GRASS

Are you so weary? Come to the window;
Lean, and look at this.
Something swift runs under the grass
With a little hiss.

Now you see it rippling off,
Reckless, under the fence.
Are you so tired? Unfasten your mind,
And follow it hence.

14

AFTERWARD

The stalls were empty in the shed;
  Nothing grazed beyond the gate.
But there was straw to make a bed,
  And the four bridles dangled straight.

We heard the water running cold,
  As she had left it, round the crocks.
Linen lay for us to fold,
  And there was pepper in the box.

The very trap that he had set
  To catch a mole that loved the lawn
Hung above the passage yet;
  Another mole was boring on.

The wounded deer still fled the dog
  Within the gold and walnut frame;
The Fishermen Among the Fog,
  And The Young Mother, were the same.

We laughed to see a boot behind
  The stove; but then you wept
At your happening to find
  Spectacles where she had slept.

IDENTITY

He knew a place on the mountain where he went
A certain kind of morning, clear and warm.
The sky was open there, and not a cloud
Came over; not a buzzard filled the blue.
The cattle never climbed so high, and the dog—
He left her in the shed. All day he walked
Without an eye upon him he could feel;
Or sat among the stones, himself a stone,
Watching an empty heaven till his mind
Passed out of him and poured the silence full.
His legs were his no longer, and a hand,
Resting upon a knee, was miles away.

All afternoon he sat, and when he moved
It was as if a stone settled a little
To firmer and longer sleep. Only the wind,
At evening, made him wake and stumble off
To stand upon a bluff over the farm.
The kitchen chimney then, and supper waiting,
Uttered his name aloud and brought him down.

GARDENER

Under the window, on a dusty ledge,
He peers among the spider webs for seed.
He wonders, groping, if the spiders spun
Beneath that window after all. Perhaps
His eyes are spiders, and new veils are dropped
Each winter and summer morning in the brain.
He sees but silken-dimly, though the ends
Of his white fingers feel more things than are:
More delicate webs, and sundry bags of seed.
That flicker at the window is a wren.
She taps the pane with a neat tail, and scolds.
He knows her there, and hears her—far away,
As if an insect sang in a tree. Whereat
The shelf he fumbles on is distant, too,
And his bent arm is longer than an arm.
Something between his fingers brings him back:
An envelope that rustles, and he reads:
"The coreopsis." He does not delay.
Down from the rafter where they always hang
He shoulders rake and hoe, and shuffles out.

The sun is warm and thick upon the path,
But he goes lightly, under a broad straw
None knows the age of. They are watching him
From upper windows as his slippered feet
Avoid the aster and nasturtium beds
Where he is not to meddle. His preserve
Is further, and no stranger touches it.
Yesterday he was planting larkspur there.
He works the ground and hoes the larkspur out,

Pressing the coreopsis gently in.
With an old hose he plays a quavering stream,
Then shuffles back with the tools and goes to supper.

Over his bowl of milk, wherein he breaks
Five brittle crackers, drifts the question: "Uncle,
What have you planted for the summer coming?"

"Why—hollyhocks," he murmurs; and they smile.

BIG MARE

The grass is deep in the field, and her four legs
Sink out of sight. She plunges lazily on
To a fresh circle, whence she lifts her head
And looks across the fences to the barn.
No voice from there, no swing of any door.
She lowers her nose to the ground; but suddenly shifts,
Looks up again; and stares into the quiet.
Yesterday, and as long as she remembers,
At this good hour there sounded a shrill cry—
"Here Chunk! Here Chunk! Here Chunk!"—and two thin arms
Were waved from a dark opening in the wall.
Now nothing; so she feeds until the sun
Comes cooler over the meadow, and starts home.
Her feet trample on clover, and her breast
Moves with superfluous might against the weeds.
She ploughs across the creek and through the gap;
Is halfway up the hillside; still no shout;
No corn upon an aged, trembling hand.
She hesitates, as if the barn were gone;
Had never been just here; and gazes long
At the half-opened door; then stumbles through.
Some stranger has thrown nubbins in the box;
Her salt is there; the timothy is down.
She munches, while no words are in her nostrils;
No feet in boots too big for them clump by.
The weak old man who never failed has failed.
Yet foolish whisperings, not of the hay, are heard;
Spidery pads of fingers now caress her,

17

Swiftly over a shoulder, down a flank,
Smoothing, smoothing her mane till evening is night.
Does a plain mare remember? And how long?
Tomorrow will come a slap and a careless whistle.
Tomorrow will come a boy. Is she to forget?

SPIRIT

A straight old woman, tall and very pale,
Moving from room to room of a musty house
No voice is ever heard in, stops, stone-white,
Her weakness come upon her. She can steer
To the kitchen only; yet it is enough.
Into a painted chair she drops, by the stove,
Reaches and lights the gas, then crumples down.
All black behind that white. Upon the plate
A kettle has been ready for the flame,
And water in it nearly to the brim.
Now, while she barely breathes, bubbles arise:
A few, then more, then many breaking fast
Until the water's face nowhere is still,
And the whole of it leaps as if to follow the steam.
Unseen the vessel shakes, untended hums;
A column pours to the ceiling, spreads, and fades;
And the woman never stirs. But now she reaches
Two thin hands to the rail of the stove, and stands
Like one of older time who worshipped fire.
The water boils for her. Water is strong.
While there is any water, it will work.
Suddenly she has smiled across the commotion.
She hears her blood again, and quietly goes
Upon the ancient round from room to room.

JAVELINS

I heard a hum grow loud in the winter woods,
So went to see. In the very furthest part
A clearing, lately cut, circled a sawmill,
A little shack that buzzed until it shook,

18

And breathed rankly of elm. I walked around;
The other side was open, whence I watched
The fat back of the sawman as he fed.
Both of his feet were hidden in the dust;
His legs were bundled tight, and his short arms
Heaved in a woolen coat that once was loose.
He stood, serving the poles, and never shifted.
I stepped to him; he turned a solemn face,
Red as the heap of elm, and only nodded.
I had to shout to make him hear at all:
"What are they going to do with these? Do you know?"
I thought his lips said "Javelins." That was wrong:
Javelins! So I screamed at him again.
This time he stopped the saw till he could tell me—
Gently, although he growled a little—"Javelins."
He started again. I waved a hand and went.
All of the way the woods were close and cold;
But as I walked they seemed to open themselves,
Spreading before me green and smooth. It was Spring.
The sky was soft, and white young men in the distance,
Posturing, flung their spears, and trotted after
To measure and fling again. I heard no sound,
But the air was swift with the darting. Then the road.
I passed a team. The field once more was forest.
A few rods on and the hum had quieted too.

THREE FRIENDS

You on the bed beside me hold
One arm straight up till it is cold,
Then let it fall, the softest part
Lying for warmth against my heart.
My fingers with your fingers' ends
Play in and out; a foot defends
Deep regions from another foot.
You turn and find my eyes. I put
A curious palm where it is seized
By a quick hand; but you are pleased.
There is a third one in the room.
See—in the sun, where the figures bloom

Blood-red on the rug—somebody kneels?
Time smiles at us, and rests his heels.
Outside a hundred horses graze.
He will drive on; but now he stays.
Soon I must follow hence, and slip
Into my place beneath the whip.
He smiles upon us. Come, forget!
He has not thought of rising yet.

MARRIAGE

No wandering any more where the feet stumble
Upon a sudden rise, or sink in damp
Marsh grasses. No uncertain following on
With nothing there to follow: a sure bird,
A fence, a farmhouse. No adventuring now
Where motion that is yet not motion dies.
Circles have lost their magic, and the voice
Comes back upon itself. The road is firm.
It runs, and the dust is not too deep, and the end
Never can heave in sight, though one is there.
It runs in a straight silence, till a word
Turns it; then a sentence, and evening falls
At an expected inn, whose barest room
Cannot be lonely with the walls forgotten.
Laughter is morning, and the road resumes;
Adventurous, it never will return.

REVERIE AFTER WAR: *1866*

I am the only man today
At the mill.
The rain will keep the rest away,
And leave me sitting on the sill
Alone:
Nothing around but my old pipe,
A bushel of bright corn crunching into meal,
Water below,
And the mountain.

The roof will drip
And the stones will grind;
I'll think and sit
Till the stones turn empty.
They don't mind.

Last winter once, in the Wilderness,
In the noise and the smoke and the stink and the wet,
All of us swore, if we got home,
To forget.
It's pleasanter now
To remember.

It's pleasant to have the leaves run rain
And you be under a board roof,
Dry.
It's pleasant to smell a hopper of grain
Cracking your food
And piling it by.
It's pleasant, the curl of the smoke
Of only tobacco.
It's pleasant to tighten the trigger finger
Warm on the stem of your pipe
And nothing go off.
It's pleasant, here at the mill,
With only your time to kill.

Down along the back paths the war isn't done.
Houses aren't built again; there isn't any smoke
Except where the long-haired men are having fun
Burning up barns: a good guerilla joke.

I could have joined a band, and had a skinny mare,
Ridden down a woodroad, held up a stranger,
Killed him for a dollar bill, or maybe for a dare;
I could have gone and been a Cumberland Ranger.

I could have joined, but I'm tired of watching men,
Guessing where they'll go, and whether they'll turn,
Crawling under cover, and crawling out again,
Setting fire to something, just to see it burn.

Scouts are not around now, bullets don't crack;
Nothing happens suddenly to make you move faster;
I can cross the mountain now and never look back;
I can go home; I can be my own master.

I've got a house now, a little patch of corn,
A plough, and a shed, and a one-eyed mule;
As ignorant and as poor as I was when I was born;
But I'm my own pauper, and I'm my own fool.

7 P.M. AND OTHER POEMS
1926

To
Joseph Wood Krutch

I

7 P:M

Slow twilight bird,
Suspended, as you sail, along the nearer edge
Of nightfall and the beechwood, are you heard
In places past my ears? Are you a wedge,

Slow tapered wing,
Driving into the outer walls of time?
Eternity is not so strange a thing,
At evening, when the towers that were to climb,

Slow searching beak,
Lie level with your progress in the soft
Dark-feathered dusk, and there are known to speak
Gentle, wild voices from the dark aloft.

MEMORIES

A child ran alone,
And nothing followed that he felt.
He never heard the sky moan
For old men. He never knelt
To call the hounds—that behind him ran alone
And searching smelt.

He did not hear their cries,
For there was curving earth between.
But he is taller now, and wise
Enough to listen as they lean
Upon the wind—that can turn and bring their cries
So clear and keen.

He still can look away
And do the business of his prime.
He has not foreseen the day
When he will sit and they will climb
And lick his face—that will never frown away
The tongues of time.

GOOD NIGHT

This moonlight lies
Like a lovely death
On the darkening eyes,
On the yielded breath

Of the earth, that turns
So quietly now;
Letting its burns
Be soothed somehow

In the widening bloom,
In the tender blight.
It has entered our room.
We sleep tonight.

APPLE LIMBS

Lay them as neatly
Away as the wind
  Lays the soft grasses
  Through which it passes.

They waited all summer,
Just as they fell:
  On gnarl and prong;
  And the time was long.

But yesterday's hatchet
Straightened their knees.
  Now nothing will cumber
  Them in their slumber.

26

APPLE-HELL

Apples, bright on the leafless bough,
In the high noon sun, with the sky above you,
Time will turn. For the white sky falls
And long, red shadows soon will shove you

Eastward, downward, into the room
Where the moon hangs low like a smoking lamp;
Walls lean in; and the studded ceiling
Shines no more; and the bins grow damp.

Apples, yellow on the naked limb,
Although you burn till the air be gold,
Time is tarnish. Skies are falling,
Noon is dead, and the day grows old.

NIGHT-LILAC

Lilac alone,
Standing so quiet, so dim, outside
Till the door-light died
On cricket and stone,

Do you sleep at last?
Or beyond this night that has taken my yard
Do you stare more hard,
In a night more vast,

At the great white things
That move the outermost world: the whale,
The stallion, the pale
High planet with rings,

The raven, the bull,
And the midnight mountain that never is black?
Lilac, come back!
My lawn is too full

Of the dark; and the fine
Impalpable shadows will never be still.
Return as you will,
Dim lilac, and shine.

27

REMEMBERED FARM

There was a line of frosty light
Along each roof and down the road.
All the rest was perfect night;
Not a field or window showed.

In my cool thought no morning came
To sweep the hills, no moon arose
To flood the meadows with its flame
As far as all this valley flows.

Now I am come, the fields are fair.
Yet not the greenest flesh atones
For when the skeleton was bare
And lightning ran along the bones.

AFTER DRY WEATHER

If the people under that portico
Are happy, and point at the pattering drops;
If barehead boys are parading below
Musical eaves of tall house-tops;

If you lean out of the window here,
Contented so with the pavement's shine,
And laugh as the covers of cabs appear
With passengers in them dressed to dine;

If all of the stones that we can see
Are licking their lips, that waited so long,
A meadow I know to the north of me
By a hundred miles has caught the song.

I am certain the clover has lifted its head
For dark, intemperate draughts of rain.
Once even I thought I had heard the tread
Of a plunging horse with a sodden mane.

ONE FALL

Time grew so thin
That it could hang
Between these hills,
Where nothing sang

Save the silence.
All those weeks
Are now as one;
And it speaks—

Sharply now—
Of a suspended
Year that died
Before it ended;

Leaving only
A blue shell,
That turned to brown,
And never fell.

WINTER FIELDS

Once they were black
And again they were green.
But the sun dropped,
And the wind grew lean,

And the crows dived
So fiercely down
That the grass blanched
In meadow and town;

And barns and fences
And rows of trees
Died to a brown
As brown as these.

Whatever can live
With the sun so low?
That wagoner there
But appears to go.

29

Soon you will look
And the wheels will stand:
Frozen asleep:
Locked in with the land.

LAND TIDE

The moon is in flood;
All things are going:
Grass uprooted
And fences flowing

Over the roads
And the meadows east
To the black immovable
Woods at least.

But the pump, there,
Knows how to resist.
The moon comes on;
It never will twist

And topple and go
As the current is laid;
With its rock root,
And pillar of shade.

EIGHTH DAY

Water goes all ways; ships go one,
And now we can see what was never there before:
The low grey line where the ocean will be done;
Though yet there is nothing, no green shore;

Nothing but a faint thing that might have been fog,
No painted houses, and no small sheep
Scattered down broken cliffs, underneath a dog
Who growls at the water; but he will never leap.

30

Water goes all ways; fields keep fast.
Let me lean and look, then, if only at a cloud.
Ninety miles in lies the meadow where I last
Walked beneath a bird, and it was bright, and it was loud.

THE TUNING-FORK

One dead tree
With arms upswung,
Silver cold,
Is the forest's tongue.

In the middle of the morning,
When the crows cry,
This oldest oak—
None saw it die—

Shrills with its far
Thin finger ends;
Till the body listens
And a scream descends

And the alleys open,
Making room
For another death
In a dateless gloom.

II

BEASTLESS FARM

The paths again are solid green
    That used to whiten in a drouth,
Whirling dust into the clean
    Heifer's nose and horse's mouth.

Stanchion-leathers crack and fall;
    Water runs, and is not heard.
No sudden thunder from a stall
    Stops a mouse, or starts a bird.

Fences might as well come down;
    Lanes are only ghosts of lanes:
Staring hither with a frown
    At smoke of rumps, at mist of manes.

TREE-DWELLERS

Ants file past
To the end of the last
Thin twig, and finding
An ultimate, vast
Green meadow, graze;
While back in the maze
Of the body are winding
Worms in the dark,
That never this bark
Shall open to show
One small bird binding
Straws in a row,
And treading them, so.

32

INFERENCE

Who made the evening made the fear
Of horse and bird and snake and deer,
Of all that do not learn they live
Till light itself, grown fugitive,
Goes breathing by; but turns about,
And the black pouncer puts it out.
Then bird and horse and deer and snake
Go posting home, before they break
The line that leads them; and their eyes
Hold all the day that slowly dies.

CROW MADNESS

There is no mandrake here to cry
As fingers rip it from the ground;
But any morning I can lie
And listen to the other sound

Of darkness tearing clear across
And fragments falling with a shriek
On lonely meadows, where they toss
And rise again with angry beak

That plucks at day and offers war
Against the green, against the blue;
Till night, returning, reaches for
All things that lost her as she flew.

RELIEF FROM SPRING

Pastures trickle and shine in this new sun;
Hill roads gurgle; and hocks of shaggy horses
Drip with the melting mud. The winter is over,
And all of the world you know is water again.
But have no fear for the grass. It will not drown.
Yesterday noon I waded the upper meadow
And saw, in the farthest field, a lonely crow.

33

Where crows will walk it has to be dryer soon.
Crows have taken the very top of the world.
They caw, and the wind is warmer, and there is a rustle
Already of weeds to please their horny feet.
Listen now. The grasses are listening too.

TURKEY-BUZZARDS

Silently, every hour, a pair would rise
And float, without an effort, clear of the trees:
Float in a perfect curve, then tilt and drop;
Or tilt again and spiral toward the sun.
They might have been a dream the timber dreamed;
But could have been a conscious thought, that cut
The warm blue world in segments. For the sky,
Unmeasured, was too much that afternoon.
It lay too heavy on us. Happy trees,
If they could so divide it, wing and wing!

DEDUCTION

So smooth a field,
With the hummocks mown;
Moss peeled
From trunk and stone;

A stunted blade
Withdrawing under
A wall, afraid
Of the herd's thunder:

Only sheep
Could have kept it so,
With nibble and leap,
And lambs in tow.

DISPOSSESSED

No hand had come there since the room was closed
To all but what could live with sifting chaff,
And dust, and pale grey webs. Mine at the latch
Startled the silence; and the wind I brought
Whirled powdery dust against the darkened panes.
No other sound; and so I went to work,
Making a room to put a table in
And sit where none could see me all day long.
No sound. I pulled a length of lining-board
Loose from the timbers, and a spider ran.
Another, and a wasp was at his hole,
Lifting an angry wing. I said of them:
They saw me, but with eyes no man can feel;
I still shall be alone; and laughed and pulled—
And did not laugh again; or go again.
For all I know the dust is quieter now
Than ever it was; with only the bright-black eyes
Of motionless mice on a beam to say if it is.

CONTEMPTUOUS

Lying along the window sill,
With a low fire to feed his purrs,
He sees a misty meadow fill
With fly-light, that only blurs

And disappears the more he turns;
But comes again and dances down
The rainy slope to where it burns
The tops of trees. He seems to frown

And gaze away at rug and chair,
And settle further from the glass.
Not for him the dripping air,
Not for him the weeping grass.

35

III

TOO EARLY SPRING

The wind is mighty in the maple tops,
And the long grass is double.
The house leans that way too; but it stops,
Like a bubble,

Swaying softly. And there you walk
With the morning under your skirt.
When blossoms blow from a tender stalk,
Do they hurt?

Does it hurt, now, as you reach the gap,
And part of you whips the wire?
Go back in and straighten your lap
By the fire.

THE CRIME

Your cruellest deed, my dear,
Was not to threaten to be gone:
Running to graze your love and my lean fear
On a strange lawn.

But as you looked away
I looked at you; and heard the sound
Of whining in my head, as if I lay
On the green ground

And, fawning, licked your foot,
And waited there for any word.
It was that you were Circe, and had put
Me with the herd.

36

CONFESSION IN PART

Though I had strength
To stand alone,
I come at length
And half atone

For my old pride,
That would not keep
You by my side;
And would not weep.

With you away
I did not fall;
But on a day—
None heard me call—

I leaned and felt
The rock give in
Where you had knelt,
And sand had been.

BY-LAWS

Never be offended
At what your love forgets to do.
Something then is ended
Between your love and you.

Seek no healing salve
That lets a wounded lover live.
Dodge the poisoned arrow. Have
Nothing to forgive.

Outwardly be hard,
To save the tenderness within.
So impregnable a guard
Is love's thick skin.

CIRCUMFERENCES

Swallows' wings
In the day are swift,
And the hawk's drop,
And the lark's lift,

And mice's feet
That run to cover,
And the sidewise look
Of a jealous lover.

Light is racing
Round the seas;
And thought can distance
All of these.

But faster yet—
And what beyond?—
Is the curving edge
Of a quiet pond,

Or any arc
As soon as drawn,
That seems to sleep,
And plunges on.

BITTEN

If ever age
Remembers youth,
Is it something sharp—
Time's tooth—

Or does it arrive
With sudden might,
Like all of the West
On a windy night;

Out of nothing,
Into the heart,
That leaps and follows
And roars apart;

Till the wind dies,
And the world is still,
And teeth begin
To drill, drill?

SEGMENTS

The first triumphant man was he that drew
His mind across a task and made it two;
And next, to be the creature nearest heaven,
Parcelled the endless mornings into seven.
Night yet unknown, nor fastened with a name,
Tomorrow and tomorrow flowed the same.
On-curving time, with terror in the folds,
Lies powerless in a hand that only holds
The clean-dividing knife, and nipping fast,
Labels the falling pieces to the last.
There are no lines in nature, false or true,
Till number cuts a door and pulls it to.

EMPLOYMENT

Who made the world was not so wise
As one that, opening his eyes
Ten thousand mornings, must again
Start making things that die with men.
Who made the world must think upon
Something never to be gone,
And his hands that never close
Are pale and dry, and his toes
Never leave their print in sand
Going to another land.
Who made the world cannot come home
Over grass or over foam
And shut his mind and so forget
All that will be coming yet.

39

IV

PARADOX

His eyes are so
Because they gleam
With an unbreakable
Soft dream.

They are stone
And they are cold
Because the world
Cannot grow old

Whereat so fiercely
Now they stare.
There was a vision
Fastened there

Before they opened
On our light,
That cannot ever
Dim to night

For one so sure
Of gilded things:
Mountains dancing
Round in rings,

Talking trees,
And never-tame
Lightning setting
Flowers aflame.

Only those
Have gentle eyes
For whom the hills
Had ceased to rise

Before they looked;
And now are laid
In rows that granite
Death has made.

Who would embrace
No sweeter breast:
Only he
Has any rest.

THE BIRD-WATCHER

He is not lifted by their flight
Across the circle of his sight;
He is cold, and he is slow
Beside the least of them that go
And never heed the silent face.
But there is something that can race
With any wing, and no one see.
A piece of him is flying free
Beyond the further forest now;
And all the beating hearts allow
A path among them to be cut
By these wings that cannot shut;
By this beak that cannot learn
Of any season to return.

SURVIVAL

He is not yet
Too solid clay
Wherein no rivers
Cut their way.

Is he cold
And is he firm?
There is something
Like a worm

41

That can awake
And drill a path
Whereinto trickle
Drops of wrath

That quickly gather
In a flood.
Then all is fire
That was mud

As the edges
Break and go
Wherever now
His angers flow.

THE GUIDE

Now to the right,
Between these bars.
This field by night
Is a field of stars.

Here I can sit
And here I can see
These boulders lit
For more than me:

For the stars on the other
Side of the sky.
Brother and brother,
Eye to eye,

They sing so long
That I have slept;
And stopped the song;
And the stones have wept.

THE PICTURE

The only thing she kept
Was not a pretty thing at all.
She brought it down one evening from the wall
And put it in a bureau, where, except
On certain cooler evenings in the fall,
It lay and slept.

She would unwrap it, slow,
And touch the formidable frame;
Whispering that her father was to blame
For nothing: for the shepherd, or the snow,
The cottage, or the children, or the tame
Incredible crow.

CORNISH VILLAGES

They are nothing but sifted
    Sand in the folds
Of round hills lifted,
    I think, from molds,

So smoothly they rise,
    And so grittily sound
The names—Pengrise,
    Trelithick, Germound—

Of the flint-grey places
    Beneath and between.
Hear the wind on their faces,
    Keeping them keen.

CORNISH CASTLE

Pengerswick then was the title of it.
Here was the lord of the hideous wit
Who laughed to her death a farmer's daughter,
And drew night-foundering crews to slaughter

43

Down by the sands, that used to lie
But a fathom deep when the tide was high.
He knew too much; the ocean came
And covered him all except for his name
And the top of the tower with the narrow slit—
Pengerswick's Eye was the title of it—
Whence he would order his evil done,
Under the moon and behind the sun.
The gulls have forgotten to pick at it now—
That deepening eye in the granite brow—
But hear them cry from the parapet:
"Pengerswick's garden is wet! is wet!
And weeds grow there that are not of the land!
Salt! Salt! Sand! Sand!"

FIRST NIGHT ALONE

He locked the window
    And lighted a candle,
Setting it where it would show him the edge
    Of the door, and the handle.

Then to the barn
    At an even pace;
Though once in the driveway cobwebs dangled
    And blanched his face.

The garden again.
    He looked to his light.
No other thing in the world was so firm
    As that tapering white.

Now on the path
    Once more his eyes
Turned to the quiet warm curtains—boy,
    That wasn't so wise.

Between the two fringes
    A circle of hair!—
Parted, as if a dead finger of chalk
    Had descended there.

44

The top of a head!
  Who bends to the flame?—
Drinks it, and vanishes, leaving the walker
  All night to his shame:

Afraid to go forward,
  Afraid to go back,
Afraid of his window, that once was so empty;
  And now so black.

THE ENCOUNTER

Between the two hedges
  As high as a horse—
Stone, with their edges
  Broken to gorse—

I walked in a shade
  That was purple and brown;
And darkly I said
  As I went down and down:

"Nothing can meet me
  In this deep lane;
Though the sun will beat me,
  Ascending again."

But, talking, I rounded
  A gentle green curve;
And something had bounded,
  Before I could swerve,

Swiftly beyond
  And out of my sight,
Tipping each frond
  Of the bracken with white,

That might have been fear
  And that might have been foam;
For the ocean was near,
  And the wind was from home.

"Why do you go so fast tonight,
In the endless dark, in the blowing rain?"
"One of these maples spat three bright
Red leaves in front of us, and the stain

"Is deepening there, though no one sees:
Blood on the roadway trickling down.
Summer is wounded high in the trees,
And red is black, and green is brown.

"Yesterday noon our lawn was bare.
So would I climb and find it still.
I am trying to beat the wind up there
That wants it lonely at the kill."

BURIAL

Nobody wanted this infant born.
  Nobody wished it dead.
They wrapped it tight as an ear of corn
  In a box of cedar and lead.

Nobody by had lighted a candle;
  No one offered to moan.
The priest and I each lifted a handle.
  The father followed alone.

Three in a Ford, that had been waiting
  Most of the wintry day.
Boys on the river still were skating;
  The wood and the road were gay:

Brown quick birds and scarlet-berried
  Twigs, and snow begun.
The priest in the back seat sat and carried
  What never saw our sun.

A blanketed horse was at the gate,
  And someone's tracks led in.

46

We entered, and we ascended straight
   To where the graves were thin,

And where, on a hill, the digger bent
   In wind and thickening white.
Snow covered the box that two of us leant
   To lower out of the light.

Then priestly words to cover the snow;
   The four of us stood bare.
Then clods to keep those words below.
   Now there is nothing there.

AMBUSH

At evening in the strange unlighted town
I sought the streets for comfort, turning down
Each covered dusky walk. There was a tree
Whereunder children swung and stared at me.
Some houses slept, with doors and windows locked.
I passed a shallow porch where people rocked;
They whispered. I went on, and met a man
Who trimmed the border where his grass began.
Across a garden, fragrant now and cool,
Three happy puppies played about a pool,
Until a boy behind them pushed them in.
The night was sweet as none had ever been.
I turned another way, to go and sleep,
When suddenly a cottage seemed to creep
Close to the walk and wait for me. I looked;
The porch was empty, and the screen was hooked;
But, dim within, two ancient women sat,
Motionless, their feet upon a mat.
I could not see an eye; but there were four
That fixed me as I hastened by the door.
Soon I was out of hearing; and I knew
There went no word between them as they grew
Expectant of the next foot that would fall.
I tried forgetting, but my thoughts were all
Of darkness, and a path before a den,
And silent, silent spiders watching men.

V

THE SAGE IN THE SIERRA

EMERSON: 1871

Because I stand and smile, and am dumb,
They reckon it was vain to come.
Because I let my Journal lie
The thoughts are dead? The stream is dry
Wherewith my fountain ran
When I was man?
Why does the world that calls me sage
Pity the silence of my age?
Only sentences, only song,
Showed I was strong?
Has no one heard that it is weak
Forever to sing, forever to speak?
I learned it from a Concord brook
Ages ago, that could not talk.
I see it now, wherever I look,
Wherever I walk.
Merely to wait, merely to be,
Is the Sierra's destiny.
Merely to stand, merely to shine.
So is it mine.

The world lies round me as it lay
In the bright morning of my day.
There is no change from what I saw
When I looked skyward for my law.
The sun paints meadows, and the hills
Happily lift their daffodils.
Mountains are tall and valleys deep,
And forests in the distance sleep.
Midnight still unrolls a heaven
Wherein the Pleiades are seven.

The volume has not lost a leaf,
Nor the proud vessel any sail.
Felicity to come is brief;
It is not frail.

What though the index to the book be gone?
Each page is new again to ponder on.
In the green days my mind was a thick wood,
Wherein perplexing branches, as I stood,
Teemed with quick birds that my yet quicker thought
Darted to fasten, and in trembling caught.
My mind is still a grove, but I advance
With steady pace, in serene ignorance
Of what deep bird springs from what hidden bough.
I weave no net of words for capture now.
There came a storm! Now, all such seasons done,
I stand, an ancient smiler, in the sun.
Shadows of passing clouds that cool my head
Provoke no sign from me, and think me dead.
I am content with this eternal place;
Who will may look for sorrow in my face.

The sentences that once I spoke
To this pure fire were smoke.
The correspondences I sung
But proved me young.
I strove to learn and teach the rest
What sang the spheres, what thoughts were best.
But seeing is forgetting speech;
The lesson learned, I cannot teach.
Come thus far forward, I have lost
Remembrance of the care and cost.
Stationed among the stars, I lack
One syllable to whisper back.

Men for themselves will find the good;
I may no longer be their guide.
Here where I would
Let me abide.

NOW THE SKY AND OTHER POEMS
1928

To

George Genzmer

I

WE COME TOO LATE

June now, like any June,
Brings up its fountains of bright flowers;
Crows rise, and beetles fall;
Wind runs in the lengthening grass;
Squirrels labor; tall tree tops
Dip all day, and a long day, there.
And so I walk where once I walked.
The grass is mine as once it was.
Evening, morning, night, and noon:
There is no change in what they are.
I watch a hawk against the white
Of an upland cloud; I enter woods;
Yesterday there I looked again
For print of deer, and—turning thus—
Beheld a fox.
June is now like any June.
But I am changed from what I was.
I see, and pass. I do not stand
Deep in the grass and lose the day.
There is no longer any ground
That flows before me down the hill.
The hours are broken that in chime
Preceded me and laughed at time.
Still I rise, and still I go;
But there is something that I know.
I cannot walk the older way.
There is something I would say.

Arc of the sky,
Northward or Westward, East or South,
There never has come any wisdom
Out of your mouth.

Waterfall sound,
And the rattle of air in the aspen above,
Language of endless grass,
And the woodbine's love

Wrapping the young
Sweet tree: no one of you ever will tell
The things in the world that are ill
And the things that are well.

The mole and the worm
Have a way, and the rain has a way, in the ground;
Birds see over the orchard,
And storms go round;

Clouds are driven,
And on to the mouse the field-hawk drops.
But here where the lesson begins
The lesson stops.

There was a boy who with the setting sun
Stepped Westward from his father's house, and choosing
One of the five worn stones within a field,
Sat there and looked away. The sheep were resting,
Grey on the nibbled grass, and all the sky
Ran down in red to where his gaze was sent.
A few small birds were disobedient still,
Circling high and black to the East and South;
And noises, far behind on the townward road,
Disturbed the looker too. But soon he lost them,
Losing himself the while; and evening came
On delicate feet that only the blood could hear.
He sat, and the same pulse, his mind believed,
Went through the wrist before him and the long,
Low, undulating veins of the warm West.
He watched the clouds that sailed into the sun,
Watching until no bones of the world remained.

The body of all the universe, he said,
Dreamed now in his own thought, that could dissolve
Perfectly with the horizon. What he knew
Always had thus been known; and what he saw
The stars, coming so pale, saw long ago.
Yet there was more if pages could be turned.
The book was big that he had opened now.
Steadily he would labor while he lived
To arrive at the hidden end. And, so resolving,
Back with a burning face and home to bed.

Sickness of heart
And the crumbling away
Of former bright edges of courage;
Dearth, and decay;

Strength of a hand
That the seasons drain
Till it withers and hangs; and the husk
Of a harvested brain;

Death, and your sisters
Weakness and hate:
There never has risen a star
Explaining your state.

Nor you, the living,
The brave one, the lover,
There never has come any sky
To be none but your cover.

Boy, in the tree
Or kicking the white
Dust of the road, you are neither
The day or the night.

Friended you come,
Friended you go;
But never the tops of those hills
Are conducting you so.

The hours of your doubt,
And your ecstasies after;
Calm, and forgetting, and sudden
Long moments of laughter;

Desperate days,
And help come soon:
Nothing discourses of these
In the yellow of noon.

Peace, peace?
The old man said,
There are two kinds of mortal peace,
And not another that I know.

There was the time
Before your birth,
And there will be a time as long
Commencing neatly with your death.

Each is deep
And each is wide,
And each is empty; which is cause,
From what I know, to call it peace.

Fill a world,
And trembling comes.
But the trembling goes; and in between
There is a space of quiet waiting.

These are peace:
Before a storm,
And after all the wind is dead;
Before the pebble breaks the pond,

And when the ultimate
Circle ceases;
When no enemy has come
And when the last of you is slain;

An open heart
To all assault,
And one, bruised, that bleeds and waits
Until the healing shall be over.

Not to know,
Or to have known
And to remember: these, he said,
Are all that be; and peace is either.

Many a dawning day and many a night,
Sitting, he looked about him for the light
That should be more than feathers from the sun:
Plumes that chance had plucked. Was no least one,
Hither so casually coming, sent to say
What feet should go in what deliberate way?
These beams that fell, was not a one concerned
With edging a perilous path until it turned?
He asked the question softly of the grass.
If that could hear, his sentences would pass
By wind and branch and cloud until they came
To where all spoken answers were the same:
All simple, and all sure. Or he would mark
The times of moonless nights, and ply the dark
With such entreaties as another sun,
Smaller and far away, could have begun
To ponder long ago when moons were not.
There was a moon, and planets in a plot
Came after one another, white and red.
All there, but separate now; and each was dead.
By nothing was he heeded, near or far;
No tuft of grasses, whispering to a star,
Took any message off or brought him back,
By twisted ways, along a glinting track,
The wisdom that he wanted. Nerveless now,
A world without direction, and a brow
Whereon no sign was branded stared at him
Through broken light that would be always dim:
All strange, with no circumference to hold
A universe of fragments growing cold.

57

When he no longer
Strove to know,
Straightway he knew.
The currents flow

Of stream and sky,
Of root and stem,
More smoothly since
He suffers them.

There is no saying,
He has said,
If there be laws
For heart and head;

Or if there be,
Another giver
Regulated
Grass and river

Long before.
We come too late
To hear the gods
Communicate.

Thus he says:
And that he finds
Comfort in
Those separate minds,

Unknowing now,
And caring little
If the greater
Frame be brittle

That encloses,
Mild and wide,
Mice and mountains
Side by side,

White and black,
And autumn red
That never misses
What is dead,

He smiling says.
Matter only
In the world
Is never lonely.

June is now like any June,
But hearing him I will not say
What seems to signify the moon,
What are the languages of day.

The earth is lovely as before;
I shall not ever cease to walk
Where it may lead. But nevermore
Shall I pretend that it can talk.

What is spoken I will speak;
What is done now I will do.
The bird had nothing in its beak
That cut my vision then and flew

Across the field, into the wood;
There was no word along the way.
So I pursue; but if I could
I would not say what it will say.

END OF TRAVEL

Here in a circle of maples I can sit
Half of a day in the sun, and before and after
Figure the speed of shadows; eastward, westward,
Going or coming, all of the shade is one.
Night, the centerless circle, widening, leaves
Me and the bounded brightness, whence I watch
Birds, coming and going—westward, eastward—
Clouds, and the smallest of all my circles, the sun.

Beyond this rounded silence there is nothing.
Roads go to the tops of hills and over,
Over to Canaan and over to all of the Cornwalls:
Eastward, westward, on to the two grey oceans.
For me they end on the hills.

                          And now there rises
Thunder of cars that pass below on the pike.
They pass, are gone; and still the Hollow is sounding.
Round and round it runs, the prisoned thunder,
Higher and higher yet in the curving trees.
I listen and follow, and laugh as the feet grow tired,
Falter, and stumble, and enter the death of hills.
Beyond there is crying of trains that people have taken,
Pointing them straight to the West. I do not listen.
Rim of the world, that cry is yours to devour.
Here am I nourished enough; remembering only
Men long gone who, never considering circles,
Straightened their eyes and pointed their steps to the West.

        Through a cool
        And speckled wood,
        Where unseen
        An Indian stood

        And asked the meaning
        Of their eyes,
        They followed hot
        Upon the cries

        Of men ahead,
        Whose going warmed
        Paths no feet
        Had ever formed;

        Until there ran
        A stiffened road
        To where the first
        River flowed.

Silver it came,
Lazily, widely, down from the North;
And one on a raft put forth
And gave it a name.

Word blew back,
Flushing the faces of men in file;
And, trotting the ultimate mile
Of the shadowy track,

Ten of them shouted,
Bringing the ferry again to the shore.
They crossed; and again there were more.
And some of them doubted;

Two of them turned,
Talking together of East and home.
But there was the river in foam,
And both of them burned

New now with desire;
Looking across where the water was walled
Once more with a wood, that called
Their feet to the fire

Laid far in the West:
Waiting for these who would touch it to flame.
So on, and ever the same,
And never a rest.

So over the biggest of rivers
And on to the plains,
Under a sun whose shadows
Were yellowing stains

On the green of the grass, and the white
Of the desert beyond.
At evening it reddened the world,
And the goers were fond

Of saying that this was the fire,
That this was the end;
Only a hundred mountains
Now to ascend,

Only a hundred valleys
And there it would wait:
Faggot and leaf and log
On an altar of fate.

The feet and the eyes drew on
Till the ocean was there.
Then silence. The hills were asleep,
And the beaches were bare,

And the sun going down in the sea
Went utterly out.
And the travellers looked at each other
And turned about.

Here in the circle of maples where I am standing
Only the bodies come back of these long gone.
Thinly they walk in the shade, and thinly endeavor,
Turning, to keep to the West. But they have lost it;
And so all afternoon I will see them circling—
Birds with a wounded wing—and never at rest.
The thoughts of a traveller never can curve and return.
Only the body comes back of one long gone
Straightly and far away. And bodies discover
Death in the hills, and death in a circle of sound.

END OF SINGING

This wind today
From the invisible West
Is the wind that carried the singing away,
Away from an Indian breast.

He sang to the four
Dark ends of the sky,
And they can remember, though song no more
Goes there in a quartered cry.

Snow tomorrow
Will blossom and fall,
Unknowing if it is the flower of our sorrow;
Nobody now will call

To the four dark ends
Of the covering grey,
To the wind, this wind, that catches and bends
The stem of no song away.

Now the corn
Stands alone
That was born
Of a green moan

From one beneath,
Who gave it milk
Within a sheath
Of yellow silk;

And the wind
Its father came,
Leather-skinned
And walking lame,

Driving throngs
Of butterflies,
That brought it songs
And gave it eyes.

Still they flutter
In the field;
But none will mutter
To the sealed,

Withered senses
Of the corn
Words that fences
Would have torn.

The parents now
Forget their child,
Upon whose brow
Will be the wild

Winds of spring
Forever dumb;
For no men sing,
And no words come.

The stallion uprears,
And softly bethudding the meadow
Beneath him surprises a shadow
That levels his ears.

They, pointing so proud,
Find only the sedulous sun,
Only the breezes, and one
Pursuable cloud.

Never a song
That will tell of the glittering grass
Beyond where the mountains pass
So gently along,

And the father of steeds,
Neighing all day in a bright
Storm of descending delight,
Eternally feeds

On tapering flowers;
Or races with clattering time,
Strewing the slopes he must climb
With the shadows of hours.

Never a strain
Of the song of the pollen that hovers
Close to his flank, and covers
The white of his mane;

No holy bright word
Of the tale of the hurrying dust:
The grains of the sacred rust
His stamping has stirred.

The stallion is lonely,
Hearing no song to his sire.
Slowly he walks to the wire.
The stallion is lonely.

There is no longer any sound
Binding men unto the ground.
There was an arrow flew and took
Its drink of flesh; the warrior shook,
And shook the ground whereto he sang,
Falling while the forest rang.
Then a whispering in his wound,
And the earth whereon he swooned
Whispered up a song of running
Over needles, after cunning
Pairs of foxes that he caught;
Or of stopping with his thought
Deer that trembled, turned, and came.
And up he leapt, no longer lame.

Wind and stars and tongues of men,
And beasts between that talk alone,
You will not converse again;
All your songs are lost and gone.

The sky is singing to another
Sky beyond that none can see;
Man is singing to his brother;
Worm to worm, and tree to tree.

There is no song that all can hear,
Coming from a silent place
Where an Indian slays his fear
With folded arms and lifted face.

NOW THE SKY

How long have standing men, by such a stone
As this I watch from on this windless night,
Beheld Arcturus, golden and alone,
Guiding Antares and the Snake aright.

The Scales were up when not an Arab walked
On sand that soon was paved with names of stars;
Boötes herded, and the Giant stalked
Past the curved Dragon, contemplating wars.

How many an open eye, bedight with dew,
Over the sleeping flowers has drawn them down:
Andromeda, and Berenice's few
Dim tresses that shall ever flee the Crown.

From such a rock whence greybeards long ago,
Forgetting it beneath them, heard the Lyre,
I watch. But there is something now we know
Confusing all they saw with misty fire.

For them a hundred pictures on a slate.
For us no slate, and not a hand that draws.
For them a pasture-dome wherefrom the gate
Of Cancer led the Lion through its claws.

For them a frosty window, painted over,
Nightly, with flower faces in a ring:
Daisies dancing up, and clouds of clover
Scenting the after way, and phlox to fling

Thin petals left and right till morning lifted.
For us no shapely flame in all the dark;
For us a million embers that have drifted
Since the first fire, and not a sign to mark

Where anything shall end, or which shall go
With which until they both shall die to grey.
For watchers once a changeless face to know;
For us cold eyes that turn henceforth away.

66

They saw each constellation take its hour
Of triumph overhead, before it started
Down the broad West, whereon the death of power
Was written by the Ram, and nightly charted.

The Eagle and the Swan, that sailed so long,
Floating upon white wings the Arrow missed,
Tilted at midnight, plunging with a song
Earthward, and—as they sank—deep Hydra hissed.

Leo had long been growling in his lair
When Pegasus neighed softly in the East,
Rising upon a wind that blew his hair
Freshly, until Aquarius increased

The stream he aimed against the Fish's mouth,
And all the stars were wet with silent rain.
The Hyades came weeping, and the South
Sent mist to soothe the Sisters in their pain.

These things they witnessed, and Orion, climbing
Fiercely with those two Dogs announcing Fall;
Then Winter, with Aldebaran loud-chiming,
Baiting the frozen Bull, that turned to call

The Bears to warm his anger. These they knew,
And knew the seasons with them, Spring and Spring;
Counting the dozen signs the finger drew
That swung the inconstant Sun around the Ring.

Slow Jupiter proceeded as they planned,
Lingering among the Twelve in stately turn;
They touched the breasts of Venus, where the hand
Of Mars's fiery love had been to burn.

The sky was then a room, with people going
Faithfully to and fro, and beasts enchained.
The sky was then a midnight wastrel, throwing
Riches away; and still the purse remained.

But now the sky is broken, door by door.
Strangers in the room obscure the hosts.
The meadow is not guarded any more
By watchers coming lonely to their posts.

The animals are never to be named
That swarm beyond our company of old:
Stragglers from the herd, that we had tamed
Unknowing the recesses of the fold.

Those were no heroes whom we once addressed:
Hercules, Orion, and the Twins.
Unwounded, they were running from the rest
Far there where only now the war begins.

There is a game for players still to play,
Pretending that the board was never lost.
But still the painted counters will decay,
And knowledge sit along to count the cost.

ABOVE THE BATTLE

Higher than hate, and the abused
Stiff bodies of men, and the stiff
Walk, close to the ground, of men not just;
Higher, yes, than the uppermost whipped head,
Than the stiff elbow of the whipper;
High in the unseen air a tree starts waving;
Waving alone, and it says to itself:
                                        I know.
Longer, yes, than the uppermost man remembers,
Longer ago than the eyes laid deepest away,
Longer ago than justice, there were trees.
The face of the world was water, and the hair—
Silk at the edge of salt—was waving trees;
But not like these.

            In a slow wind
            They rose and fell,
            Laying them down
            To sleep so well

That, standing to look,
They still would sway
In the bent wind,
In the curved day.

With a slant wind
They fell and rose,
Slowly, slowly,
And never a close

Of the circle of soft
Unended motion—
Silk at the salt
Stiff edge of ocean.

The low grass at our feet was a forest too;
The wind in it was a snake with indolent folds.
The wind in us was the word the white sky sang,
Sending no more than one slow syllable down.
All of them long are dead, and none remembers.
Not even a root remembers; but I know,
I know what none of the men there huddle and cry.

The salt came,
And talking sand,
And north snow,
And man's hand,

And my slim fathers
Fled and stood
In a coarse fear,
In a loud wood.

We straightly rise,
We stiffly fall.
We do not listen
If men call

On ignorant winds
To set love right.
That was our day.
This is our night.

II

DEFEATED FARMER

Lift as he will a wordless face
To an earless wind, to a sightless sky,
He is not told if meadows lie
Beyond the rumor of the race
He ran and lost; and found disgrace
With common trees that standing die.

He can no more escape the scorn
Of day, that loathes a failing thing,
Than the stripped oak can beat a wing
And fly the wood where it was born;
Falling at night in a forlorn
Contrary wood where mold-worms sing.

Once he thought the wind conspired
With wet and dry and hot and cold
To slave for him. But he is old,
And long ago the year was tired,
And if the wind was ever hired
It bustled off to better gold.

Once he felt the city's eyes
In envy on him as he swung
Ill storms away. But not a tongue
Proclaims him lately weather-wise,
And he has heard towered laughter rise
From throats that in their turn are young.

He still can lift a lidded gaze
And count the mornings light and dark.
So the stripped elm with fallen bark
Receives the days. But not its days.
The greener wood has private ways
That posted death may not remark.

CIVIL WAR

The country is no country I have seen,
And no man goes there who is now alive, and no man
Ever is going to leave there. But they try;
Waving a million beards that on pale faces
Blacken with time and spread.
It is a field of bodies of blue boys,
And gray boys, grown half way into the ground.
The wind is dark that sways them;
All of them bending with it, south or north,
All of them straining here; but no one knowing
Of any fellow by who gazes too.
It is a field of legless bearded boys
With bright unnecessary buttons on their breasts,
And skirts of coats that hold them in the sod.
The bodies twist,
The circular, small eyes are mad with being;
A million mouths fly open without sound;
But none can tear his coat up, that must come
With roots and worms or come not up at all.

Away in Carolina, Maine, Wisconsin,
Boys who kept their legs walked long and long.
They set their feet in furrows, or in aisles;
They strolled with girls, were taken, and were fathers;
Had old companionship; and last were covered
Quietly with smooth boards, and grass, and stone.
Stiffly now they hold society;
Forever thus they lie without a want.

In the forbidden country where the sod
Grows down and down, with restless blue roots, gray roots,
In the dark windy land no one can leave,
Separate necks yearn homeward;
Separate hungry shoulders pull and pull.
Wind, oh wind, I did not come to stay;
I must be there tomorrow, not to miss—
But the dark wind is earless, and the day
Is endless, and the grasses hiss and hiss.

THE ORCHARD GHOST

Strictly at noon the mist was there,
Between two pear trees like a web.
There was no other mist abroad,
There was no other hand to grab
And tackle nothing but the sun,
Beneath the blossoms making fun.

He put it safely out of mind,
And sauntered home; but came again
Upon another shining day,
Upon another whitened noon.
And there it was as thin as dew;
And the sun was coming through;

And there were two rows of ribs
Around a heart that shook and glistened,
Like a poppy that the sun
Within a web of beams had fastened.
And there were elbows; and a face
Smiled transparently in place.

He closed his eyes and struck the thing;
He opened them and it was dancing:
Left and right, a little stiffly.
And it bowed, and with a mincing
Gesture came; but he was gone.
They found him lying on the lawn,

And they say that he will never
Leave the door while there is light.
After sunset on the mountain
He can start; though he must wait
And watch the west a fearful minute
Lest it have a spider in it.

TIRESIAS

There goes the man with yellow eyes
That see within, and see too much.
He was blinded by a god
That he might prophesy and touch.
So he takes a crooked rod
And peers with it as with a crutch.

Propping so his yellow eyes
He can discern the speeding day
Whereon a hundred hills shall fall,
And every city shall decay.
Ask him now and have it all.
Would no one hear what he can say?

They can say, those yellow eyes,
What both a man and woman are.
Since the morning he was cursed
The breasts have shrunk; but not so far
As to forget the teeth they nursed,
As to enfold the bitten scar.

Will no one bid the yellow eyes
Revolve again? Or call the tongue
To witness women in that pain
Wherewith their filaments are strung?
Will no one touch the whirling brain
Of him who is both old and young?

Tiresias, damned with yellow eyes,
Pursue your endless road alone.
What you see beyond the night
Is but a frame of bloody bone.
We were wiser, yet we might
Come never there without a moan.

MAN WITH GLOBE

In the mornings of my strength
The world is tin upon a table.
Standing from it, I am able,
Fingers firm upon the pole,
To spin the whispering breadth and length
Of its small, rounded soul;
And I am whole.

Then descends an afternoon
Of fallen walls, of panic light.
Staring out, I hear the night
Pursuing seas and breaking land
On spheres too far to cry in tune;
And my once stony hand
Crumbles to sand.

THE DISGUISE

Groper up the narrow landing
Past the invisible voiceless clock;
Then to the left and higher again
Till the carpet ceases, and shadows rock
Of linden leaves on the moon-white floor:
Suddenly stop; for this is the door.

Grasper of club and turner of handle
And prowler as far as a darkened bed;
Feeler of hair; and beater and beater
And beater and beater until he is dead:
Man, descending through the night,
How is it forgotten that flesh is white,

That eyes on a pillow had much to see
On mornings that never are now to come;
That there is silence worse than all
When even death is stricken dumb?
Man upon another stairs,
What is the cap your madness wears?

74

Has it a visor slanting down
To let you look and still be blind?
Is it a jester's bonnet, chattering
That deliverance may be kind?
Or is it Time's old drooping hood:
Saying all that goes is good?

ESTRANGEMENT

They were not old enough to be
Two musty mows that nothing joined:
Darkening places strange with mice
That never caught a foreign sound.
They were not separated yet
By moldy mortar wrath had set.

They were still a single room,
But longer now than once it was;
And in the middle quiet spiders
Worked unseen on certain days.
What they built she twice removed;
But the third time it was proved.

Each aware of something hung there,
He rebuked it; then was still.
If it stung their meeting faces,
He could wait along his wall.
Neither was old enough to know
How wide and high a web can grow.

THE RELIC

It is something that he handled;
It is something gold and small
That he dandled

From a button of his vest;
And his fingers never learned
To fall and rest

Until they died. But it lives,
Lying on a shaded table,
And it gives,

For me who look, no lie to death,
Though a pale pretence of hands
Is there like breath;

Though a flutter as of fear
Tries to say around the room
That he is here.

Deeper proof of death is none:
That all the ghosts keep abed
Excepting one.

DEATH

He never had heard of it. Then it was there;
And still he would not talk of anything
Save walking on and seeing; rolling an eye
Right, left, as if there still were nothing there.
And nothing was: that now is what he knows.
He knows that men are walkers through a wood
Filled with a light from nowhere; and the trees
Stand shadowless. He knows them, few and clear,
Companions of a morning no sun makes.
The walkers on bright feet, the happy men,
Forever, until a day, go straightly through,
Or wind a little, swaying as they pass.
Then on a day a shadow falls, and rising,
Stands like a tree; and then another stands,
Twisting the paths of walkers till they falter,
Circle a while, and cease in striped shade.
The trunks are there—thin intervals of light—
But not for mind or foot was that way made.
Death is not knowing what is not a shadow.
And nothing is. That now is what he says.

DEATH OF LIGHT

The winter face of wisdom, the slow eyes
Opening never widely lest surprise
Come with the first snow and whitely shed
Whispers where the hard truth should tread;
The grey ears that, hearing, disbelieve
And fallen cheeks all time will not retrieve—
The wary eyes of wisdom are too changed
From the green year when straight the vision ranged
And straight accepted seeing. Then the lines
Led ever on and on, with no designs
Woven upon the world of false or true.
Light was a bird that too much looking slew.
Dropping upon a wire, it sat and sang
And trembled.
                    Only feathers of it hang
For shaded eyes of wisdom to see now.
Safe are the ears, and deep the careful brow
Of wisdom, counting riches. But the tale
Is one of losing, and of lids that fail.

DEATH OF OLD MEN

When they no longer lean there,
And leer, and hold a sentence in;
When they no longer fix the air
With a grimace, a grey grin;

When they are gone, a stiffness goes,
As if a post were pulled out.
The wire is down, and wind blows
Uncut to where the young ones shout:

Tall and bending, green and free;
Looking up at only light.
But that is not enough to see.
They will weary of the height.

They will say a word for old
And crooked men beneath a cape
Of nights and stars; and for the cold,
That fastens faces into shape.

77

III

MAD SONGS

I

That chime I hear
And you do not
Is the singing of fear
In the rope, the knot

That I with a knife
Go forth to sever.
You of this life
Through me shall never

Stumble again
In a circle of dust.
The four gates then,
With a crying of rust,

Will equally swing
And will equally pour
Mouths that will sing
In the rain evermore.

And the wind will unsay
That I ever was blind.
That was your way.
Now follow behind.

II

You did not come;
How could I keep
Four winds awake
When one would sleep?

78

I hurried by;
Another slept;
Then all were gone,
And I had stepped

Before I knew—
It was your will—
Into a night
Where, dark and still,

I heard you walking
Round and round.
Not any other
Sight or sound

Until you laughed
And led me back
To touch my brain,
Crack after crack.

Still your fingers,
Pressing tight,
Hurt what could heal
In wind and light

Would you but come
As far with me
As to the singing
I can see.

PHILOSOPHER'S LOVE SONGS

I

My one love has lighter loves,
And taller ones, and merrier.
Still my love has less than I,
Who having her, have only her.

Having her, who has those others:
Him, and him, and flowers, and horses:
Having her is having sometimes
Jealousies and loud remorses,

Which to punish with her eyes
She turns her head, as if to see
What is to see—and, stepping lightly,
Come those loves more light than me.

Having me that have no other,
She has others; but the sum
Of all her halves is less than my
One that is compendium.

II

Her changing eyes
Knew me too well,
Wherefore they fell;
And now as they rise
They look for lies
No one can tell.

No one. But where
May not be nine
To smile and whine?
So ten are there,
As thin as air;
And she is mine.

I learn at last
To wait alone.
She is my own,
And tethered fast.
But to no mast.
But to no moan.

Death is a tall horse
With large white feet,
Coming on a slow walk
Down the long street,

Nudging with a soft nose,
Opening the gate.
Up you must climb then,
Lest you be late.

Starting on a slow walk
And never looking round,
He moves; and the great feet
Never make a sound.

Soon it is a road
With the houses far between,
And when a farm is there at last
Children come and lean,

Shouting over fences;
But not as if they knew.
And not a word arrives
Of what they say to you.

On beneath a bright hill
Is water in a trough.
But he is never thirsty,
And you are looking off,

Thinking of the afternoon,
Thinking of the night.
But all the sky is green there,
And all the hours are white.

He will never halt again,
And you will not descend.
You will be content there
Without any end.

THE CROWD

There were six children in a house,
And there was one across the way;
But when he joined them he was more
Than making seven in the play.
They were six and he was one:
A single flower among the hay.

They remarked the careful stem,
And felt an envy for the face
Of one who, flourishing alone,
Grew out of hurt and rose to grace.
But he among the roughened heads
Bewept his nakedness of race.

He had come as if to cover
All he lacked; for he had lain
Beneath the body of their wind,
And sweated with them in the rain.
But he was white and slender still;
And still they coveted his pain.

THE ORPHAN

In the same moment, child,
With death upon a train,
You walked, and with a wild
Clamor walked again.

I was not by them, boy;
I know not how they fell;
But I beheld the joy
Of you that stepped so well,

And, stepping, never knew
What made us weep to see:
Lightning in the two
Branches of a tree;

Lightning leaving only
Sky above your head,
That still is not so lonely
As the stricken dead.

COMPANY GONE

Mountains, stand again,
And flowery hay, put up your head.
They are gone, the ten
Men
That flattened you with nothing said.

Lilac, come alive,
And coreopsis, turn about.
They are gone, the five
Wives
You always shun because they shout.

Rambler, tie your shoe,
And Emily Gray, go on along.
We are here, the two
True
Mouths that move but to your song.

THE DINNER

Jupiter and Mercury
Among the Phrygian hills
Envied even sparrows
That picked the window sills.

Not a door was open
To show a table laid,
Till Baucis and Philemon,
Startled as they prayed,

83

Answered godly knocking
And bustled at the board,
Giving all to strangers
Either could afford.

Baucis plucked a salad,
Philemon brought a chine
Of bacon moulded over,
And set it by the wine;

And nodding to each other
They ran—but it was hard—
And slew the only gander
Walking in the yard.

Jupiter and Mercury
Glistened as they went,
And quickly all the valley
Whispered what it meant.

Water flooded inland,
Filling every field,
And everyone drowned there,
Even as he kneeled.

Except in the cottage
Where the four had dined.
That rose up,
And the gables were lined

With a thatch of gold,
And Philemon poured
Wine forever
From a silver gourd.

IV

MAN

Brown as the glade he moves in,
Entering out of the sun, the slayer of eyes,
He walks; and the blind shadows,
Hearing his soundless feet, awake and arise,

Bending with him and parting
The pale hair of ferns, pretending to see;
But while he looks they leave him,
Becoming the portion of earth himself would be.

He still can forget his fingers,
Softly he says—and a toad is there on the moss.
He stoops; and the greyling stays,
Panting, with only half of the rock to cross.

Patiently settling earthward,
One of his hands, unfolded, touches stone:
Rests, and cannot remember
If arms are there or if it is a leaf, alone.

Cold are the rock and the lichen,
Cold are the quieted eyes, and the palm, and the wrist.
Around is a thick stillness—
Save for his suddenly hearing, out of mist,

Waves of an old awareness:
Blood in his hand come back, and bone returning.
Wisdom is underground.
So to the sun again, and the fever of learning.

THE TRANSLATION

Ant and shrew
And marmot, going
Safely there,
The time of mowing

Comes tomorrow.
Meadow lark
And banded snake,
Then the dark

Sky will fall:
What is green
Above you now
No more be seen.

What is single
Will divide.
And as you run
The other side

Of all the world
Will drop its blue
As if it looked
For none but you.

Toad and cricket,
Worm and mouse,
You will find
Another house

That not a hand
Was there to build.
My own sky
Has never spilled,

Right and left,
And shown a new one.
Night and day
Mine is the true one.

Would it were not,
And could lie
Thus to the sickle
As I die.

DESERTED HOLLOW

This valley sends another sound
Than was delivered of its rocks
When they were seized and set around
The cloven feet of little flocks.
The sheep were taken long ago,
And fences wait a wilder foe.

There is no hushing of the wind
Between the blows of axes now.
No breathless timber-lengths are pinned
And shingled fast to make a mow.
There is not one expectant eye
Upon the purpose of the sky.

It was a race of silent men
That taught the clouds to hesitate,
If only to upgather then
A blacker heaven-full of hate.
Riders up and down divided
Weather since grown single-sided.

Winds that strike upon these stones
Hear not an angry voice among them.
They have smothered their old moans
Against the hairy hands that wrung them.
Boulders, grass, and border-trees
Supinely harken. Fences freeze

And crumble wider every spring;
They will yet be flat again.
There is not a wilful thing
In all this patient mountain-pen.
There is only the dead sound
Of slowly unresisting ground.

RAIN ALL DAY

The sky is laid as low again
As once it was when fearful men
Heard the hoarse chime
Of moving time.

Over me now unmuffled feet
Trample the blue, and flatten the sweet
Flowers of day
That sang him away.

As up they sang the distance grew
Between our faces and these two
Merciless heels
My forehead feels.

Space is fallen, time is found,
And we are nothing but the ground
On which he walks,
Mashing the stalks.

CONTEST

The east wind I worked in,
And endless black rain—
Working with a wet axe
As long as there was wood—
The rain, the wind, and I
Argued which should die.

The chopper never looked up,
Behind him or around;
Only at the wet log
His blade fell and warmed;
Hoping heat would spread
Until the dark was dead.

The wind never looked away,
But, always coming on,
Drove the rainy knife edge
Deeper in and in.
It was the day that died
With blue in its side.

DECEMBER 22

Noon today, and the earth swings high—
Swing low, you sun whom once she loved—
Noon, and her body is trying to die;
And horses stop, and men go gloved.

Noon in the north, but never an end—
Look far, you sun whom still she knows—
Try as she may, she cannot bend
Backward enough for the eyes to close.

Stiffly at noon now, under the lids—
Look in, you sun, and remind her now—
She stares once more, though her will forbids;
And mice dream on in the darkened mow.

JUNE 22

Up and around as far as her old eyes,
Opening young and warm, can see they swing;
And swing; and swallows
Take them a little farther, daring the wind.
They are off there now, in the quiet,
And here she sits indifferent, playing blind.
One smile she has for all of the rounded day;
One face she turns, and says that this is the time
For sitting and letting the mind go run with the hours.
There is nothing to fear, she says;
In a field so wide and white no body could die.
She smiles and fingers flowers and, lifting her head,
Listens softly; and swallows
Take her a little farther, daring the sun.

DARK BARN

Windows, dying, left for dust
The wings of flies that spiders trussed
And waiting speared. The door is held
With weeds that not a blade has felled,
With vines that thicken since the last
Inlooker shut the shadows fast.
It is a piece of darkness saved
Against the summer, and the waved
Bright hair of harvest, brought to shear.
Nothing will cut the darkness here,
That grows and fills the rafter spaces,
Hangs, and wraps the rusted traces
And blind bridles on their pegs;
Stares between the stanchion legs;
And is the only thing to know
That running mice bear pretty snow
Upon their bellies, which they hide
For joy beneath them as they glide.

THE DISTANT RUNNERS

> Six great horses of Spain, set free after
> his death by De Soto's men, ran West
> and restored to America the wild race
> lost there some thousands of years ago.
> —LEGEND.

Ferdinand De Soto lies
Soft again in river mud.
Birds again, as on the day
Of his descending, rise and go
Straightly West, and do not know
Of feet beneath that faintly thud.

If I were there in other time,
Between the proper sky and stream;
If I were there and saw the six
Abandoned manes, and ran along,
I could sing the fetlock song
That now is chilled within a dream.

Ferdinand De Soto, sleeping
In the river, never heard
Four-and-twenty Spanish hooves
Fling off their iron and cut the green,
Leaving circles new and clean
While overhead the wing-tips whirred.

Neither I nor any walker
By the Mississippi now
Can see the dozen nostrils open
Half in pain for death of men;
But half in gladness, neighing then
As loud as loping would allow.

On they rippled, tail and back,
A prairie day, and swallows knew
A dark, uneven current there.
But not a sound came up the wind,
And toward the night their shadow thinned
Before the black that flooded through.

If I were there to bend and look,
The sky would know them as they sped
And turn to see. But I am here,
And they are far, and time is old.
Within my dream the grass is cold;
The legs are locked; the sky is dead.

THE PULSE

One thing is sure
When most are not:
That there is cold,
That there is hot.

There is no error
In the frost;
With warmth away
No warmth is lost;

Waves are coming
Of a time
That has been written
In slow rhyme:

Hot and cold,
And cold and hot;
All things may fail,
But this one not.

Though hate and love
And mercy cease,
Under the rippling
Vapor fleece

Of earth goes warmth
Pursuing cold;
And neither is young;
And neither is old.

PASTORAL

Fleeing the town where every face
Was long and pale in the lamplight,
He sighed for any simple place
Of minds round as midnight;

And thought he came to such a valley
Westward by a hundred miles;
He sat with Ed, he lay with Sally
Underneath the rooftiles;

Concluding in the autumn, though,
Returning to the pantomime,
That country faces, ticking slow,
Tell too strictly noontime.

EPISTLE TO TOWN: FEBRUARY

Go to your table, in the lined room
Outside of which four ashmen used to bark.
Go to your table, to the lettered keys.
Send me words quickly, on small hard feet,
Tapping this snow that is too soft and wide,
Dotting this white that is too everywhere.
The trees stand out of it, and bushes blow
Thinly, as if they meant to creep indoors.
Yet nothing moves; all things are waiting here,
And the sky waits upon a dance of words.
Let them say anything, so they are black,
So they come suddenly on little heels,
Dropping like seed upon this table cloth.
Say I am a crow, and have a hungry eye,
Fed now too long upon an empty field.
Think of me hovering. Tell me a taxi
Halted just now and let a lady out,
And she went into Number 45.

FAREWELL TO FIELDS

Bird, tree, and cloud, and all you creatures going
Under upon four feet, and shadows showing
Of things behind, put so for none to see:
Fold up your pipes, for you are done with me.
This is the seventh summer we have played;
The end comes, and all the sounds are made.
You were the slender instrument I took,
Blowing until the rooted grasses shook,
And the crows cried, and nodding horses came;
But ever now the tangles are the same
Of the mazed steps that once our rhyme unravelled.
There is another wildness to be travelled,
And I have set my feet to go alone.
Over no grass, and by no greying stone,
I now would hunt new music out of bare
Hatred, and quick love, and old despair.
Where I am going men and women go.
Fold up your pipes, that have instructed so.

JONATHAN GENTRY
1931

To
Allen Tate

I

OHIO RIVER

1800

Jonathan Gentry, with an English heart
Broken in two high places that must heal;
Jonathan Gentry sailed, and told the sea-winds:
"Your meadows are green with salt and endless anger,
What you look down on, flying, is flat death.
I could have died too, sea-winds, sea-winds,
I could have bled too long from either bruise.
But over the American mountains
The American meadows wait.
Broad with good breath,
Sea-green with only grass,
And heaving with God's promises to men,
The American meadows, faint from so long calling,
Still bring their voice to me. Here now I have it"—
Holding his heart—
"And here it makes loud music for the mind
To feed on and be wrapped with and grow well.
Already, winds, I smile at my forgetting
Figure and name that in the suit of friendship
Stole my white love at midnight from a room;
And bursting the door outward, burst two chambers
High in my side where he and she had been.
No, no—not quick to close. It has been empires.
Or has it been a fly's life in the sun?
But in good time the meadow-song
Came, and I straightway heard;
And straightway come."

Standing among the taut ropes and the seamen,
Courteous like a knight with hidden wounds—
In the deep, shaded center still they flowed

And solemnized his glances, till each smile
Came out of him as gentle as abstracted—
Jonathan Gentry sailed,
And told at last the sea-gulls:
"Shore-birds,
Dwellers upon the dead edge,
Criers above the white line of salt and beaten sand around the
    world,
Wing watchers
Sick of an old sameness—
Gulls, it was not you I sailed to see.
Lead me to land and go again,
Ruefully rising, rising,
Desolate up and up, forever behind me.
Birds of an old world,
My eyes are shaped for newness, and for wings
Of paradise above an inland river.
·Over the inland mountains it commences,
And flows a thousand miles
Along the meadows of the mind:
Deep in my heart I hear it round the bends,
Taking new thought of bluff and ripple and pool;
Dreaming among the flats;
Rousing, rousing again;
Then pulling in daylong peace—nightlong, daylong pulling—
Past gentle and old gigantic and thoughtful trees.
Birds of the salt beak,
Line-criers,
My taste is all for freshness, and for free
New-going wings above an inland valley."

So land, and stripling cities
Aproned from the sea.
So coaches, carts, and cobblestones and faces,
And doors that shut and opened as he waited—
A week, a month he waited—
Then the long jolting out of Philadelphia,
West and a little north, and west again.
Like a tired tortoise,
Clambering up old slopes of rock and weed
To nothing at the top, then down and on
And on and up once more, and on and down,

Went the filled wagon.
Jonathan Gentry rode, or walked and rested,
Over the endless hills, and told the driver:
"No, I am never weary. No, I am going
Only for curious reasons. Yes, I am married.
No, I am going alone"—till the driver spat,
Reaching an end of words. But hairy eyes
Still crawled the length of Gentry, and a tongue
Rolled in its cheek unwillingly confined.
The couple from New England with their baby
Talked in a tavern once, before the fire,
Of where the new land was, and how they went there
Hoping to find a country young as milk.
Jonathan Gentry loved them, and he whispered:
"Yes, we are done with oldness, done with men
Pressing too hard upon us"; but they stared,
And Gentry ever after smiled alone.

One more mountain lay there,
Looking the other way, and Gentry said:
"Nothing will ever move you, nothing make you
Turn your old head to see who comes so late.
All of it in your eyes! You have it all there,
And had it when there were no men to weep.
You had it when there were no women either:
Women to weep and laugh and run away.
Is it a world ancient beyond all error?
Is it too young to know? And will it know?"
The horses leaned;
The wagon, gritting its last gravel,
Groaned, and they zigzagged up.
Too steep, the driver said, and so they rested
Where a bright spring, refusing to go further,
Tumbled down past them backward, laughing loudly
At labor and all good purpose. But they left it,
Took a long breath and toiled, and wound thrice more
Right upward, till the trees
Opened; the mountain stopped; and all their faces
Fell on the broad Ohio, soft below.

Like a white dream this beautiful of rivers
Lay in its forest folds, and if it moved there

99

None of them knew it now. They too were moveless—
High, little gods of momentary stone—
They too were dreams the mountain dreamed, old father
Of flocks of dreams that circled each day and fell.
When they could see again they wept and wondered,
Turned to each other and chattered, and wiped their eyes.
But Gentry's eyes had nothing for the others.
They still were stone as the path tilted down,
Dragging the jolted wheels;
They still were fixed on air as the slow road
Slanted all day and night,
And another infinite night,
Crookedly down to the clearing and into the town
Where smoke rose, and houses of new logs
Huddled away from hills;
They still were sightless eyes until he wandered,
Leaving the unhitched horses tossing their hay,
To a smooth bank and stood there, while the river
Moved at his feet, and moving, brought more water
That followed and flowed and followed, and stopped in eddies
Only to go again.
So Gentry stood and trembled, and his eyes
Melted, and his mind
Entered the faithful flood.

Nine days the hammers rang, the sledges thudded,
Saws whined, and swarming men along the shore
Fitted the fragrant timbers of an ark
That floated on the tenth day and received them—
The couple from New England with their baby,
A preacher with a brown beard and a brood
Whose mother lay in Maryland under a hill,
Two men with silver watches and cigars,
A blue-eyed woodsman swinging gun and fiddle,
Twelve boatmen, lanky-jawed; and Jonathan Gentry.
Then came the bags and bundles, and the stove,
And chairs tied two together, and the beds;
Then, timorous in their ropes, the seven sheep
The preacher could not leave, the fiddler's pig,
Two heifers, and two Jerseys big with milk.
The creatures in their stout pen at the stern
Bawled as the bugle blew; the cabin people

Crowded the clumsy bow, and the languid boatmen,
Languid no more this morning, heaved at the sweeps.
The flat craft, swinging slowly into the middle,
Moved to a dwarfish music; for the woodsman,
Climbing the cabin ladder, scraped his bow
Thinly upon the strings; it came back thinly
And sadly now to the shore as the sawmen shouted,
And down at the stern the sheep called faintly too.
But the small music, rising between the mountains,
Moved as the long oars moved; and when they ceased,
The ark come full to the current, wavered on
Like the lost voice of birds.

> Over the mountains, boys,
> Into the land of grass;
> Down the big river, boys,
> Stand up and pass.
> > With a heave-la-ho,
> > And a heave-la-hum,
> > Bend and go
> > Till kingdom come.
>
> One time there was Adam,
> One time there was Eve.
> Can it come again, boys?
> What do you believe?
> > With a heave-la-ho,
> > And a heave-la-hum,
> > Bend and go
> > Till kingdom come.
>
> Eden's up ahead, boys,
> And the golden age.
> Not a lawyer there, boys,
> Or parson in a rage.
> > With a heave-la-ho,
> > And a heave-la-hum,
> > Bend and go
> > Till kingdom come.
>
> No one's very bad there,
> And no one's very good.

It's the promised land, boys,
Land of livelihood.
    With a heave-la-ho,
    And a heave-la-hum,
    Bend and go
    Till kingdom come.

The mountains folded in upon the full, unconscious river;
The shoremen heard no more, and turned away and said:
"Where is it now, the wailing barge? Only the sun sees;
Only the hill night knows, and a few stars overhead.
Well, let them go and stay forever—and these new ones too."
Was this the shaded river? And these the waiting dead?

More people stood upon the bank to go;
Others had gone before; and thousands came.
But Gentry in his ark,
Proud at the low bow, lifted his forehead high
And watched the waveless water, knowing nothing
Of men before and after. So the shades
Crossed once the final stream. But Gentry faced
Straight downward, shores forgotten.
This was the flowing earth he came to find,
This earth with no men on it; or if men,
They kept an equal pace and a sweet distance:
All going smoothly down against the sun.
The twenty-two companions of the voyage—
He smiled at them indulgently; and smiled
With the same eyes upon the patient pigs,
The heifers, and the ewes. All riding down,
All keeping a dumb distance; though they stared
And whispered who he was; and some of the children
Mimicked his stately walk, with hands behind them.

So thirteen days and nights, and the rough hills
Grew gentler, and the willows
Waved at the edge of meadows whose deep grass
Was walked on by a wind of falling flowers.
Some days the mountains sharpened, and the shadows
Stood with an awful stiffness.
Then the mild slopes again, and opening sky.
Once, where the river widened,

Suddenly dogs barked; cabins smoked in a clearing,
And children in a low line by the shore
Stretched like a fringe of weeds, and would have hailed them;
But nothing could be heard beyond small cries
And piping little laughter, that the ring
Of axes in the forest and deep bells
Of happy-throated dogs, and idle screams
Of jays and red-birds mingled with and lost.
More settlements; and Gentry,
Straining his eyes and ears, would have beheld
Joy on the new-born faces, and heard songs
Never before let loose from mouths of men.
But still it was too far; so he was left
To his own shining thoughts, and to the river;
While on the shore young men and women lounged,
Envying him that floated like the summer—
Suspended a long season out of time—
Envying him the soft air and the clear,
Unchanging gentle current, south and south.
Storms came; windy rain beat up the water,
And thunder from the hills
Dropped down as if to break them, boat and all.
But sun came always after, and he said
This only was to prove the land was old;
Longer ago than men it had a voice—
And used it now, remembering. If a gorge
Threatened them in the night, and rapids roared,
And the tired boatmen cursed like evil birds,
Gentry in the morning smiled and found
The smooth way only smoother, south and west.
And now the days were longer, and the trees
Taller along the shore, and thicklier hung
With vines and ranging moss; and now the river,
Rounding the great slow bend, went west and west.
But Gentry now was done with his own thoughts,
That, living too long inward, drooped a little,
Dying unless he spoke.

The preacher with the brown beard, praying loudly,
Ceased, and sending his circle of children off,
Turned a big face toward Gentry: "Brother in trouble,
Brother in mortal need of the touch immortal,

What of our days ahead? What night has cast them
Into your face's shadow, that no smile
Lightens, and no morning may expel?
Tell me; for your silence is a load
Like sin upon us all, and thwarts us all."
Gentry, as if awakened out of years
Of stiff and standing sleep—startled a little—
Frowned; but when he thought of the humming woodsman,
And thought of the pair of men that even now
Smoked at the other rail and hung white hands
With rings upon them over the roughened wood,
Smiled:
"Brother? But not in trouble are we brothers.
What burden could bear these down?"—watching the rail—
"What night? And what of the fiddle? We move in song.
The days ahead are waiting, and their brows
Are bland with perfect ignorance of our past.
Sadness is forgotten here; we bring
No seed of it to sow in any meadow."
But the small eyes in that big face looked shrewdly,
And the brown-bearded mouth said "Nevertheless
Something is sore inside you, something is hard,
Moveless and smooth like stone." So Gentry thought:
"He can be told"; and told of the man and woman
Lost in a London moment; but concluded:
"All of it left me lightly when I landed;
Nothing remains of them I have forgiven—"
"Forgiven!" the preacher groaned, and bit his beard
In anger at a word so mildly made;
"Forgiven! You were not just to end it so.
Evil sometimes is monstrous, and calls out
For monstrous good to take it by the throat.
You should have stayed and salted with your wrath
Such love-wounds, such red flowing mouths of hell!"
Gentry, in mingled shock and pale dismay,
Knew that the others heard, and turned to see
Wry, empty grins twist over the rail and down.
The two men there bowed promptly, and one said:
"Now that you know we listened, let us argue
Half of the sermon sound. You might have stayed;
But not to do as much as one weak deed.

You could have stayed and lived. It didn't matter.
Nothing was new in that. Nothing is new
In anything men can manage; and this world
We poke through now is no calves' pasture either.
Isn't it so, musician?" For the fiddler,
Mending his bow, had wandered along to hear.
He kept a kindly eye on Jonathan Gentry—
Standing in sudden trance—and picked his strings
Mock-soberly a while before he sang:

> Over the mountains, boys,
> What came you for to find?
> Look ahead and see, boys,
> And never look behind.
>> Bend and go,
>> Then stop and stay
>> And get you ready
>> For the Judgment Day.

> Over the mountains, boys,
> You'll work as hard as ever;
> Except the very lazy;
> Also the very clever.
>> Bend and go,
>> Then stop and stay
>> And get you ready
>> For the Judgment Day.

> Over the mountains, boys,
> We're starting in again;
> And what eternal pity
> We're doing it with men.
>> Bend and go,
>> Then stop and stay
>> And get you ready
>> For the Judgment Day.

> Over the mountains, boys,
> What came you for to find?
> It soon will be the same, boys,
> As though you looked behind.

105

Bend and go,
Then stop and stay
And get you ready
For the Judgment Day.

The mountains fell away, and now the full unconscious river
Slowlier moved west, or idly slid along the south.
The bottoms opened farther, and little rounded hills
Divided where a northern stream washed a muddy mouth;
But over warm forests, beyond the mingled waters,
Turkey-buzzards floated in circles from the south.

Watching them tilt and spiral, Gentry said:
"These are the birds I dreamed of, yet their slow wings
Mock me, as if to say I knew too much,
Dreaming of Eden then, and know too little,
Dreaming of Eden now. Slow birds,
Wind-sleepers,
Writers of lazy lines upon the sky,
You taunt me with your aimlessness, you tell me
Not to inquire the meaning in an up-sloped invisible wing-stroke,
Not to demand the purpose of a plume.
Therefore you high drones,
You lofty, tongueless inlanders
Cutting a higher circle as I talk,
I ask you nothing more, but only ask
Of men henceforth, and women. They must answer."

So day by day, the still shores drifting past,
Off to the north and south, and the great sycamores
Sunning themselves in patches where no shade
Darkened their silver sides, and turkey-buzzards
Counting the indolent hours and losing the count,
They told him, one by one, wherefore they stood there
Riding upon his river.

The pale-nosed pair behind their long cigars
Grew solemn now in praise of bottom soil.
They came to see their hundred thousand acres,
Bought with a piece of paper months ago,
And take its virgin measure. Was he buying?
A bargain there. They talked of the Muskingum,

106

Scioto, and Miami beds of salt,
Of iron that could be floated on these waters
Down to the mouths of coal mines, and of mica
Glittering underground for picks to take.
They talked, and Gentry listened; yet his thoughts
Turned even while they talked upon the preacher:
Perhaps he had a reason one could hear.

But all he got was thunder from the beard—
Broom of the Lord, that went to sweep the west
And cleanse it for the righteous feet to come.
No dance, if this could help it, of bright heels
Of change across those meadows; no loose growth
Of loveliness unpruned, and innocent vine.
This son of wrath was marching with a face
Furious against old sin, and bound to find it
Planted upon the prairies with the spring;
But stamping would destroy it, and strong hands
Would follow, sowing winters of old faith.
He saw a country filled with stiffened feet
That trampled flowers in rhythm with cold bells
Ringing beyond the mountains through all time.

No hope in him, said Gentry; or in these—
The couple from New England passing by
Almost without a question. Yet he asked it,
And once again was quieted with a stare
Half timid and half proud, as now the husband
Bragged of the hard days gone and of the new ones
Flowing ahead like honey, in whose hive
A boy might feed, and not a father fail;
While Gentry thought of little burrowing beasts—
Two marmots and their young one—nosing westward
Into a thicker pasture they had smelled.

The woodsman, taken last, was short of words.
He only came to try the river once
And see what kind of people floated on it.
Somewhere along Kentucky he would change
And work his way upstream again by fall.
The fall was when he got his little living
In Pennsylvania woods with trap and powder.

No house had ever held him. "But the pig?"
He took it for an old friend who was married
And lived on part of an island farther down.
He said he chiefly came to see the river.
He knew the songs but hadn't heard them sung
On water. What he wanted was the water,
With people going on it mad as mice.
And he would tell them so, and scare them home,
If he were some one better than a fiddler.
The fiddle fooled them all; the cat was belled.
"But you," he said to Gentry, "I can talk with.
You are the maddest of them all. You look
For something that was never in the world.
It wasn't where you lived and you grew thoughtful.
It won't be where you will live either, Mister.
Not that I mind such madness. Do you see?
I like it. I am only walking, talking;
Waiting till you say your say yourself."
He winked, and Gentry let him pull the others
Round them in a ring, as if to hear
A peddler, or a hatless politician.
So when they all were there, Gentry began
Half talking to himself; yet half to them.

The sun was soon to set upon the full, unconscious river;
It came along the water now, wide and ripple-red.
The long, low shore lines sagged with the silence;
Not a bird sounded, settling into bed;
Not a wave went there, so steadily they drifted
Down the middle water, cool and straight ahead.
A dozen people standing, small in the twilight.
This the final river? These the waiting dead?

"Sleep-walkers,
River-mates,
Ohio-blinded, groping two by two
For ever and ever onward, westward, penned in a careful ark;
Mountain-swarmers,
Valley-finders,
Drift-logs and meadow-men with pollen in your eyes;
We are the shades of an old race;
These are the final ferries down the dark stream

That may flow into morning; and may only
Deeper and deeper drop into the night.
Creatures crated together
And floating out of an old time;
Remnants,
Dream-passengers,
We go perhaps unto the death of deaths.
You—and you—and you—have spoken easily
Of a new life, a clear day
Dawning this side the mountains, a flowered field
Waiting for men to walk it and be dusted
Angel-wise with powder of pure gold.
But you I tell—and you—that time is old;
Time withers even now upon its stalk,
Waiting with us the planted end,
Leaning to watch us die. And we shall die,
Raft-riders,
Ark-fugitives,
Unless we fall like rain upon the dry,
Wide harvest of burnt death that spreads and spreads,
Licking the borders of this valley now.
Chosen people,
Noah's men,
What use to bring the old world on our backs,
What beauty in baggage here?
When the dove flew,
And the rainbow rested high on the steaming hills,
What gain from an Ark that opened and let forth
Stale fools,
Fortunate knaves:
Creatures the same as ever creatures were?
When the crow flies,
And the shores draw near to receive us, lords of the land,
What good if we step not forth new men,
New minds in the cool of a day untouched of time?
The American meadows wait,
But not for us if we come there
Unchanged, unbright, and unanointed.
They were not made, I hear them cry,
To be another width of waste: the weary edge of a tramped range
Already weary and too wide.

And so they wait for us to choose,
And multiply, and plant the choice
Within a million minds to come, and some day reap—
Some day reap death?
Who now says death?
Who now has the worm in his heart, who dares
Step forth and carry contagion?
Who knows?
I knew my grief, then stumbling here
Knew my great hope; and have it still.
Who now has more?
Who now sees harvests ahead of men not hollow, not stuffed
    white husks, not snake-skins left on a rock, not moth-shells,
    fragile as amber, found on trees?
Who knows, and says to go on?
Who feels? Who sees?"

No answer; but the sun upon the full, unconscious river
Spread a sudden purple; then the empty west.
The people moved away now as dumbly toward the cabin
As sheep before a shepherd, driven into rest.

Not a whisper told him, tall by the low bow,
What his mind desired; nor could he hope to hear.
All he had was silence, slipping up the river,
All he had was night, lapping from the rear.

All the silent night had, and the endless river,
Was something small and dark there that floated like a leaf;
And others coming after it; but not a sign to say now
Whither they were drifting, or whether into grief.

Not a whisper told the sky whether green or brown,
Whether these were spring-drift or offal of the fall.
Only up from one of them, hidden down the dark stream,
Rose a tiny wailing, drowsy over all.

It rose upon the soft tide of stillness flowing by,
Came a little way along, and then as quickly ceased.
This is what it said against the night above the river;
This is what it sang before it died beneath the east:

Over the mountains, boys,
Come long lonesome way.
Morrow morning, boys,
Be a different day.
   Go sleep now
   And shut your eyes;
   Let whatever
   Got to rise.

Over the mountains, boys,
Don't know where to go.
Morrow morning, boys,
Some us bound to know.
   Go sleep now
   And shut your eyes;
   Let whatever
   Got to rise.

Over the mountains, boys,
Can't see far ahead.
Morrow morning, boys,
Maybe dark and dead.
   Go sleep now
   And shut your eyes;
   Let whatever
   Got to rise.

Over the mountains, boys,
End old river road.
Morrow morning, boys,
Lift a different load.
   Go sleep now
   And shut your eyes;
   Let whatever
   Got to rise.

I I

CIVIL WAR

The sun upon two generations falling
Fell on the bones of Gentry, in a grave
No wider for their being prophet's bones,
No longer for the length inside the eyes.
The ark had paused; the waters had gone on;
Gentry, moving northward over land,
Had found the flowery prairies in the spring;
And forty flowery springs, with forty winters,
Had made him an old man whose prairie children
Forgot him in a grave that was too small
To hold so large a hope, however silent.
Silence was all he had between himself
And seven sons who loved the present time,
And, laboring the green ground, had other sons
Who loved another present.
                  Yet in one
Was something like a memory remaining
After the mind had closed, some nerve surviving
Out of a body otherwise put by.
Jonathan Gentry Third had eyes within him,
And a slow tongue, deep rooted in the heart,
That grew not out but up, and wrapped the brain.

Jonathan Gentry Third this winter morning
Waited upon no dawn, but in the stillness
Climbed the dark stairs and found his brother, and shook him.
"Charlie, it's time."
The boy in the cold bed laughed. "I heard you coming;
I knew by the army shoes, the iron slippers.
Anyone else up yet?"
"No, and you mustn't wake them. Come to the barn.
I'll have the horses ready. And be fast.
They say the train won't wait a half a minute;
They'll call the roll and miss us, and go on."

Powdery snow had drifted in the night
Like sand against the door, that opened groaning—
Opened and suddenly shut with a windy shriek.
The harnessed horses, nosing the warm hay,
Lifted a pair of faces to the lantern
And blinked as if they knew the narrower face—
Big in a mist of breath now, but they knew it—
The dark-eyed face that came along and spoke:
"Yes, Prince, yes, Billy,
Time for us to go;
Time for two to go;
Time for team of horses now to take a team of men;
Take a man and boy—Charlie—put 'em on the train;
Time for them to leave you home and ride so far away
There won't be any horses there as good as you, as you—"
He stroked the pair of noses as he talked,
Then dropped his hand again; and dropped his voice:
"Star face,
Bald face,
Gentle and sideward eyes, and coats furry with cold,
Warm necks and shoulder-skin, and belly and tender flank,
Warm hearts, pounding on, pounding on, pounding on,
Prince Boy, and Dappled Billy,
Wait for us and keep the farm,
Keep it well and warm for us, and keep yourselves, and wait."
Holding their heads as if they had not heard,
They let themselves be led to the sleigh; then, starting,
Beat a monotonous music on the shrill,
White ground to where the boy at the opened gate
Stood yawning.

The crusted road before them in the first light
Had lines of black upon it, of old ruts;
But all the way was smooth for them in the robes,
And day came on them merrily as they passed
Two houses set together among barns.
This was the day; and one of the houses knew it,
For out of an upper window a hand fluttered,
The fringy curtains trembled, and a face,
Small in the snowy distance, watched them go;
And watched an arm of Jonathan wave slowly.

Charlie looked straight forward, playing his white breath
Smokily into the wind; but soon he stopped that.
"What did she have to say last night especially?
Anything fit to tell?" He grinned, and Jonathan
Tried to be careless too as he answered "No."
"Didn't she even send me her goodbye?"
"Yes; she said to take good care of Charlie.
But now be still and drive awhile, or talk—
Well, if you have to talk, begin with the war."
"I would, if I knew anything about it.
You are the politician—you begin."
But Jonathan said nothing, and the miles
Slid quietly beneath them on to town.

The engine had grown quiet with its waiting;
Out of the clumsy funnel, like a flower,
A curl of smoke was held beyond escaping,
And hung with all the people on the hour.

The Nineteenth Illinois was soon to waver
Down the unfinished track ahead and south;
But now the captain put aside his saber,
And many a girl was giving him her mouth,

And many a girl was weeping at a window,
And many a soldier's face within was red;
The little town boys kept their arms akimbo
And marched; or stiffly tumbled, playing dead.

There was an ancient woman who had squinted
All morning up and down, and counted caps.
And there were Prince and Billy, nearly winded,
Waiting another driver, gone for wraps.

Jonathan and Charlie stood together
Inside the foremost window of the train;
One beheld the horses at the tether,
But one beheld the boys, and laughed again,

And laughed to see the hats, so high and silky,
That moved upon the heads of solemn men.
"Our engine is a man," he said, "or will be,
And one of these can make the funnel then."

114

The engine bell rang suddenly;
Steam was roaring somewhere up ahead;
Over the dead-white field beyond the depot
Went the brown shadow of smoke.
There were commands, a settling into place;
The town increased its voice, and women crying
Ran with the started coaches; then the whistle,
Smothering voice and bell; and then a silence.
The silence was of watching eyes, and lasted
Only as long as glances go unseen.
But when the people turned upon each other,
Quietness all at once again—and the singing,
Down the long track,
Of soldiers:

> The girls we left at home, sir,
> Are very warm and kind;
> There won't be any smile ahead
> To match the tear behind;
> But John Brown's eyes, sir,
> Are lying cold and blind,
>   And we must stay
>   Until they see
>   Old America
>   Stand free.

> The land that we have left, sir,
> Is where content was born;
> There won't be on a southern field
> Such green and yellow corn;
> But John Brown's eyes, sir,
> Lie fallow and forlorn,
>   And we must stay
>   Until they see
>   Old America
>   Stand free.

> All of us that go, sir,
> Want to come back together;
> There won't be any rebel camp
> With fellows of our feather;

115

But John Brown's eyes, sir,
Are lonely in this weather,
    And we must stay
    Until they see
    Old America
    Stand free.

Should a brother fall, sir,
And not come home again,
There won't be any rebel ear
To hear complaining then.
John Brown's eyes, sir,
Look out of dying men,
    And we must stay
    Until they see
    Old America
    Stand free.

The train went on, the wooden coaches creaking
Endlessly past the farms that lay in the white day
Scattered beyond all gathering; save for a village
That huddled along the tracks, then opened again,
Losing itself in a blank no mind could measure.
Inside the soldiers, finishing their song,
Fell to a round of talk, and some of them tramped
So merrily up the aisle beside the brothers,
Charlie could sit no longer, and he joined them.
Jonathan followed his voice awhile, then lost it,
Mingled among a dozen not so clear.
Jonathan sat alone. He too would join them—
Soon he would be there, saying a hundred hellos—
But now he sat alone by the pictured window,
Letting the whiteness whirl inside his eyes
Until there came a death of sound and color.
Only the white was there for color, and only
The click of the frozen rails for sound; and only
Jonathan in the world to see and hear.
Click, click, clickety click, clickety clickety clickety click,
Click, click, click, click, clickety clickety click;
Prince, Prince, Billy and Prince, Agatha, Agatha, Agatha Rowe,

Barn, road, bin, tree, Charlie O Charlie come home;
Agatha, Charlie, Billy and Prince, timothy, timothy, timothy tops,
Spring, summer, winter, fall, Jonathan, Jonathan Gentry;
Agatha, Agatha waving her hand, goodbye goodbye goodbye in the
    night,
March, April, May, June, and summery summery corn;
Three things, a triple of things, I had and I haven't, I had and I
    haven't,
Agatha, Agatha, home, and Charlie—but there'll be Charlie, I still
    have Charlie;
Charles, Charles Gentry and brother, answer to roll call, Gentry
    and brother,
Where is the boy his brother would keep? Under the cotton fast
    asleep;
No one to wake him? Yes, I can wake him, shake him, wake him,
    take the boy home,
Home, home, by Agatha's window, Agatha come right down;
Spring, summer, winter, fall, Charlie and Jonathan Gentry;
Click, click, clickety click, clickety clickety clickety click,
Click, click, click, click, clickety clickety click.

"Twenty-five miles already," Charlie informed him,
Coming back suddenly now with a green cigar.
"What do you look for? Nothing to see out there.
Summer's the time to see."
                      "I wasn't looking."
"Well, winter's the time for thinking. Was that it?
Jon, you're the politician; you begin
And tell me what the war so far's about.
That song—is that the reason we are going?
Four hundred thousand fighting for a blind man?"
"The war's about as many things, my boy,
As there are men to think of it, and women.
There are as many wars as there are leaves
On trees, and who can say what leaves are for,
Or which of all that hang there is the true leaf?
John Brown hangs there, and many that are marching
Go beneath a corpselight, with madness in their eyes.
I think the war is not about a man, though,
And least of all about another man
They hope to hang in a sour apple tree—
The sooner then the better; yet his breath

Would sweeten it, and half of us would cry.
I think it isn't either about black heads
That bend all day in the cotton, and come home
To pitiful beds, and bleed from a dirty blow.
The war is about ourselves, and who we are
Depends on what we love, or cannot love.
Harry Camargo couldn't stand his wife,
And so he went the first month, and he marches
With a charmed life and shines among the faithful:
Happy because it's treason to come home.
And there was Ira Benjamin; his law books
Leaned a little crazier every day;
He went and is an officer, and hopes
Jeff Davis won't be caught for ten more years.
Some of the boys here go because the going
Is wonderful in itself, for they have heard
Songs sung, and light was bright along a barrel.
The war is about ourselves: you, Charlie, and me.
We go because we love the land we live on;
Somehow or why—I mean to find out how
Down there in the other land, the bitter country—
It's threatened, the way we live, the first idea.
The man that I was named for—not our father—
Came west with some new country in his mind.
And so it is with us who never saw him;
The way we live, loving the quiet land,
Each place a gentle kingdom, yes, a fourfold
Eternity of square seasons—that's the way
He lived it in his mind; and since we have it,
We have to keep it, Charlie, whole and sound.
Something has made it sick, and it could die,
And will die if we lose. But we'll not lose.
Every man a year from now will enter
His kingdom, north or south, and sit with wisdom
Safely upon the center of a world
Where kingdoms are as many as the men
To rule them and be wise in the slow way
Good farmers from the end of time were wise.
It is the world of farmers that will win:
Good farmers, slow and wise to the end of time.
The war is about ourselves, Charlie, ourselves."

"It may be so for you," said Charlie, waiting
More than his usual moment for the words;
"But not for me. You want to know my reason?
Only that you were going, and I couldn't—
I couldn't—Jon, do you want a cigar like this?"
They rose and found the fat boy with the tray,
And puffed among the others, or walked back
To feel the swaying platform, and to count
The curves that now came oftener; for hills,
Snowy and small, began around them here.
They said they knew the train was getting south.

They knew it even better when the sheds
Of workmen gone for winter slept in snow,
And piles of ties, with rusting tall machines,
Waited upon the season. Here the rails
Ended, and here the ending afternoon
Was darkened by low orders to fall in.
Down a grey road they marched, the column stumbling
Over uprooted lumps of ice and mud;
Down a long way they went, with not a sign now
Of people in any world; and some of them said
They soon would reach the river, the Ohio.
But just before the full of darkness fell,
Barns loomed like little mountains on the right;
Sheep bawled, and lantern light across the snow
Showed a wide doorway opening into rest.
They climbed the ladders laughing, and found hay
Like feathers underfoot—or so they said
Who but the night before in papered rooms
With curtains and washed covers had lain down—
And laughed again, and rolled their blankets round them.
There was some talk and tumble, but it ceased,
And night took up its watch under the rafters.
It waited above the rafters, too, and farther
Beyond than any could know; but here, unheard,
Invisible in sweet darkness, lay the hundred.
Jonathan, trying to think and keep awake,
Thought of the boy beside him—a small heap,
Rounded under the darkness, of wrapped flesh,
And bone, and the inaudible circling blood—

And thought, or tried to think, of three good things
The click of the rails had told him still were good:
Charlie and home, and Agatha, Agatha Rowe;
But could no more than name them, one two three,
One two three, like children in a game.
One two three. But these were older things,
As old as all the world. So one two three
And one two three, till night grew tired of numbers.

Jonathan Gentry, with a country heart
Waiting in three warm places for a wound;
Jonathan Gentry crossed, and told the Ohio:
"Your water is cold and yellow with thick anger,
What you are dreaming stiffly here is death;
You move, and the banks beside you,
Standing, groan as of iron;
You move, and the chains along you
Rattle;
I hear them rattle who heard them singing—
Not I, but the first-come Gentry, heard them softly
Rustle with spring, and singing,
Tell of young time before men came with their measure
And counted the years; dividing summer and winter;
Dividing the north, the south.
Cold river, angry and yellow water,
We cross you here with iron inside our eyes;
Winter is on us too, and on the land,
Bitter and black, behind us and before.
Changed river,
Threatened world,
We march upon salt dust and poisoned clods,
Through woods that wave and hiss upon us, passing.
Ohio water,
Altered with aging time, he floated on you
Otherwise, in sweet spring, in childish peace.
And peace will be:
But peace grown into manhood, and returning
All of us here safe home that should come home.
Again there will be void without division;
But not a void of men, who will increase,

120

Each one upon his kingdom, in the center
Of seasons—four strong horses—
And of love, the deathless grass."

The barge that bore them, sidling into place,
Touched earth a little eastward of a town
Whose children, black and white, came out to watch them:
The dark ones standing backward of the rest,
Haltingly up a hill, but all grown silent;
Though soon they chattered loudly in the cold
As first the column formed and then departed
Down the old eastern road. The chatter, rising,
Followed upon the wintry air a way,
Then met the soldiers' singing; and died there.

> Over the river, boys,
> Come now and take a stand;
> Over the river, boys,
> In the strange land.
> > Hayfoot, strawfoot,
> > Tramp right through
> > And make one country
> > Out of two.
>
> Over the river, boys,
> Plenty of southern mud,
> Mixed already, boys,
> With northern blood.
> > Hayfoot, strawfoot,
> > Tramp right through
> > And make one country
> > Out of two.
>
> Over the river, boys,
> Buzzard, looking down,
> Can't make up his mind
> If that's John Brown.
> > Hayfoot, strawfoot,
> > Tramp right through
> > And make one country
> > Out of two.

Over the river, boys,
John Brown sure enough,
Playing with a buzzard,
Blind man's buff.
    Hayfoot, strawfoot,
    Tramp right through
    And make one country
    Out of two.

Over the river, boys,
Into the strangers' land.
We call them kin, but they
Misunderstand.
    Hayfoot, strawfoot,
    Tramp right through
    And make one country
    Out of two.

Over the river, boys,
Wait and hear them yell.
But there's enough blue heaven
To hold all hell.
    Hayfoot, strawfoot,
    Tramp right through
    And make one country
    Out of two.

On they went and left behind the cold, unconscious river.
On they went, and turned, and swung around a little hill.
The children watched the last man; then into their houses;
And now the flowing river worked its old unseeing will.

It flowed as it would always flow, without a thought of rivers
Sliding from the south to make it wider as it went.
It never saw the hidden country past the little mountain
That took the hundred in now, closing like a tent.

The river never knew of any valley, east or south,
Wherein a wintry wilderness of tents and greying men
Waited round a nightly fire, waited for the spring;
The river never sent a sigh for what would happen then.

No one standing here beside the cold, unconscious river,
No one could have seen the hidden country of the war.
But many a hill was posted there, and soon the time was coming,
The green and bleeding season death had lingered for.

On beyond the little hills Kentucky, Tennessee,
Cumberland, and Shenandoah nestled in their names:
Dark and ancient syllables, lords of an old language,
Lords of an old fire that long ago put out its flames.

They flickered in deep caverns now, perhaps as old as time,
But only rock was there to see, and cold and sleeping trees,
And meadows up from winding streams descended from the hills;
Meadows, and the campfires smoking over these.

It only was a little while that such a light would live;
A day would come again of darkened slopes and the cool grass,
With peace upon the mountain-heads, and silence in the plains.
But here a party tramped to reconnoiter up a pass,

A file of teams was plodding there, and on the farthest pike
Guns glistened in the mud; a messenger rode forth;
He met another messenger; the bayonets stood still;
Then slowly on again, these newest comers from the north.

Slowly down the valley there to make another camp,
Light another square of fires, and wait upon the spring.
Winter wasted slowly now, but rain was in the air,
And birds; and thoughts, set upon a fearful thing.

In April, in Virginia, when the rain
Came softly, with a coolness like the breath
Of new-born haze upon the mountain-heads,
And mud was round the tents, and sentries coughed
Like sheep in a wet wood; on April evenings,
Charlie being gone three tents away—
The boy was restless, and the candles soothed him,
Dripping upon the blanket and the cards,
Shining upon the foreheads of new friends—
On April evenings Jonathan stayed in,
Reading a letter. He would light his torch,
Unfold the fingered sheets, and lose the world
In lines he knew already; but he read them.

123

He read them for the way they had of making
Daytime out of nighttime, and of turning
Half of the tent wall back: the northern wall,
Towards Agatha, towards home, the only home.

"Dear Jon:
I just saw Prince and Billy going by.
You wouldn't know them, they're so fine and fat.
The boy from town's too good to them almost.
You wouldn't say so, though. Too good to babies!
Half past ten, and I should think of dinner—
Jon, what do you and Charlie eat I wonder—
But now I won't awhile. Well, yesterday.
Your father and my father walked and talked
Between here and the barn, and it was you—
I didn't see your father, I saw you.
And yet it wasn't you, for you are different—
More, being mine, and less too, being younger.
Then afterwards I thought I saw us two there,
A tiny girl and boy, held by the hand
Between them, and I had the oddest feeling,
As if we two were only parts of them.
And yet it's only you I am a part of.
I know it now so well. And so I guess
I felt that way because it was your father—
My father and your father. I was excited;
I had that happy heavy feeling here—
You can't see where, and wouldn't know—but, Jon,
All this is one more way to say I love you.
I love you, and I love you, and I ride
Quite often past your place. It's just the same—
House, barn, and little barn, and the wide walls
Of hedge around the fields—so cold and brown,
But the first thaw has softened them, and soon
I'll write of greenness everywhere, and wind
Like feathers, and the little building birds.
I went in once. Your mother let me read
What you and Charlie wrote her from Virginia.
She lives on letters, Jon, and so do I,
Though when they come I have to stop pretending
You're just a mile away from me, at home.
I do that all the time. I love you, Jon."

124

He read it every night, till others came—
Three of them tied together with brown string
And dropped somewhere in the mud, but he could read them—
And then he bound them all in a thin bundle,
Just thick enough to feel inside his coat,
And read them when he could. He even read them,
Hastily, for one nervous noisy hour,
The night the army moved; and Charlie laughed.
But it was frightened laughter.
                            Fierce commands,
Though spoken low, as if death walked and cursed them
Out of the corners of a whiskered mouth;
Commands that ran along, low on the ground
Like lightning laid on hills; the breathing of men
In fear, yet more in hurry, the father of fear;
And horses splashing by; and rifles clicking—
These cracked the tune of his mirth, these left him silent;
So when he spoke at last the words were husky.
"Well, Jon, we're off."
                        "All right, but we're together."
Both voices had a strangeness as they started.
Both big and little boy, the brothers Gentry,
Moved as the dark line moved, against the morning.
No singing now; but day in another valley,
Brightness under another noon, and rest,
And rumors that the war was farther away
Than ever—would it be there when they got there?—
And cooling water lifted out of wells
Behind the shuttered houses: then was song,
With Jonathan to join it, for he found
New lightness in his feet now, and he sang.

> Another damnation day, boys,
> Another damnation night,
> And maybe we don't come up, boys,
> And maybe we dassn't fight!
> Never you worry, Johnny Reb;
> Take a long breath and hold it tight.
>   Yankee Doodle went down south
>   To get him a stick of candy;
>   He stuck it in his Sunday mouth
>   And came home Doodle Dandy.

Another damnation ridge, boys,
And then the enemy's there.
Another damnation slide, boys,
Out of this mountain air.
Never you worry, Johnny Reb;
Look up and let us part your hair.
    Yankee Doodle went down south
    To get him a stick of candy;
    He stuck it in his Sunday mouth
    And came home Doodle Dandy.

Another damnation song, boys,
And then forever quiet.
Another damnation rumpus, boys,
Before the biggest riot.
Never you worry, Johnny Reb,
We got a tune, and you're to try it.
    Yankee Doodle went down south
    To get him a stick of candy;
    He stuck it in his Sunday mouth
    And came home Doodle Dandy.

Another damnation inch, boys,
And see them give a mile.
Another damnation hour, boys—
Eternity then awhile.
Never you worry, Johnny Reb;
Old John Brown'll rise and smile.
    Yankee Doodle went down south
    To get him a stick of candy;
    He stuck it in his Sunday mouth
    And came home Doodle Dandy.

A pair of peaceful mornings, and a pair
Of afternoons with houses going by,
And Jonathan to watch them, one by one.
They sat so idly there, and the red road
Went on so warm and winding, farm by farm,
That Jonathan half wondered where it was—
The evil, the cold danger. Not in houses;
Not in the budded hedges; and no barn,
Empty of beast and wagon, but looked long

At Jonathan, who looked and turned away.
So on the column tramped, and Charlie's feet
Ground the same dust as Jonathan's, or rested
Quietly by their side on grassy banks
Where honeysuckle gathered; and they talked—
Strange talk, compact of laughter and low fears—
But all the time in silence one was saying:
"The evil, the cold danger,
It isn't in these windows; it isn't in the weary way
These houses lie and look at us, it isn't
In any patient barn.
The country is good country, for I see
Good barns in it. Good barns,
Good boys, we used to say;
Good people all.
Good people, come and listen while I tell you—
Tell what? And who would listen?
And where are all the people gone today?
All fled? All fighting?
The fighting is to come. It will be strange,
Fighting this country of the harmless barns:
Good barns, we said, good boys.
We're in it now, this country, and it lets us
Walk, and talk, and sleep, and wake, and sing.
We're in it, and the fighting hasn't happened.
It's strange, as if a dream
Dragged at my feet and made them very
Drowsy; a very
Dream."

So when it happened he was unprepared,
His mind and heart conversing in the shade
Of his wide-branching nature, murmuring there
While he stood dumbly by, and while the woods
They marched in—not the forest of his thought—
Rang with a sudden shot.
               Then a mad chatter
Of rifles ahead, and a pause, and the guard retreating.
They came where he could see them—a pale huddle
Of running and stumbling things—and now he heard
Commands along the column to deploy.

"Take cover! Corporal—corporal—cover your men!
Cover yourself, you fool!"
                              The battle was on.
Jonathan by a low rock in a gulley,
With three strange men in blue beside him firing,
Tugged at his rifle too, as they had taught him,
And peered beyond the rock, and aimed, and trembled.
But all he saw was new green branches falling,
Leaves cut and floating down, and on the rock
Fresh ferns, the April growth, torn up and dead.
"Where's Charlie now!" The bullets coming over
Said nothing of any Charlie, and he looked
At nothing, left or right, but flying dirt,
And balls of smoke, and spreading legs of men
Who peered like him and fired, and maybe trembled.
"Where's Charlie? Where did they put him? Will he be careful?"
The questions all were useless, but he asked them,
And, asking them, lost count of the hot hours,
That ended now as suddenly as they came.
The woods ahead, no longer smoking trees,
Turned into men who leapt and yelled, advancing—
Advancing now, a grey and angry wave,
Foaming upon them. They could see the eyes,
The long hair and the hats; and they could fire,
And many of those could spin and tumble there;
But now they ceased to fire, and falling back,
Fled, for the day was lost.
                              And more was lost.
Jonathan, remembering as he ran
How when the time for four to leave the rock
Had come and gone—how one of them had stayed there—
Jonathan, remembering his surprise,
Felt nothing now as his exhausted feet
Stumbled on corpses. Some of them were bleeding,
Some of them had no hands, or any eyes;
Some of them lay without a wound to show:
Boys in blue coats, asleep. He counted them,
Unconscious of the counting, till he came
To safety, and the camp, and the tired hundred.
"Where's Charlie!" Asking blindly, he was answered—

"Here, Jon!"—and fell to laughing over-loudly
As now the brothers fumbled for each other,
And found their hands, and wrung them, and sat down:
Both home without a scar, and weak as children.

Time rested then, while day on quiet day
Brought warmer, dustier weather; and brought there,
To Jonathan in his tent, another letter,
With maple leaves laid freshly in the fold.
"They were so green, and made so great a sound
The day I talked beneath them with your mother—
The end-of-May winds tried to blow them down,
At your house and at my house, but they stuck—
They stuck like me to you, if I do say so,
And sassed the wind as I would sass the war—
I would, but I am here and it is there,
Doing I don't know what to you and Charlie.
Some nights I dream I have it where my hands
Can wave it way away, and I can scold it,
And shame it for the thing it wants to do.
Then other nights I can't as much as dream;
I only lie there wondering what it wants,
And hoping it can't have it. All the having
Must be between you, Jonathan, and me.
The roads are dry, but not too dusty yet,
And the big cornfield downward from your house
Is perfect black, with long green lines upon it—
The baby corn. Your boy from town was plowing,
Yesterday when I rode the sorrel by,
And bragged about the stand. He'll keep it clean—
And keeps our Prince and Billy like a pair
Of dudes on Sunday. Do you think of church?
I don't. I think of Jonathan and Charlie,
Two boys that go as one, but they are different.
You are the whole, the rather solemn blackbird,
He is the wing, the red wing, by your side.
Goodbye, and fly away home. I love you, Jon."

He wrapped it with the others, and would read it
In its own turn by night; but once by day—
The morning of the day the dozen died—

He read it. For the twenty had been picked,
The skirmishers to clear the Afton road,
And Jonathan's and Charlie's names were there.
They had an hour till ten, the time of going.
Charlie had whistled, and the red-haired boy
He knew from Indiana had strolled over,
Laughing, as if to lay the ghost of danger
In such a day ahead, and such a duty.
But Jonathan, stone silent when he joined them,
Pressing the under pocket of his coat,
Laughed not at all, though Charlie thought he smiled.
At ten the party left in two divisions,
One for the right-hand fields and one the left.
At twelve they still were plodding, left and right—
Charlie among the woods now, where he walked,
Indian wise, from tree to sheltering tree
And listened for loud noises on the road;
But Jonathan, who led the right division,
Had only open meadows, where he hid,
With seven men behind him, under walls
Of rail and rock, with honeysuckle down them.
At twelve the woods were innocent; but now,
At very noon, with white light everywhere,
And warmth upon the meadows like a room
Wherein old people move and smile and nod,
Jonathan stopped.
        The house and barn ahead
Were empty if the captain had been right;
But if he had been wrong those little windows,
High by the eaves, and staring at them now,
Commanded all this wall and had them covered.
He thought: but then the captain had been right,
Captains are always wiser than we know;
And there was a quick instant when he saw
House, fence, and barn as if they had been his,
Jonathan Gentry's, in another day;
Under a northern noon; as if he crept
Home now with cap and rifle to surprise
His people, who were clasping hands and weeping;
And Agatha was coming on her mare;
And Prince and Billy whinnied.

130

                         Then the sun
Told him. Something shone a dreadful moment
Out of that upper window on the left.
His house—but not his house—was armed against him:
Windows with bright eyes in them, of guns;
Bright hatred pointing down at him from home.
He crouched, and seven crouched, and missed the first
Wide shot. It hissed among the honeysuckle,
Flattening on a stone. But now a volley,
And one two three four skirmishers went down.
Another; then a yell from the sharp woods:
Charlie and they, the twelve good men, were coming.
"Hurry, my boy! For God's sake though be careful."
They came, and three of them fell; and now the fire
Dropped hotter upon the few, with no escaping.
And now the raid was ready.
                         So they charged;
And so the elder Gentry, turning to see
If one too young ran still among the rest,
Staggered and almost fell; but kept on running;
Then staggered again, and slipped into black water
Over his head, and floated among cool caverns
Down from the sun and down, and down, and down.

The stream that brought him back flowed on forever,
Swiftly and very smoothly, up and on,
So swiftly that it sickened him sometimes
And blurred the little picture of the sun
That hung in a square frame, the cavern's end.
Then he would have it bright again—burning
His buried eyes. But now the end was coming.
The current pulled more strongly at the last,
Sweeping him on so swiftly that he fainted
Just as the picture altered, and a window
Hung in its shining place.
                         He opened his eyes
Slowly, in a cabin, to the voice
Of an old man who came to him and said:
"Hello, my boy."
"Hello."
"They left you in July, and this is August.

The war went on and left you—"

"Where is Charlie?"

"Charlie?"

"He's my brother. Was he—too?"

"A dozen altogether. They believed
Thirteen, but here you are. So I was right.
I don't remember such a name as Charlie."

"Maybe he—"

"Yes, let's say so. Now be quiet,
And sleep again."

He slept, and when he woke,
They talked; and many a sultry day they talked
Of how the house was his, the tall old man's,
And how it burned that day, and how the barns
And all the little buildings went but this:
"The mansion of the wronged," he smiled and said.
"Yet I myself had freed them. They were gone.
All of them here were gone but me. I stayed.
It was my house and ground, my little—kingdom."
He looked at Jonathan's eyes, that watched the word
Half fearfully, as if it were a spectre.
"Kingdom. It's your word; the only word
You gave me for a sign that I should like you.
You know I ought to hate you."

"Yes, I know."

"But how can distant kings destroy each other?
There is your kingdom. Here is mine; or was.
They didn't so much as run with the same rain.
Mountains and miles between them, and a river.
You lived on yours, I lived on mine, and only
A war like this could make us any different.
Yet hearing you I know we are not different.
You came for the same reason—fearing me—
That my three sons went—fearing you—and fought.
Each to preserve his kingdom, that was safe
Already. There was never any danger."

"But how could such a war be such a fool?"

"I wonder. Yet it was."

"Then where is Charlie?
Charlie has got to be somewhere alive.
He's got to, for I brought him, and he's guiltless!
Charlie—"

"Now you ought to sleep again.
Be patient. Word comes slow, and in good time
The best of all good words—excepting home—
May come; it might be lame, and have to crawl."

He slept, and mended slowly; till the day
They heard some voices laughing at the door.
They opened it for Corporal Charles Gentry,
Who waved a stripèd sleeve in wide salute,
Then ran as small boys do unto their fathers.
"Sergeant Jonathan Gentry, I believe;
Hero of Afton Road, and"—then the tale
Of how the raid had ended, and of how
This old Virginian stayed against full orders.
"Now, sir, he'll go along if you'll allow him."
No word from the old man; but as they went
He stood, a single pillar of a house
That otherwise was level ashes, watching.

Charlie had brought a letter that began:
"Dear Jon, where are you now and can you hear me?
Not me so much as all these loving locusts,
Loving the trees and letting it be known
As nothing I can whisper lets you know.
They love the going summer, as I love
All going time—it's going, Jon, it's going,
The war is getting older every day.
There never was a war that wouldn't die.
I used to dread the growing old of seasons;
I died a little with them, and I knew
How hard it is to die when every morning
Meets you a little later, like a friend
Deserting you by gradual degrees.
It used to leave me heavy, and it leaves me
Heavy as ever now—but now I love it.
I loved your maples yesterday at noon,
Hung with the full of summer, holding on
For dear life; but there's something dear in death.
I speak of seasons, Jon, and afternoons
Dying of too much time. I love you, Jon."

133

Time dragged a weary foot along the far,
Thin edge of a spent summer, waiting now
On fall, and on another waste of winter.
It was an idle time, but Charlie bragged
Of battles still to be, or grumbled, laughing,
Because so many chosen men decayed
In a slow camp—corn rotting in good fields.
He knew they had been chosen by the fact
That here they were still laughing and alive;
He said they were elected to be missed
By any bullet coming. He was safe.
The sharpest rebel claw had never scratched him.
Jonathan believed him, though he said:
"Be careful, nevertheless; luck isn't a fool."
Jonathan, believing the bright lingo,
Had yet no faith in fortune; luck was lazy,
And tended only a few, and couldn't remember—
Luck certainly couldn't remember who were brothers.
They talked; and winter wandered down the hills,
And days went by uncounted, as if sheep
Should keep on coming after the eyes were closed.
They talked, or Charlie came with noisy friends
And cut the cards for poker, while the blanket
Warmed to the candle light, and spread its brownness
Under the waves of song—the doleful song.

> Four long, long, long,
> Long and weary winter-years.
> Told the war to stop, but thunder
> Deafened him; he never hears.
>   Dig a hole;
>   Make a bed;
>   Nothing now but
>   Night ahead.
>
> Four old, old, old,
> Old and sorry summer times.
> Told the war to weep, but he was
> Busy with the Widow Grimes.
>   Dig a hole;
>   Make a bed;
>   Nothing now but
>   Night ahead.

Four rainy, rainy, rainy,
Rainy, windy equinoxes.
Told the war it's wet, but he was
Yelling in the wood for foxes.
    Dig a hole;
    Make a bed;
    Nothing now but
    Night ahead.

Four long, old, rainy
Roads from here to there and home.
Told the war to pack, but he was
Playing on a paper comb.
    Dig a hole;
    Make a bed;
    Nothing now but
    Night ahead.

Time dragged a frozen foot along the far,
Thin edge of a spent winter, waiting now
On spring; and spring arrived, and letters came
To quicken the slow blood of time and man.
"Dear Jon: There is a newness in the wind;
Old age has died again, the mangy lion,
And where he laid him down a little lamb
Struggles to stand; he will, but now he wobbles,
And his thin knees are colder than he likes.
Nothing is here for him but folded grass
And black and broken weeds, but he is breathing
Sweetly against the ground, and grass will rise
Like rain to taste the sweetness and be tasted.
I know it, for my appetite is fed
On hope, that still is small, and hardly green;
But I can feel it growing, and I know
Why grass comes—it is wanted by the wind,
To taste of it, and in good time be tasted.
There is no need to tell you what I hope for.
Maybe it wouldn't come so quickly then.
You guess, and Charlie guess. I love you, Jon,
And you must let me see you soon, and soon."

In middle spring,
With battles all around them, but they held
A quiet hill, they waited;
In middle spring, one morning with the round,
Warm, life-bestowing sun
Their battle came:
Faintly at first,
Like horns of early hunters, moving trees
To frosty music, melancholy mirth;
Then louder, and less musical; and now
Full cry upon them, ranged along a wall
Midway within a forest down the slope.
Midway it struck them, and confounded most
Cool Jonathan, who listened and remembered
Nothing but one old man; and looked along
For no one now but Charlie in the line.
He found him with his eyes, and smiled; but turned
Full face to meet the monster, loose at last.
There was to be an end of it, and soon;
But while it breathed, the many-headed beast,
Its breath was to be hotter, and its reach
Longer, and the murder of its claws
More awful than the oldest there remembered.
Backward awhile the battle moved, and fell
On earthworks farther up the bleeding mountain;
Backward again, until on top they panted,
Firing like blind men—and so Jonathan,
Whose eyes were fixed on nothing as he fired,
Lost now from every soldier he had walked with,
Or talked with in a tent—through all that smoke,
And noise of ripping branches, and burst shells,
No Charlie to be seen. Then forward, slowly,
Down the wrecked hill they reeled; then swiftly, swiftly,
Howling in shrill pursuit; until the woods
Cleared, and the thing was over, and he heard
Wailing, as if the monster, deadly wounded,
Lay in the forest somewhere, lifting its heads
One after another, bloody, and spent, and blind.
The monster—but he paused.
The monster! His exhausted mind
Came back, and he could see; and he could hear

Men, crying men, bestrewn like colored birds,
Tumbling after a volley, brought to ground,
Wingless and still, or pitifully moving.
Men everywhere, and some without a sound.
Men everywhere—and where was Charlie Gentry?
Somewhere safe, he said; it was to be.
But when the searchers passed him he went with them,
And looked a long hour, and looked, and looked:
And found,
There in the middle morning, in a forest,
In spring, beneath a white,
High sun that warmed his back as he stooped over,
Death in a smiling boy—
Smiling right up and up toward nothing at all—
Death in a guiltless boy.

He lay as he had lain so long ago
That Jonathan remembered through a mist:
How the sun loved him, and he seemed to know,
And laughed at lady-bugs along his wrist;

And slept; and how the April afternoon
Went slowly over both of them at rest;
How Jonathan stood up, and how the tune
Of blackbirds took them hunting for a nest.

> Where is the boy that looks after the sheep?
> Under the oak leaves, fast asleep.
> Will you disturb him? No, not I.
> If he laughed now, I'd surely die.

He lay as he had lain another day,
In winter, on a rug before the fire,
Warming himself and watching the slow way
Heat crept along a poker of old wire;

And slept; and it grew dark around the floor,
And cold, except where Charlie stretched his hand.
Then Jonathan came calling at the door,
And Charlie jumped, and answered the command.

137

Little Boy Blue, his brother's lamb,
Had thoughts as white as snow,
And everywhere the brother went
The lamb was sure to go.

He followed him to war one day,
Which was against the rule.
There never went a whiter lamb
Beside a blacker fool.

They laid him under many leaves, and one uplifted rock;
They laid him in a peaceful place, and walked to war again.
But now the war was over; everywhere a stillness now
Answered to the other stillness, buried with the men.

It was the very end of it, the dark years were done—
Four of them, to count the bitter corners of the land:
One for north and south, and one for east, and one for west;
Four of them as one now, the fingers of a hand.

Four of them as one, yet there was anger in the grasp,
As if the hand would hurt itself, crying with new pain.
But Jonathan was going home, indifferent to the end
Of any life but one now, lying through the rain.

Jonathan had wandered north and west between the hills;
Jonathan had watched the wide unconscious river flow;
Jonathan had crossed and wondered what a man had said,
The other Gentry, floating there, years and years ago.

Jonathan said nothing to himself or to the river;
Jonathan said nothing to the train that took him back.
The soldiers going home with him had noisy, pleasant voices.
He liked them, but he leaned and only listened to the track:

Click, click, clickety click, clickety clickety click, click.
He listened, and it told him of a bullet singing true.
Click, click, click, click, clickety clickety click—
Click, and one was coming home instead of two, of two.

Click, click, clickety click, clickety clickety click, click.
Three good things, and one was gone, and two good things re-
    mained.
Click, click, click, click, clickety clickety click, click.
Two; but he could only see the one, the bloody-stained.

Click, click, clickety click, clickety clickety click, click.
He listened, and it told him of a bullet singing—here.
Click, click, click, click, clickety clickety click—
Click; but it had never come, and Agatha was near.

Click, click, clickety click, clickety clickety click, click.
Home and waiting Agatha; he wondered what to say.
Click, click, click, click, clickety clickety click, click.
Kingdom come. Will be done. Death another day.

Click, click, clickety click, clickety clickety click, click.
Death has had its day at last, and little kings can live.
Click, click, click, click, clickety clickety click, click.
Forty-acre kingdoms now, with nothing to forgive.

Click, click, clickety click, clickety clickety click, click.
Nothing to forgive now, but never to forget—
Click, click, click, click, clickety clickety click, click—
Charlie in the realm too, Charlie, laughing yet.

Click, click, clickety click, clickety clickety click, click.
The rails were very happy now, and as he leaned along—
Click, click, click, click, clickety clickety click, click—
He listened, and his lips were open, to the soldier-song.

> Rolling home, rolling home,
> Rolling home across the corn;
> Rolling up, rolling up,
> To the place where I was born.
> Black, black, between the green:
> Plenty, plenty, blow your horn.
>   War, war,
>   Go away
>   And never come
>   Another day.

Through the gate, through the gate,
Through the gate, and what I see?
Through the gate, through the gate,
They are coming out to me.
Well, well, well, well,
Hello, hello, and how you be?
  War, war,
  Go away
  And never come
  Another day.

III

FORECLOSURE

Jonathan Gentry Fifth, descended long
From him that dreamed a river, and from him
That crossed it and recrossed it in the dark;
Jonathan Gentry Fifth, descended straight
From farmers, and himself the farmer now,
Stared at the April stream. The deeper grove
He stood in had been feathered overnight—
Jonathan could believe it—with high, pale
And singing new green branches; where his boots
Slipped on the stony bank small ferns unfolded;
And here the listless creek, late numb with ice,
Swelled like a serpent, rolling its colors on.
He watched it pouring full between the oaks,
Coming above him smoothly till it fell,
Here at the rocks, and roared; then watched it moving
Busily round the bend that brought the pastures.
He thought of it there, with the sun just risen on it;
He thought of the morning round him; felt the wind
Filling the new-born leaves, filling his eyes
With coolness and the strength of a cast fragrance;
Stared; and remembered breakfast. She was waiting.
It warmed him to remember: a dry warmth,
With nothing of awakened woods about it,
A dry and indoor warmth, as good to keep
Inside him as this other one, of ferns.
He walked a few more rods to find the ewe:
And found her, big with lamb, where twisted roots
Had caught her like a rat; so in the flood,
Sometime between an afternoon and dawn,
She drowned. He freed the foot and dragged her up
To lie on last year's leaves—the belly full,
The eyes washed almost empty, a weak blue—

141

And dropped a word of pity; but turned now,
Hurrying home to the other eyes, the well ones.

Up the white stream he went, and through the green
Black grove that still was young upon the year.
The youth of it rose rankly; Jonathan walked,
Smelling the potent odors, minding the will
That worked in dampness round him, through decay.
Jonathan, in the might of such a morning,
Hastened awhile, then tempered his pace and said:
"Uprising fingers, palms—
The forearms still to come, and the wrapped shoulders—
Upspringing world, you speak,
You sing your power already, and you bring me
News I have needed—I,
Jonathan Gentry Fifth, who love the coming
Of day, and the thrust of spring, and the standing again of stems
    that taper and wave.
I love you. But I love you less
For what you show me now than for the places
Under the leaves, the rocks,
Under the homes of worms, the print of snakes,
The places where you come from, as you come
This morning, now, after the warm long rain.
What I can see is nothing for my wonder.
I have it too; I stand; I drink; I live.
I love you more for having what I may not—
What no man may have had, yet there were times
Before my time; I think they had it then—
For having what I may not have, a place
To die into and thence be born again.
Upclimbing vine-tips,
Folded, uncurling ferns,
Buds, ready to burst,
I envy you the womb that cannot wither,
I envy you the jest of a November
That only plays at dying: as he falls,
Pretending all is over, he can drain
Green blood into the April cup beneath him,
The buried cup that sleeps and never spills.
I stand, I walk, I live,

And men of some good kind will live beyond me;
And sometimes, world—deep world—
I think we have your secret, we who walk
On furrows in the fall, that can uncover
Burial-place and seed-bed there together.
Even this moment, maple,
I thought I had it fairly from your fingers,
Gift of the small green gods. But it is going.
Most of the days it goes, and I—and we—
Stand rootless, with no future
Underground."

He left the woods and walked into the sun,
That came now like a reaper over the cool,
Flat fields between the last tree and the house:
Reaping the dew, reaping the level shadows.
The longest of the shadows made a lane,
Running an even course beside the high
Black hedge that cut the farm into its halves;
The eastern half was cornfields, but the western
Pastures started here where Jonathan walked,
Spreading unto the grove, whence water tumbled
Quickly, and quickly slowed, and now meandered.
He left the sun and took the lane of shadow,
Watching the light strike over his tall head,
Flooding the right-hand fields until the woods
Stopped it; so he watched it glancing backward,
Downward along the bed of the bright creek;
And watched it settling softly on the faces
Of seventeen hundred sheep a man was driving
Out of their winter shed.

Soon the lane ended where the hedge gave way
To posts and woven wire, that followed down
As far as the wide pickets bounding the barn lot.
Jonathan, through the gate, stopped in a moment,
Having to see the horses at their breakfast.
They lifted their long faces as he came:
Dolly and Dick the Belgians, plump and mild,
Bob and Mahomet, roans, and Jack the Western,
Daisy the freckled white, and Plug the puller;
All of them smooth and happy, and his friends,

143

All of them chewing soberly, and blinking;
All of them so but Jack, who rolled a white eye,
Snorted, and jerked his rope; yet soon forgot,
Plunging his nose once more in the nervous hay.
Jonathan smiled and watched them, still as wood,
Then went as suddenly out as he had come.
Breakfast was waiting. He could see the door,
Ample and white, between the pair of maples.
He stamped his boots, approaching, and he thought:
"Laura won't want to hear about her ewe.
Pity it wasn't mine; a special pity."
He mounted the muddy steps, and would have called;
But heard:
At seven in the morning Jonathan heard,
Coming from the horses and the hay,
Coming from a dewy lane of shadows,
Coming from the wet woods and the ferns,
The new song—thump—upon the phonograph;
The brand new words. He loathed them, but he listened:

It was a band of city boys—
And girls, we must confess—
One night along a lonely road,
A rustic wilderness.
The picnic walk was ended now
But they had missed the train.
The latest bus had left for town,
And this was their refrain:
    Bright lights, bright lights
    Shining on the square,
    Don't go out, we're coming home;
    We're done with country air.
    Don't ask us how we'll get to you,
    But when we do we'll know
    There's nothing sweeter in the world
    Than bright lights in a row.

The day had been a laughing day.
They said, between their smiles:
"You wouldn't guess a city lay
Within a thousand miles."

144

But now the road was black ahead,
And stony where they stood,
And this was what they sang to the
Mosquitoes in the wood:
    Clean lights, clean lights,
    Shining on the square,
    Don't go out, we're coming home;
    We're done with country air.
    Don't ask us how we'll get to you,
    But when we do we'll know
    There's nothing sweeter in the world
    Than clean lights in a row.

They started walking, two by two;
Sally and Tom McCloud,
Bess and Hal, and Larry and Jean:
All of the homesick crowd.
They stumbled on—not even a moon
To show them where to tread.
And this is what they grumbled to the
Fireflies overhead:
    Big lights, big lights,
    Shining on the square,
    Don't go out, we're coming home;
    We're done with country air.
    Don't ask us how we'll get to you,
    But when we do we'll know
    There's nothing sweeter in the world
    Than big lights in a row.

Laura, bending her brown head,
Pouring the coffee smoothly into the white cups,
Looked not up to see what manner of husband
Stood in the doorway.

Jonathan, notwithstanding,
Crossed and lifted her face, and kissed the warm mouth:
Warm with the odorous breakfast she had made him;
Warm with the song.

Laura, quietly smiling,
As if she need not say what thing had pleased her,

Opened her eyes a little wider, and kindly
Suffered his kisses.

Jonathan, hearing the needle
Scrape on the finished record, hurried and stopped it;
Closed the shiny machine that neither mentioned,
Now at their coffee.

Nothing was said between them.
Laura, busy with bread, wove with her brown hands
Figures against the cloth for him to see;
And against her apron.

He cleared his voice reluctantly, beginning:
"I found her in the woods. Along the creek.
The farthest up she ever went, I think.
Up by the big rocks, under the sycamore,
Lying—"
                "Oh, was it twins? Tell me, tell me!"
Suddenly she was straightened in her chair,
And the brown eyes were black with narrow fire.
"Jonathan! Was it twins? And was she sick yet?"
She stopped, for it was plain now.
                                "She was dead.
Jonathan! She was dead. And not a lamb there?
Can there be nothing young of any kind?"
"Listen. It wasn't her time yet. Not for a week.
You knew that, didn't you, lovely? Can't you guess?
The sycamore, remember, is a trap—
Always the roots were coiled as if to catch you.
We said so when we waded up last August.
Well, all this rain had washed them worse—and Laura,
They caught her. She was drowned. But she is dry now.
I pulled her on to the bank, on to the old leaves.
Her eyes—"
                "Don't! I can see them. I have eyes."
But they were closed, and Jonathan beneath them
Guessed the full tears that gathered. So she wept,
Hiding her face with hands too quick, too quiet,
Not to be now the garment of a storm.
She wept, and Jonathan watched, and heard her saying:
"Nothing has ever grown in me, or will grow.

146

Pass me over, bee-wings,
Seed-showers;
I am a barren bed—and worse—
I am a poison-weed-bed;
I can kill.
I have no children, Jonathans or Lauras,
So my four-footed creatures, when they swell,
Come to the dead end. Drowned!
Nelly, I talked of twins for you. And drowned!"

Jonathan sat and waited for a word
Denying her and healing her; with proof
That nothing was yet so bad, or ever could be.
He waited, watching; but the word was lost.
Perhaps there were no sentences to say,
Here in the open country of the storm:
Nothing to make the wind hear, and the rain.
He only could divert them; so he offered,
Calmly, as with a stranger's voice tossed backwards:

"Let's see, it's April now, and time for Joe—
Isn't it? Doesn't he always come in the spring?
The last midwinter visit he was snowbound;
But that would hardly hold him off in April;
April, and he's no lawyer any longer;
April, and he comes flying; he remembers
More of our boyhood here than ever I do—
Doesn't he? Don't you think?"
                                        He watched her slyly,
Seeming to be most busy with his bread.
She had grown doubly quiet, but her dark hands
Still were upon her eyes—that heard, perhaps.
"There ought to be a letter."
                                        She was quieter,
Suddenly, than the room, and farther off.
"There is a letter, Jonathan. To me.
He's coming Friday morning. I misplaced it;
Burnt it, maybe—careless. But don't bother,
He's coming Friday morning for three days."
"Good. Wednesday, Thursday, Friday. In the morning."

So Jonathan and Laura in the long house,
The house that every Gentry had increased,
Waited upon the brother, and made ready
The room he stooped and entered like a priest.

It was the little low one on the wing,
The last one toward the trees, beside the well.
The first of all the Jonathans had built it,
And hung above the door a silver bell:

The only English thing that he had brought there;
He hung it up to ring his wedding in.
And there they all had left it, under the shingles;
It tinkled in the wind, that wore it thin.

The second of the Jonathans was born there,
But he had builded farther; and the third—
After the war, with Agatha—had finished;
So now there were no hammers to be heard.

The fourth one merely mended what had fallen,
But widened both the porches for the play
Of Jonathan and Joe, his only children:
Two sons, with whom the place had had its day.

They were the last to run from room to room,
Shouting and hiding faces; till the time
They grew afraid of corners in the long house
Where still the spiders drop, the shadows climb.

Their father locked the doors, and filled the wing—
The oldest room of all—with sacks of seed;
And nailed the oldest door; and still the bell
Swung rustily, without a present need.

The boys would come and wipe the dusty windows,
Peering into the first, the little house.
But all they saw was spider webs, and hanging
Bags above the reach of squirrel and mouse.

Jonathan forgot, but Joe remembered.
It was the room he wanted when he came.
They opened it and washed the little windows,
And roped the ancient bed upon its frame.

They brought the table back, and two of the chairs,
And hung old-fashioned curtains on a rod.
It was the room old Jonathan had slept in,
And bred his sons and daughters like a god.

All gone now, and their children's children too.
Jonathan and Laura lived alone.
The upper floors were musty, the grey shadows
Starved at last to skin and silent bone.

The stairways both were darkened at the top,
As if a day had walked up there and died.
They slept below, and ate, and wound their music
Out of a box, and let the shadows bide.

What Laura thought was more than Laura said,
Then, or the next long day, in the dusted room.
Invisibly the shuttles rose and glided,
Inaudibly, upon a wordless loom,

Weaving an expectation past the hour
Merely of someone's coming. That was soon;
But she was getting ready the trailed garment
Of a long night beyond the present noon.

What though a certain head was coming swiftly,
Behind a glass, behind a polished wheel?
What though a triple day of happy silence—
Faded then, with nothing left to feel?

A slow and perfect garment had been gathered;
The thread was being tested on the years;
The silk wherein her bosom would be buried
Was yet both soft and strong, against her fears.

The throat was low, for courage to be born;
The waist was not the slender one of maids;
The skirt was full and blowing, where the shears
Cut roundabout with bright and reckless blades.

And there would be a mantle, like the sky
At night beyond the stars, a fall of black;
And under it a face of Hyades,
With seven summer sisters glancing back.

What Laura thought was more than Laura said;
But what she thought was nothing of all this.
She never knew, in April, of the rise
Of any constellation in her kiss.

She only was preparing, out of sight,
And out of flying time, a thing to do.
But now it was the hour. The gate was there,
Wide open, and a car was coming through.

Jonathan in front of her was waving;
Joe was slowing proudly to a roar;
Then the stopping engine, and the gift
Of hands, the brown and white ones, at the door.

Jonathan gave all he had to give;
Laura kept the greater part, and laughed.
She told them she was laughing at the new
Brown roadster; it was longer than a raft;

Too much good metal there for single men,
Too much red leather, rounding empty space.
Joe smiled, and if he could have answered further
There was no means to tell it by his face.

He only bid them both climb in the rumble.
"I'll be unselfish instantly," he said,
And took them with him straight across the barn lot,
Into the darkened hollow of the shed.

They left it there, gleaming among the cobwebs,
A bolt of lightning haltered in a stall;
They left it there, each portion of it mocking
The dusty pegs that watched it from the wall.

They watched, and through the quiet of partitions
The horses raised their noses from the hay—
Listening; but the motor's mouth was hooded,
And now the going footsteps died away.

Jonathan, behind the other two,
Could hear the horses listening, or could think,
Swiftly, of all between them: the furred ears,
The softly blowing nostrils, and the clink

Of pistons on the temper of thin steel;
Jonathan could think of this and pause.
But Joe and Laura rose to their own laughter,
Swinging on—while streamers of dark gauze

Moved through her mind and draped it like a garment,
The mantle of the dress the moments wove.
It seemed as if the farm itself were flowing
Up and away, and hiding in the grove.

The day was fair, with breezes coming over
Close to the ground, and cool, yet streaked with warm.
The spring-dam up the world was open, letting
Trickles of life—that promised the full flood—
Run tentatively, gently, over and down,
Nosing the loam, curling along the fences,
Nudging the undulations of parched land.
Jonathan, the current at his feet,
Smiled, and felt it rise in him as far,
Filling the wintry veins, as ever an ending
April had yielded, breathless, her permission.
Jonathan, the season in his walk,
Stepped freshly, finding greenness at the root
Of the old stalk, himself, and at the base
Even of dead white stones and pitted stumps.
Jonathan, the spring among his thoughts,
Saw the wide summer coming in himself—
This only the infant year, the sweet beginning.
There would be more for him. So he was quiet,
Waiting.
          And Laura waited, but not so.
The gale of her first laughter, passing over,

Left her, as if the spring should last a day,
Blowing to utter madness, and so die;
As if the most of time were a ringed desert,
An herbless field, that waited; and for what?
She laughed to see the car, and in the barn lot,
Going, she laughed again; but after that,
Laura, with wider eyes than he was used to,
Watched, with hardly a word, with never a sound.
She watched the brothers talking, and her eyes
Stared; but what they saw was not for Jonathan
Anything he could see. They widened round him,
Beating a nervous flight to another world's end,
Windy and far away. And they were darker,
And moister, as if the motion of their going
Circled them with soft tears.
                                   "Yet happy tears.
She never was so happy. Strange," he said,
"That wanting something nameless and impossible,
Something beneath another bounded sky,
Should warm her so, and wake her; as if a life
Could live on what it lacked. Or is it strange?"

Joe drank the season deepest of the three.
He had come wearily, an endless winter
Laying its load still on him, and his face
Older beyond its time than they remembered;
He had come drooping; but the miracle
Of wind, and last night's water, and deep sky,
Working upon him now as if it only
Saw the one there, the palest of the three,
Straightened him on his stem. "A cellar growth,"
Jonathan looked and said; "something forgotten,
Something almost too late remembered—brought
Suddenly into the sun upstairs. And see?
It darkens, it uncurls, it all but dances."
Joe led them like two older, doubtful children
After him up the hedge row, where the shadows
Shrank to a narrow lane; it was eleven.
"At noon," he said, "we had to crawl clear under;
That was the only shade there was for miles.
Remember, Jon, the big hedge apples dropping,

And almost braining the well hidden boys?
If there is any brain about a boy,
Or such a boy as you were. Laura, look!
We took our hatchets here and trimmed a room.
You still can see the shape of it. An oval.
We lay inside like rats. Oho! the creek!
It's roaring!" So he hauled them suddenly out
Into the blinding light of the west pasture;
And so the morning ended in the woods.
And so the house again, and the slow dinner;
And so all day they followed him, with Laura
Staring between the two at something, nothing.

Jonathan pitched the hay down,
And stopped at each dark manger with a word:
A word for Dick and Dolly, and for Daisy,
A foolish, friendly sentence for the roans;
A slap for Western Jack.

"So you roll your eyes, eh?
Why? To brag that part of you was white?
I knew as much, you rusty good-for-nothing.
I knew it all the time, you woolly runt.
You with the hairy ears!"

Jonathan caught the halter rope,
And pulled, and brought the broncho to his hand.
"There. You needn't treat me like a stranger.
After the second summer men are friends,
Jack old boy, old codger."

Jack, crunching a mouthful,
Blinked his eyes and suddenly was tame.
"That's right; and now remember. Well, here's Plug.
Who let you in, Plug-ugly? Who are you?
Any of this for you?"

Jonathan tossed it all in,
Pressing down a mangerful and more.
"You'd take a field of hay, including the fences.
But then you'd try the forks—and where'd you be?
Good night!" And so to supper.

Jonathan in the twilight,
Slowly walking sunward to the house,
Looked. For Laura waited by the low wing,
Lifting both her hands to swing the bell:
Lifting them, and waiting.

Expectant as the evening,
Tilted like a shadow toward the night,
She leaned, as if she wanted to be pulled there,
Drawn against the door, and in, and in.
"Why doesn't Laura call him?"

Then she jerked the bell-cord.
A jangle, cracked and musical, that stopped her—
Standing straight as iron, and coldly flushing.
He told himself he felt the icy warmth,
Flowing within, within.

Joe in the doorway then,
Nodding; but she had warily withdrawn.
A backward step, a waiting, as in terror;
A look; until Joe laughed and came along now,
Taking the path behind her.

He waved, and Jonathan waved—
Jonathan now at the gate, and the three together.
It was the end of twilight, the beginning
Of a cold April darkness, after the sun;
And it was time for supper.

"Well, that was good—as good as ever, Laura.
And I am tired; as tired as we were, Jon,
The night we dragged our legs in—you remember?—
After the day we drove to town, and the team
Broke, and galloped home with a piece of the wagon.
It was the first time father let us go;
And the last time for years. He didn't like it.
But I have always liked it, being tired
Like that, and like tonight. It's a complete
Feeling, to be remembered under your dreams,
A charm put under your pillow when you sleep

154

Alone, alone, alone. Let's play the song—
Laura, you haven't heard it; it's the latest,
A very good silly song—and then to bed.
All right?"
                    She cried him "Yes!", and Jonathan nodded.
Why not a song—a silly one, a new one?
And so he went and brought it, and it sang:

> Over the traffic, boys,
> Over the red, the green,
> Alone, alone, alone, boys,
> A bachelor sits unseen.
>> Nineteen windows up and never married.
>> Elevators, sliding up and down,
>> Don't you click and stop, for he's the buried
>> Bachelor-mummy-king of all the town.

> Over the honk of horns, boys,
> Over the taxi lanes,
> Over the whistling cops, boys,
> He sits and entertains.
>> Nineteen windows up and never married.
>> Elevators, sliding up and down,
>> Don't you click and stop, for he's the buried
>> Bachelor-mummy-king of all the town.

> Over and up and up, boys,
> Who is the evening guest?
> The Lady of the Pyramid?
> The envy of the rest?
>> Nineteen windows up and never married.
>> Elevators, sliding up and down,
>> Don't you click and stop, for he's the buried
>> Bachelor-mummy-king of all the town.

> Over the silver spout, boys,
> Who sees the coffee glide?
> Give a little guess, boys,
> But let it wander wide.
>> Nineteen windows up and never married.
>> Elevators, sliding up and down,

Don't you click and stop, for he's the buried
Bachelor-mummy-king of all the town.

Over the velvet rugs, boys,
Who's moving, arm in arm?
Why, it's the villain
And his killin'
Pretty, brown, and very willin'
Victim off the farm.
      Nineteen windows up and never married.
      Elevators, sliding up and down,
         Don't you click and stop, for he's the buried
         Bachelor-mummy-king of all the town.

Laura laughed, and Jonathan at last
Laughed too, but why they did so neither said.
"Of course it is the tune; the words, as usual,
Crazy," Joe expostulated, looking
Chiefly at Laura's eyes, that blazed again;
"They come by chance out of bright rattlebrains—
If there is any brain about a song man;
He shakes his head and words come out like those;
The very first he gets go down on paper.
And now why not to bed? Good evening, Jon.
See you tomorrow, Laura."
                    But she rose,
Saying she wasn't sure his room was ready.
They disappeared, and Jonathan heard their feet,
Two and two on the gravel, till the door
Opened under the bell; he caught its tinkle,
Down at the other end of the silent house.
He listened, and the silver sound again
Came; and Laura came; and crossed, and kissed him.

Saturday and Sunday yet.
The three of them were children still:
Joe among the woods again,
And they behind him up the hill;
And if they thought of him ahead,
Nothing anyway was said.

Laura spoke to Jonathan,
But not of Joe. Was she afraid?
Was she safer with the tale
Of where the angry hen had laid?
When he spoke it was the garden;
Time for harrow and for spade.

Joe led them down again, and wandered,
Wearily, beside the brook.
He was old again—a chapter
Finished in the fairy book.
"See the ashes in my eyes!"
But neither one of them would look.

"See the scythe. The bearded man
Has come and gone, and done his mowing."
They only laughed, but Laura looked
And saw another river flowing.
Time was rapider, that spring,
Than any other going thing.

Even then she only spoke
Of supper waiting—the last one.
End of Sunday. Milk and bread,
And then the holiday was done.
She turned and led them, faster now
Than either's feeling would allow.

The brothers called her, but she ran.
They let her go, and picked a way
Across the pastures round the shed.
It was the death bed of a day,
They walked and watched it slowly dying;
Walked, and found a woman crying.

They found her so, but she concealed it swiftly,
Setting the three bowls out and cutting the bread.
They supped in a half silence, until Joe
Spoke of his going soon, and sighed, and said:
"It wasn't long enough—three days, three minutes;
Only as long as one deep breath; but then,
I breathed it; there is that; and it was good."

"Do you remember," Jonathan began,
"The time you talked of staying? Not for days,
Not for another breath or two, but always?
Always! We could talk of that again."
"No."
        "I say we could. This isn't a house
Merely to be brought forth in, learn to walk in,
And then to walk away from and be homesick.
This, with the land it looks on, is a life,
Something to own as utterly as air.
It's yours, it's mine; I love it, and you love it;
I stay, and why not you? Do you remember
The way we two were boys here? How we planned
Those letters on the mail box—J. and J.
Gentry, Incorporated?"
                "I remember.
I studied my first steps here, slow and well.
This is the place for walking. But the race
Runs swifter where I watch it, and I learned
Too long ago to love it to be changed.
I knew it better yesterday than ever.
I know it now so plainly I am sad—
Almost. You see I do remember things,
And it is melancholy, living lives
That overlap, one dead beneath the other.
This one is dead. It breathes a little for me,
Here on the very ground, if I come tramping.
But that one, there, the one you never saw—
Even when you came you didn't see it—
That one is always running, with me on it,
Midway the polished road, midway the stiff
Banners of stone and steel, and the many windows:
Millions of windows, Jon, and I can miss them.
I can be homesick too for all of that."
"For this, too, sometimes?"
                 "Yes, for both. But listen.
Happy is not the word for that—for the close
Press of an upright universe, a tilted
Brick and glass rectangle of horizon,
A cornered mountain round me of white faces:
All·with a love behind them that is my love,

A madness, if you must accuse it so.
The stars above us there, and the smoked sun,
Are never again the same. The roof is nearer,
Studded with neater cunning; and it catches
All of the flying wonder of our talk;
It rings with the deathless din of human voices
Crying across each other and coming back—
All human; we have shut the forests out,
And the dumb fields, and every beast abounding.
It is our place: a carnival, a manhole.
If still we love the country, it is love
Not of the first old Gentry's kind, who came,
Blessing the soil and promising a kingdom.
Those kingdoms are a little rusty now—
For me, for us they are—those backward patches
Lying beyond our empire. Yet we love them.
We love them to go out to, and remember:
We love them to come back from, and be mounted
Proudly again upon the bannered steed,
The iron horse, the animal with rivets.
And so we clatter sweetly, and forget;
And then remember you; and then forget.
I have been happy here, but this is why
I'm going. Do you see? And are you angry?"

Laura, in the half-light of the window,
Silent all the while, but with her eyes
On fire between the two, watched Jonathan now—
Waiting, with his hand upon the table,
Waiting, with his eyes upon his hand.
"No," he said. "Why angry? But I'm glad
You said it all, or something of it all.
There's more, I know.
There's more of it, you Gentrys
Lying with your old faces up, and looking
Into a small black sky,
A narrow lid.
The bigger top beyond is not for you now,
Grandfathers,
Grass-lovers,
Walkers slow and slow across a kingdom yet to come.

It's come; you had it round you all the time;
And gone. It's fading
Sandwise into a desert—I can feel—
A desert where the dry, indifferent winds
Blow, blow, and all the rain of men's regard
Goes round to fall with laughter on the towers
Of towns—the splendid towns!
I've known it, and forgiven it;
I've watched it here, the finish of a race:
The light feet lagging now, and the far eyes
Failing their old horizon. I have seen
What you will never see, you happy old ones,
Raft-riders,
Sod-breakers,
Steppers upon a garden shore, and singers
Loud of an ancient song,
An over-the-mountain, Eden song.
I've seen the garden wither in the rain;
I've felt the roots unwrapping their strong fingers,
Laying themselves away in a strange
Ground. It's not the ground you walked on, fathers.
Still it is what it is, and I will stay.
Laura and I will stay, loving the least
Vestige and green remainder: loving horses,
Loving a lane of shadows, and the four
Corners of every year. Not angry, Joe,
No; and come and see us when you must."

Soberly then he rose, and Laura, listening,
Wandered into the light, circling a little,
Mothwise in her helplessness; but now
Nothing was left to hear. The brothers smiled,
Soberly to each other, and went out.
She followed them over the grass and through the gate,
Whose posts, in the black of evening, moistened her hand,
Feeling the way. She followed, and they found it
Waiting among the spider-webs—the bright car,
Flooding at once the dusky shed with its silver.
A last goodbye to both of them, and Joe
Backed, and swung the stream of his great lamps
Over the barn, the picket fence, and the house trees,

Over the lane to the road. And now they heard him
Humming between the hedges. So they stood there,
Separate in the darkness, till the sound
Died, and the light was gone.

Separately, slowly,
Each of them familiar with the way,
The two of them walked in without a word.
Separately, slowly,
Each of them possessing a lone thought,
Jonathan and Laura crept to bed.
Jonathan, exhausted,
Stared into the emptiness above him;
Stared, and seeing nothing, fell asleep.
Laura, too awake now
To make a single sound—for she was careful—
Stared, and seeing something, stared again.
Into the void, the ceiling,
Through and into the upper night she gazed,
Narrowing there her eyes, stricken with stars:
Stricken with another light
That poured across another earth, and showed her
One in a stately garment, topped with gauze.
Herself without a name there,
Herself, with light around her like a sea,
Herself alone, waiting upon her day.

The end of April was a dry end, bringing
Never a night of rain, with mornings after
Glittering in the glances of the sun.
Clouds lay, sometimes so low that a tree touched them,
Drenching its budded head; and the rolling sky
Frowned from a little distance; but no rain,
And Jonathan, each evening by the clock,
As if he were the day itself, and the dial,
Spoke of the needed showers.
                                   "A dusty April
Never can do the pastures any good;
No matter what the May, we want a spring month
Wetter about our feet than we might like
If we were not a yoke of farmers. Laura,

I am a farmer here because time passed
And put me so; and you because I asked you.
We are a team in harness, though we pull
Unevenly sometimes; which is to say,
You pull as often back as you do forward.
And yet the brutes are matched; I still can think so.
Still, Laura, we can hope for rain together—
Knowing the pleasant pain of being played with.
Weather's a game, and the sky uses us:
Up with the wind and down with the wind, then lying
Patient upon a corner of the board,
Waiting to be picked off with a wet finger.
Some would want to make the moves themselves;
But then the board's a very small indoor one,
And the mind, playing, sharpens till it hurts.
I like the big one better, even so;
Even if I'm the jest of it, the dummy.
At least it is a long joke; I roll slowly;
And there is something deeper in the pockets:
Deeper than disappointment."
                    "Jonathan,
You're thinking more of what Joe Gentry said
Than what you say yourself. So. Was it true?"
"I am, a little. But I spoke of rain.
At least in the beginning it was rain."

May came with warmer winds, and the sky softer.
Lazier now the scud of white and blue,
Lazier, out of the west and over and down.
It was a gentler month than they remembered;
It was a finer world above them, blowing,
Than either of them could answer to. But rain
Came not through any night, or through the long,
Tired days of Jonathan's labor, that redoubled.
"And that's all right, but where's our summer hand?
I've looked, and asked, and talked all over town.
He doesn't seem to be there any more—
The boy, the man who waited till we came,
Smiled and said he would, and climbed the wagon.
It's work and they don't like it; or it's far
From the red fronts of stores, and from the car line.

162

Well,"—and he would mutter to the sheep
More than he ever said at home to Laura.
Between the sheep and horses and the corn,
And the new field of oats, and the alfalfa,
He faltered; but went on, and was so late,
Some of these lengthened evenings, that she kept
Supper for him alone in the high oven—
The "waiting oven," Laura learned to call it—
Over the nickeled stove. He came, and stamping
Dust before the door, looked in at Laura;
Cleared his throat and entered, and sat down
Some days without a word. For he was tired,
And his tongue too was tired from its slow moving
Silently by the side of his slow thought;
So weary that it would not trust itself
With words, that might come edged with anger now.
No time for anger, Jonathan believed,
Though inwardly they rubbed him—the raw words,
The other words outside him he could hear,
Often in the twilight, as he stumbled,
Wearier than ever, from the stalls.
He held his tongue and sat, and ate, and rested;
Except that once the legend of the needle,
Scratching around the disc with frantic zeal,
Provoked him past his patience, and at last
He spoke. But he had listened to the end:

> She told him she was lonesome.
> It was in the summer time,
> And the day was long agoing.
> But he only had a dime.
> So he thought until it struck him—
> An idea like a rhyme.
> > "There isn't any better fun
> > (With nothing else to do)
> > Than going arm in arm, hon,
> > Up the avenue."

> She told him he was crazy;
> Better sit at home and talk.
> But he had slipped into his coat,
> And so they took the willing walk;

And the first new thing they noticed
Was the children with their chalk.
  "Sally Jane McArthur
  Loves Big Bill McGrew."
  Going arm in arm there
  Up the avenue.

They strolled, and now the shadows
Of the roofs across the way
Fell upon their quiet faces,
And the windows in display;
And she read the printed words
She never bothered with by day.
  "Awnings fitted anywhere."
  "Cables to Peru."
  Going arm in arm there
  Up the avenue.

They passed the shuttered banks,
The restaurants along the Row;
Looked, and saw the people dining,
Heard the music playing slow;
And they watched a dirty kitten
Sniff the grating down below.
  "Meow, meow, let me in;
  Open it, and let me through."
  Going arm in arm there
  Up the avenue.

They almost said "Good evening"
To a tailor by his door.
But it began to rain now,
And it began to pour;
And this is what she said to him
Above the subway roar:
  "There isn't any better fun
  (With nothing else to do)
  Than riding arm in arm, hon,
  Down the avenue."

"Inane, preposterous syllables!"—
Jonathan was saying it at last—
"Why do you let them chatter at me, Laura,
Now in the hopeless hour of a dragged evening?
Why do you sick them on me? To insult me?
They do, I tell you—jabbering little jokes,
Twittering little fingers in my face—
They do, and I am weary of it. Trying
To make me sentimental about sidewalks!
They are beneath you, Laura, words and tune.
It used to be *Drink Only*, and *Abide*,
And *Aberdeen*, and *She Was Passing Fair*.
It used to be that you could sit and sing
Those old ones, the grave sweet ones, with a something
Solid in them, like a golden wire.
You sang, and it would tremble and commence
Another humming round you; I could feel it,
Even if it was never to be heard.
You were the one I heard. But something happened.
I heard all music too, and heard the heart
Of an old time, a better one than this time,
The strong and pretty worktime of the world.
Why do you, Laura? Why?"
                              But she was waiting
More for the end than for a suited answer.
"Inane," she only said, repeating dumbly;
"Inane"—but then she blazed a sudden moment,
Strangely, and she was more surprised than he was.
"They aren't any more inane than—"
                              "What?
Than what? Than what? You've got to tell me, Laura.
Maybe I need to know. And I'm already
Sorry for what I said. Than me? Than this?
They're good enough for us, the way we live?
They keep you well enough reminded, do they,
Of the bright other place you ought to be?"
But she was silent now. And she was sorry,
And kissed him where his hat had left a red,
Straight mark across his forehead. "You are tired.
Here's your supper, Jon, as warm as ever.
There. Oh when, I wonder, will he come—

165

This necessary fellow we can't find?
When, to save the summer, and save you?
And me? And when's it going to rain again?"

Still the dry days, and still the lonesome labor,
Still the dumb truce between them, and no end.
But then one afternoon as May was going—
Culprit, with the sign of dust upon her—
One afternoon, with not a cloud for comfort,
The gate clicked twice, and Laura, looking out,
Saw a long back unbending from the latch,
Saw the low gate swing open softly; and saw
A tall, straw-colored man glide over the grass.
He came, and she awaited him; and wondered,
Even as he stood capering there and smiling,
Whether it was a man at all, or whether,
Strung so and oddly dangling, he was oatstraw.
Or both, she said almost aloud, and asked him
What he had come for; asked, but got no answer.
Only the blue eyes, under the lonely forehead,
Smiled, and the light lids fluttered, and a long
Grimace, as when a slow wind strokes a hay field,
Rippled across the rest of him. The silence
Startled her all at once; he had not answered.
She stared and stepped away from him, and ran.
"Jonathan!"—she traced him to a far field—
"There is a crazy fellow at the house.
Come with me, I'm afraid."
                              "What kind of crazy?
Isn't he the kind you can take care of?
I'm busy."
            But he came, and the two found him
Exactly, Laura said, where he had been.
"And been forever. Can't the fellow move?
I saw him move at first—a blinking cat,
Purring and putting his paws out over the tall grass.
There he is, though. Now what to do with him?"
He heard them coming, and a look of woe
Escaped from him to vanish up the trees:
A curl of mist returning to the sky.
They came, and Jonathan called: "How do you do!"

No answer yet, and Jonathan, amazed:
"Who are you? Where'd you come from? Do you know?"
The long legs bent a little at the knee,
The sideward eyes grew sober, and the lithe feet
Shuffled, as with a sigh the new one sang:

> Way down south in the sycamore timber.
> That's where I come from, that's why I'm limber.
> Went and cut a sapling, threw it in the air.
> Where's it goin' to land, you white man, where?

"Who are you, though, and what's your name? You got one?"

> Tom, Tom, the son of a gun,
> Stole my gal and away he run.
> I'm Tom, too.
> Stranger, do you chew?

He spat and took tobacco from a bundle
Tied high upon the string about his waist.
Jonathan stepped closer: "Do you work, Tom?"

> Never hitch me up, boy,
> I'm no mule.
> Let me wander free, though,
> I'm a workin' fool.

"What did you come away for? Were you tired?"

> Pluggin' on a farm, boss,
> Never got me weary.
> Then I tried the cotton mill—
> That'll leave 'em bleary!
> Sal ran away with the foreman's brother;
> I started round the world, one end t'other.

"I need a man to help me. Will you stay?"

> Let me make a hole
> In the middle of the straw,
> Show me where the well is,
> Feed me somethin' raw;

167

Give me piece of balin' wire—
Pipe won't draw—
And I'm the little man
You been a lookin' for.

It was no use. Laura could hear it coming.
She hummed a cautious sound, and pulled at Jonathan;
But he turned straight away, leading the long legs
Up to the empty hand's house in the orchard.
"He had to stoop to get himself inside,"
He told her, coming back almost at once;
"And yet he didn't shorten; he uncurled
And entered like a snake. I left him sleeping,
Coiled like a length of rope—I think a strong one.
Lucky, my Laura. But you don't believe it."
"He's horrible! Not dangerous, I mean—"
"Yes. He is unnatural. No words;
Nothing but jigs and nonsense. But I'll try him.
He'll sleep all day and night—he said he would—
Then wake; and we can see if he's not faithful."

Tom stayed, and was as willing as the wind—
That blew too much that summer, and too warm.
He fed the sheep with singing as he trailed them
Busily back and forth between the pastures—
Nibbled almost to death now; but with resting
They grew a little greener. Then he came,
Swinging his arms behind the puzzled creatures.
They bobbed before him, wondering, yet they liked him.
"Of course. Tom's silly too. So they're at home,"
Laura would frown and say; but Jonathan smiled.
Or he would wrap himself around the corn plow,
Riding a cloud of dust, and sending nonsense
Up to the horses' ears—that never caught it,
There in the wind that wafted all away.
Jonathan was pleased.
                    "But what about him?
Doesn't he ever tell you of himself?
In prose, I mean, and standing halfway straight?"
Laura with her loathing still was curious.

168

Two months had passed, more terrible and dry
Than either dared complain of, doubting the other—
Doubting his temper, doubting her content.
But she must ask the question, there in the poor
Parched garden, on this side the orchard fence.
"Don't be too loud. His ears are like a fox's,
And though it's been a long day he's awake.
Be careful. No, he doesn't let me know
Anything more than both of us could guess
That day he came, the crazy day. He sings,
And doesn't expect attention. What they mean—
His words, if they are words—I never know.
I don't know what to say of him, or to him.
But then, why talk at all? The substance is,
We're lucky. He was sent us by the gods."
"And like the gods, to send a simpleton!
I hate him. It's as if—"
                                    "Well, what?"
"As if—and I can tell it to you now—
As if one thing too much were added here;
One leaf too many, laid upon my back,
Breaks it. I go mad sometimes I think,
Without you ever knowing that I do,
From the hung sky and from the waiting earth
Under it: you waiting, and I waiting,
Barrenly, a pair of patient boulders.
But one of us is not so patient lately.
It is as if I'd rolled out here and stopped,
Clear at the edge of things. And how go back?
The only cloud above me is a cloud
Of moments, and they drop relentlessly,
One after another, regularly paced,
To bury me. And now this zany comes,
And sings his death's accompaniment, and grins,
As if my fate had taken the small form
Of a grey, foolish sheep. Oh, I get over it—"
"Do you, Laura, do you? Listen, Laura,
Mustn't go on like this. We'll move away."
"No, we won't. You couldn't. As for me—
I'm sorry, Jon. I'm sorry once again.
And now that I have said a little of it,

I never will say the rest. You know there's more,
But let it be. Let's bury it."
                              "All right."
Yet Jonathan could only look away,
His hands, his feet as moveless as the plum trees
Over the orchard wall, and as the window,
Open to the twilight, of Tom's house.
Jonathan could see it through the leaves—
One window staring at him, the unlidded
Eye of a dead, useless evening. Then he listened,
And Laura listened, silently behind him,
To the cracked words that floated down around them:
Fragments of a song, Tom's sleeping song.

        There was a bird
        Of solid gold.
        So I've been told.
        At least it was yellow.
        And it did sing
        With a silver sound,
        Until it was found
        By a foolish fellow.

        He carried it home
        And builded a cage
        Of lettuce and sage,
        And slippery ellum.
        People came by.
        "See here, see here!
        But not too near;
        It's shy," he would tell 'em.

        Some looked in;
        But the golden bird
        Never was heard
        With its song of wonder—
        Missing the woods,
        Missing the rain,
        And the old refrain
        Of sweetened thunder.

Sits there still,
Long hour by hour,
And the sky grows sour,
And the wings are folded.
Better let it out,
Take away the wall.
Feathers goin' to fall
And the heart be moulded.

Whatever it meant to Jonathan, he kept it;
Whatever it meant to Laura, she was sad.
But there was not a song that would have given
Comfort in a season going mad.

The fall, without their knowing it, was round them;
They looked, and on a day as dry as ever
Haze upon the grove was trailing signals
Of a lost year, yielding its endeavor.

It died head downward, leisurely converting
Tips of green to umber one by one.
Nothing now to hasten it, and nothing
To check the flowing fall till it was done.

And it was done, and the dead year, suspended
Blue and dusty brown beneath the sky,
Clung, as if the shell of a great locust
Waited upon the wind, itself to die.

The season had grown old beyond departing;
Time was dead, and yet it could not go;
And the turned earth was beautiful; or would be
If any easy mind were there to know.

Laura, like the branches, fixed in fever,
Hanging too, and waiting for an end,
Laura in her silence only wondered
What sudden deed October might intend.

Jon nudged the horses' noses of an evening,
And led them every noon to where a pool
Of water in the creek was growing stagnant—
He himself, or sent the cheerful fool.

Tom went, the drove behind him in their halters,
Seven thirsty faces gazing past.
He went, and he must always sing a mournful
Song, as if it were the very last.

        Rain crow, rain crow,
        Heard the saddest rain crow
        Ever, ever seen
        Since the world was green.

        Rain crow, rain crow,
        Moanin' like a rain crow:
        Never turtle dove
        Lost such a love.

        Rain crow, rain crow,
        Never such a rain crow
        Sobbin' in the hedge
        By the brown field edge.

        Rain crow, rain crow,
        Mortifyin' rain crow,
        Who, who's gone,
        And left you all alone?

        Tall boy, tall boy,
        Leadin'-horses tall boy,
        Look inside and see:
        You're the same as me.

        Tall boy, tall boy,
        Good-for-nothin' tall boy,
        Walkin' there apart,
        Bleedin' through the heart.

        Tall boy, tall boy,
        God-forsaken tall boy,
        What's the time o' year,
        And where'll you go from here?

Tall boy, tall boy,
Cotton-headed tall boy,
Home folks gone,
Trampin' all alone.
Tall boy, straw boy,
Pokin' all alone,
All alone.

When the grey corn, more stunted on the stalk
Than any moon remembered, rustled nightlong,
When the shorn lambs grew coats again, and dipped them
Frugally every evening in the dew,
When all the mows were filled with powdery hay,
And Jonathan, his dry-imagined throat
Lined with a long defeat, was few of words,
He said once during supper, when the wind,
As impotent as ever round the house,
Whirled the white plaything, dust, above the dark road:
"Laura—Joe. It's been six months, and more,
Since either of us saw him. Overdue.
Didn't he tell us then it would be three months?"
"But it has been a busy season for him.
I don't know why, in summer, but he says so;
And says that he is coming—very soon."
"You've heard from him. Well, when is very soon?"
"Tomorrow, late; maybe at midnight; maybe—"
"Good. Oh, that's good news. And so he wrote you.
When?"
            "I don't just know. I can't remember."
"I didn't mean it mattered. Does he say—
But then there will be time enough for that.
Three days this time?"
                    "Yes, yes—it has to be!"
He looked at Laura sharply, in surprise.
His mind was long ago made up to wonder
At nothing. "Nothing ever must be strange,"
Jonathan had told himself, and sworn it.
Nevertheless he wondered at these words,
And looked. But she had turned as far away
As the lamp light could follow; so it ended;
So talking for them ended, and the night

Passed over the cool chamber that contained them,
Passing before another day, and dumbly
Joining another night. And now the night.

Eleven, twelve, and half past;
Jonathan was dozing.
Laura at the window still,
With eyes too wide for closing,
Turned and saw him; turned again
And said it softly: "When, and when?"

Not a rattle on the road,
Not a light above the hill,
Spreading forward in a fan,
A narrow dawn, until, until
There it broke—she saw it plain—
And swept the valley like a rain.

There it tilted and descended,
Coming downward swiftly now;
Oh, so swiftly, Laura, swiftly,
As your brow,
Pressing hot against the glass,
Shuddered, fearing it would pass.

It did not pass. The long lights, swinging in,
Startled the barn lot, where the shadows ran,
Awakened and bewildered, all one way—
For safety, Laura said, escaping so
Into the farther darkness of the fields,
The aged darkness, free of these young fears,
This new excitement coming, as it came
Now, this midnight moment, unto her.
She stood, expectant, rigid, her two arms
Risen above her, holding the window frame;
She stood, her beating forehead on the glass,
Longer than death, longer than any world
Would take to turn its silence into sound;
Longer, yet it only was a moment.
When the dark engine died, already Laura
Stood at the shed's high entrance, watching Joe,
Who came; and seeing Jonathan behind her,

Blinking a pair of brotherly, tired eyes,
Laughed; and kissed her quickly, her hands hanging
Straightly beside her; laughed, and said to Jonathan:
"Sorry I wasn't later, so as to let you
Sleep the night out. Now it's badly broken:
Cracked across the middle, like a plate.
I will not say I'm sorry, though, to be here.
It's better than you know to come again.
Six months! And—well, how are you?"
                                        "Hello, Joe.
Stranger, you'll excuse this dust before you.
Don't kick it, for it flies and fills the face.
I didn't have time to sweep the farm this morning.
How are you, Joe? Been busy?"
                                        "Yes—here, Laura,
Guide me. It's new country, and I'm awkward.
Got a small bite to eat? I took no time out,
Anywhere on the road, for supper. Really?
Good!"
        So while he drank the pleasant coffee,
They talked: three of them there, with none to say
The only thing that waited to be said,
The painful thing that might have lost its pain,
Clear in the lamplight, with three faces round it.

They talked; but not of anything; till Jonathan,
Weary beyond all words, got up for bed.
"You take him, dear, and turn him in. Goodnight."
"Goodnight!" and he was gone. They heard him go,
Heavily down the narrow hall, to the end.
They heard him; but he heard them, too; their silence
Followed him and surrounded him, and pressed there
Hurtfully at his ears, as if the walls
Came closer than they ought. He stood a moment,
Staring at all or nothing; then undressed,
Drew the familiar blankets over, and slept.

He woke in the same darkness—in the same
Hour, if any hour was still alive.
He lay, and all his body was in labor
With a dim question, that would turn and strive,

175

Meaning to find a way unto his tongue:
Was she come back? Was it the bell that rung?

It reached him now, and asking of himself:
Was Laura there beside him, and asleep?
Jonathan could answer: No—the silence
Never had been so terrible and deep.
And yet this very stillness gave him doubt,
Till he turned, so, and put his fingers out.

He found her by him, moveless in her place;
Asleep already—long ago, perhaps.
He drew his fingers slowly home, and smiled,
Playing in his mind with harmless scraps
Of hope. But soon her silence, breath and limb,
Stretched beneath the blankets, bothered him.

He rose without a sound and struck a match,
Holding a hand between it and her face.
In the half-darkness she was whole and white;
But the dark eyes, like apertures in lace,
Stared at the ceiling—open as she slept,
Unseeing, though the world went by and wept.

Morning, and Laura waited by the table,
And when Joe came looked eagerly to see
What lines of rest lay crosswise of his face—
And seeing none, was happy, Jonathan thought,
Watching them both, and wondering how her gaze
Could feed so on the bones of that distress.
Yet feed it did, till Laura, new-exalted,
Busied herself with breakfast, singing low
And listening not at all. So, if he spoke,
It merely was to lead his mind away,
And Joe's—but not her mind, already room-loose.
Joe's mind was here or nowhere, for his eyes
Never were off of Jonathan, and never
Comforted even there. What word last night,
What sound between them, silent beyond the bell,
What thing was he afraid of, Jonathan wondered.

"Well, have you seen our Tom?"
                              "I have."
                                      "And did he—"
"Yes, he did. A song and dance. 'The Rain Crow.'
Afterwards I tried to make him talk.
Doesn't he talk?"
                    "Oh, no, he doesn't need to.
Jon can understand him as he is.
Songs, you know. And real ones—maybe old ones.
Not the silly stuff you like, and I like."
Jonathan grew patient. "He is silly.
I never said he wasn't, or have praised
His songs, although I like them secretly.
They're silly too—and make a perfect match
For these that come on rubber."
                                "I'll agree.
Laura, Jon, there isn't much to choose.
But now I have to know one thing about him.
Where did he come from? Did he happen here?
I asked him, and I gave him time to answer—
Vainly. Does he understand a question?
What does he understand?"
                          But even then
A shuffle in the pantry made them listen,
Startled, till it ceased, and Tom began:

> Over the mountains, boys,
> Come long lonesome way.
> Over the mountains, boys,
> This many a day.
>> Didn't like them goin's-on
>> A little bit, a little bit.
>> Tied my yellow handkerchief
>> And out I lit, and out I lit.

> Over the river, boys—
> Big one runnin' west—
> Over the river, boys;
> Thought that the best.

Didn't like them goin's-on
A little bit, a little bit.
Tied my yellow handkerchief
And out I lit, and out I lit.

Over the open country,
Good roads runnin' north.
Look for better people;
See what these are worth.
    Didn't like them goin's-on
    A little bit, a little bit.
    Tied my yellow handkerchief
    And out I lit, and out I lit.

Over the open country,
People about the same.
Everybody ornery.
Don't know who to blame.
    I don't like this goin's-on
    A little bit, a little bit.
    Tie my yellow handkerchief
    And lickety-split, and lickety-split.

Over the lakes and yonder,
Injuns may be good—
Whittlin' red new babies
Out of cedar wood.
    I don't like this goin's-on
    A little bit, a little bit.
    Tie my yellow handkerchief
    And lickety-split, and lickety-split.

"A sample!" Laura cried, and looked at Joe,
Who only looked at Jonathan and said:
"Bring him in here. I want to see his eyes."
But Tom had ceased as simply as the song.
No sound of going, yet the pantry, searched,
And afterwards the kitchen and the barn lot,
Brought no tom cat prowling. "He's a tom cat—
Slippery, young, and long," said Laura shrilly;
"I for one don't like his meowing much.
Do you? Do you?" But neither had attended.

Afternoon, and what was now to say?
Four o'clock, and where to send themselves?
"I'll tell you. Don't we need to go to town?
Jump in. I'll take you. Jonathan, come on.
There's room for you up here."
                              So off they sped,
The three of them, with Laura in the middle,
Fingering at the gears and crying "Fast!
Eight miles, eight minutes—can you make it, Joe?"
"No hurry," Jonathan said; but up the long hill,
Over and down, and round the Johnson curve,
Round, and then straight on they roared, till the town,
Lying upon the left, lay there to see.
At the cross-roads they slowed. "Too sharp for speeders.
We're speeders," Joe was saying. "Now, tomorrow,
I'll go to the right here, won't I, driving back?"
For a quick moment, turning, Laura swept
The way they had not taken. "Yes, you will.
You will. But there's this half a mile, remember.
I think you'll never make it"; though they did;
And bought their few unnecessary things;
And turned for home. "Now slower," Jonathan said.
So all the way in silence, in the last light.

The sun had lingered long above the house,
Yet not too long for Jonathan, who watched it
Going, red, by the grove, and when he lost it,
Shivered a little, suddenly, with a dread
No one would know the name of. "And it's nothing.
Nothing but a fear of nights," he said:
"These nights, when things can happen. But they won't."

It was the night of all his nights if Jonathan had known;
A true alarm; but now he sighed and laid it well away:
Down among his oldest fears, forgotten with his hope.
But that would be remembered, too, upon a certain day.

He stood, if he but knew, within the call of certain hours
That soon would ring him round with voices, pitiful at last.
He stood beside the current of a bold, unconscious river;
Stood, but could not see what it was bringing there so fast.

179

He only felt the night around him, dark, without a star,
Heavy, like a fur; and then he felt a drop of rain.
Another, and another; but they stopped, and while he waited,
Nothing came at all, and nothing came that night again.

"I couldn't have expected it; the drouth is not to break
Till something else has broken here—what? and who? and how?
Nothing will declare it." Yet the weight about to fall
Hung above his head and snapped a cable even now.

He walked indoors and found them wildly opposite each other;
A table's width between them, but a world between their eyes;
Space that Laura looked across and trembled, leaning toward it;
Something though that frightened him, as when a shadow flies.

Something there had frightened Joe, staring at it still.
Something there had fascinated Laura. Yet she turned:
"Jonathan, be careful. We were walking on the edge—"
"Of what?" But she had caught her hands, as if the fingers burned.

"What I was saying, Jonathan, was nonsense.
I meant to tell you simply of an errand
One of us has to run, and that is me.
I left the most important of our packages—
Spice for Sunday dinner—at the store.
How could I be so foolish? But I was,
And it is there; and since it's Saturday night
I'll have Joe take me in and get it. So?
You're tired. You stay."
                              "All right. Go on along."

When Laura, coming slowly forth at last,
Murmured that she was ready, Joe had gone.
There at the gate, his lights along the road now,
He idled. She could see him through the glass;
Or see the lights, enough of him to know;
And here could see her husband, tall and friendly,
Coming to button more of her brown sweater.
She met him as he came with both her hands
Upward, as if to hold him there, and kissed him.
"Goodbye," she said, and ran;

And that was all.
But the hung weight was hurrying to its fall.

Jonathan, alone among the shadows of the room,
Heard the minutes pass, but heeded not their starting back;
Heeded not the panic that was on them as they ceased—
Stiffened there with something seen, trembling on the track.

For Jonathan the time was dull; for them the time was dead.
The hour had come, the weight was down, and still it would not
    rise.
A desert space before them with no river going round;
The stop, the awful end; but none of this was in his eyes.

He closed them, and the circle of the silence was complete.
He opened them, bewildered. Joe and Laura. Were they here?
The car had stopped. Or had it stopped? Why the humming still?
And why those deeper voices coming near, and near, and near?

Jonathan, awake upon the instant, filled the door—
Shutting in the light, but soon his shadow leaned and spread,
Enclosing her at last, embracing all of her together;
Possessing her forever now, beautiful and dead.

"I loved her, Jon; she was my brother's wife;
I loved her therefore only, and that much.
It was not little, either, as you know.
So I have been unhappy this dry while,
Watching her love go out of her and wander
Like a lost star that would return its heat
To some familiar cluster in the sky—
Familiar if she found it; but she didn't.
Better than you, standing away a little,
I saw the search, I felt the cold around her,
The perfect cold wherein her eyes, so warm,
Burned to a black unnaturalness. I felt it,
Touching us too with frost. And felt her eyes.
In April, yes, they found me, they declared me—
Me!—the mist they had been searching for.
How wrong they were, and—may I say it?—mad,
I shall not try to tell you. But believe.
Believe me when I say I would have saved her

Had she been any other girl alive,
And had I been as free to do the thing
She wanted as a thousand, thousand more.
She told me then to take her—and I knew
The reason, the unreason. Not me only—
Not me, Jon, at all, and you must see it—
Nothing but cities; she had fallen in love
With cities, and though broken on the spires,
Dashed like a windward bird, she still must cling there,
Loving the very edges of the stone.
Sometimes they find a swallow thus, and drop it
Over the side, and watch a bloody wing
Fluttering down and down. I otherwise.
I did my best to pet the panic out,
Smoothing the plumes and talking past the sun.
She did not hear me. She would watch the wind
And fly again, and enter me, and stay.
She told me that. And so I talked to you—
I talked as I was going, there in April,
Of cities and the love of cities—thinking,
After I left, how Laura would defend you.
In her own mind at first. And then with words.
Therefore I was silent these six months,
Coming at last in hope. But it was worse then,
After the drouth, after your tuneful bumpkin.
I found her different only in degree,
And that the top. I warned her, and she struck me—
So! And tonight. There wasn't any package.
I knew there wasn't any, yet I took her—
I—to the fearful end. For at the cross-roads,
Even as she had threatened, it was 'Right!
Right! And away forever! Or I'll jump!'
I faltered then, but not the wheel, that followed
Left, and left—and pulled us on so swiftly,
Who would have thought a woman could stand up!
It was as if the wind had wanted Laura.
Maybe it had; or one mistaken star.
At least—well, there's no more. You want me, Jon,
How long? For I can stay or I can go.
How long? Or are you done with me, as she was?"

"Done? Nothing is ever done with. Nothing goes
But goes too soon, too soon. Yet I'll not beg you.
There never was enough of Laura stayed;
So go. My word to her was always 'Longer,
Longer, Laura, longer.' If she went,
Maybe it was a word too much that moved her.
So go. But you are welcome, Joe, till Doomsday."

"Jon—what if you went with me? This is finished."

"Nothing is ever finished. Nothing fails
But fails before its time. It's not my time yet.
When that has come I shall have more than failed—
My kind and I then perished altogether.
To cease is not to fail, and may be honorable.
At least I see some honor in an end
Not hastened, not escaped: an end accepted.
The first old Gentry would have had me stay.
I think he must have been the kingly kind
Who dies with what is left of a long staff:
A stick, a piece of nothing, but his hand
Holds it, and his voice goes through the kingdom,
Bigger than ever, bidding the dust come down.
The first old Gentry—Jonathan his name—
He would have told me stay. And I shall stay.
It is the only word that has a meaning,
Now in our death of names."
                                        "It is a good word.
Listen."
              For the night was marching off,
And the slow feet were awful till they ceased.

"Listen."
              For the morning, come again,
Moving the trees apart, was there to calm them.

"Listen."
              For the semblance of a song,
Meeting the day, meeting the dawn and falling,
Quickened the separate brothers; and it sang:

Over the mountains, boys,
And down the river middle,
Took long lonesome way
To solve old riddle.
   Adam and Eve,
    They dug and spun
    Till the Lord got tired.
    Then where'd they run?

Over the mountains, boys,
And down the river middle,
Ask that fellow there
With the broken fiddle.
   Adam and Eve,
    They dug and spun.
    And so must every
    Other one.

Over the mountains, boys,
And down the river middle,
Won't learn nothin' new,
Hey diddle diddle.
   Adam and Eve,
    They dig and spin
    Till the Lord he's tired
    And turns 'em in.

A WINTER DIARY AND
OTHER POEMS

1935

A WINTER DIARY

This was not written then, when measuring time
Ran smoothly to unalterable rhyme;
When even song—but still it is unsounded—
Kept the pure tally that has been confounded.
This was not written then, when sudden spring
Not yet had threatened winter, and no thing
Stood colder than the skin of apple trees.
Now every top is bursting into bees;
Now all of them, solidified to light,
Reflect a cloudy fire, as high, as white
As any sky in summer; and at last
Sharp edges of a shadow have been cast.
Thus sudden spring, with sudden summer near,
Has made a certain winter disappear:
The winter of all winters I would keep
Had I the power to put this warmth asleep
And make the world remember what I saw.
But who has power against a season's law?
Who lives a winter over, who is proof
Against the rain of months upon his roof?
A certain winter fades that I had thought
Forever in live colors to have caught.
A certain moveless winter more than moves:
Runs backward, and oblivion's great grooves
Lie deeper in the distance, and tomorrow
Nothing will be there save mist and sorrow.
Therefore must I fix it while I may:
Feign records, and upon this single day
Tie months of time together, in pretended
Sequence till they once again are ended.

. . . So it is autumn, when the city reaches,
Pulling us home from mountains and from beaches;
Down the curved roads and from the crescent sands
To oblong streets among divided lands.

Yet not us four. It is the year we stay
And watch the town-returners pour away.
Now the last stragglers of the stream have gone;
Here now we stand upon a thinning lawn—
The shade wind-shattered, and the cut grass sleeping—
Here then we stand and to the country's keeping
Tender four faces. Not a leaf that falls
But flutters through a memory of walls;
Flutters, with more to follow, till they weave
This solitude we shall at last believe.

. . . October sunshine, and a summer's day!
Yet not the heaviness long wont to lay
Slow skies upon our heads and bind us round
With the full growth of a too fruitful ground.
The morning sun was southerly, and noon
Came swiftly, and the day was over soon:
An airy thing time tossed us for our pleasure,
Blue, and wide-blown, and rich with gold leaf-treasure.
The solid green is gone, the trees are fire:
Cool fire, and top-contained, without desire;
Not caring if it lives, for lo, all day
Wind bullied it and bore the sparks away.
October sunshine and red-ember drifts;
So the long burden of a summer lifts.

. . . November rain all night, the last of three
Dark nights and mornings. We have been to see
The brook that piles grey water down the meadows.
Grey water, and there is no sun for shadows;
No wind for bare tree-talk, no thing but spreading
Rain; no thing but rain, wherein the treading
Crow-feet leave thin tracks, and grass is drowned
With a contented and a final sound.
Safely indoors now, with a fire to dry us,
We hear a whole long year go slipping by us—
Backward to die, with nothing left ahead
Save solitude and silence, and a thread
Of days that will conduct us through the cold.
The window-panes are waterfalls that fold
Small misty visions of our valley's end.

188

The rain is sewing curtains that will rend
And rise another day; but shut us now
In such a world as mice have up the mow.
Thus do we know ourselves at last alone;
And laugh at both the kittens, who have grown
Till here they lie, prim figures by the fire,
Paws folded, aping age and undesire.
The boys would have them up again to play.
But they are sudden-old; it is the day
For dreaming of enclosure, and of being
All of the world time missed as he was fleeing.
They think, the furry fools, to live forever.
So then do we, the curtains lifted never.

. . . It is December, and the setting sun
Drops altogether leftward of the one
Long mountain-back we used to measure by.
The maple limbs swing upward, grey and dry,
And print the lawn, now naked for the snow,
With lines that might be nothing. But we know.
We see them there across the bitten ground,
Dark lace upon the iron, and catch the sound
Of half a world contracting under cold.
Slowly it shrinks, for it is wise and old,
And waits; and in its wisdom will be spared.
So is the frosted garden-plot prepared.
The withered tops, arustle row by row,
Fear nothing still to come; for all must go.
That is their wisdom, as it is the horse's,
Whose coat the wind already reinforces,
There in the blowing paddock past the gate.
The four of us a long day, working late,
Confined her where she grazes, building the fence
She leans on; yet she would not wander hence.
She drops her head and nibbles the brown grass,
Unmindful of a season that will pass;
Long-coated, with a rump the wind can ruffle;
Shoeless, and free; but soon the snow will muffle
All of her four black feet, that study a line
Down to the ponies' corner under the pine.
So have the field-mice, folding their startled ears,

Burrowed away from owls and flying fears.
So have the hunters ceased upon the hills;
The last shot echoes and the woodland stills;
And here, along the house, the final flower
Lets fall its rusty petals hour by hour.

. . . So, in December, we ourselves stand ready.
The season we have dared is strong and heady,
But there is many a weapon we can trust.
Five cellar shelves that were but layered dust
Are wiped to kitchen neatness, and confine
Clear jellies that will soothe us when we dine:
Crab-apple, quince, and hardly-ripened grape,
With jam from every berry, and the shape
Of cherries showing pressed against the jar;
Whole pears; and where the tall half-gallons are,
Tomatoes with their golden seeds; and blunt
Cucumbers that the early ground-worms hunt.
The highest shelf, beneath the spidery floor,
Holds pumpkins in a row, with squash before:
Dark, horny Hubbards that will slice in half
And come with pools of butter as we laugh,
Remembering the frost that laid the vines
Like blackened string: September's valentines.
Firm corn, and tapering carrots, and the blood
Of beets complete the tally of saved food;
Yet over in a corner, white and square,
Is the big bin with our potato-share.
Then seven barrels of apples standing by.
We brought them down the ladder when a high
Stiff wind was there to whip us, hand and cheek;
And wheeled them to the barn, where many a week
They filled the tightest chamber; but they found
More certain safety here below the ground:
The Baldwins to be eaten, and the Spies;
But Greenings are for betty and for pies.
A dusty cellar window, old as stone,
Lets in grey light, a slowly spreading cone
Sharp-ended here, and shining, at the shelves.
All of the other spaces wrapped themselves
In darkness long ago; and there the wood

190

Remembers a great sky wherein they stood:
The twenty trees I walked with Louis, marking,
Once in a mist of rain; then axes barking
Through the wet, chilly weeks, with ring of wedges
Under the blows of iron alternate sledges,
Louis's and Laurier's, of equal skill.
These were the two woodchoppers whom the still
Small faces of the boys watched day by day.
They sat among brown leaves, so far away
We barely could hear their shouting as the saw
Paused, and the great trunk trembled, and a raw
Circle of odorous wood gaped suddenly there.
Now maple and oak and cherry, and a rare
Hard chestnut piece, with hickory and birch,
Piled here in shortened lengths, await my search:
Coming with lantern and with leather gloves
To choose what provender the furnace loves.
From wall to wall a dozen resting rows:
We shall be warm, whatever winter blows.
So for the range upstairs a mound uprises,
By the back fence, of birch in sapling sizes.
Old Bailey cut them through a lonely fall—
He and his axe together, that was all:
They in a thicket, and the white poles gleaming;
Now a high frozen pile the sun is steaming.
We shall be warm, whatever north wind catches
Any of us outside the rattling latches;
Down the sloped road, or where the yard descends
To the barn's angle with its gusty ends,
Or higher, beyond the garden and the orchard—
We shall not be snow-worried or wind-tortured.
The armor we have sent for has arrived.
The great book spread its pages, and we dived
Like cormorants for prey among the rocks;
And chose, and duly ordered; and the box
Came yesterday. A winter's woolen wraps:
Thick-wristed mittens and two stocking caps;
Three fleece-lined jackets that will turn all weather,
And one cut neat for ladies out of leather;
Red sweaters, nut-brown shirts, and rubber-soled
Great workman's shoes for wading in the cold.

We shall be warm; or we can stamp indoors,
Wool failing, till the supper and the chores.

. . . So quietly it came that we could doubt it.
There was no wind from anywhere to shout it.
Simply it came, the inescapable cold,
Sliding along some world already old
And stretched already there had we perceived it.
Now by this hour the least one has believed it.
Snippy, the lesser kitten, lies entangled
Deep in the fur of Snappy, where a dangled
Feed-sack drapes a box inside the shed.
I found them with the lantern, playing dead:
Those very creatures, Snippy and her brother,
Who in the orange sunset tumbled each other,
Lithe by the stepping-stone. Through such a night
How often have they put the frost to flight;
How often, when the blackness made them bolder,
Have they confounded time, that grew no colder.
Yet not this night; they recognize the god,
As in the barn the black mare, left to nod,
Stands in her blanket, dozing. I have come
From tending her, and heard the ominous hum
Of branches that no wind moved overhead;
Only a tightness and a stealth instead.
The stiffened world turns hard upon its axis,
Laboring; but these yellow lamps relax us,
Here in the living-room at either end.
She by the south one, I by the north pretend
Forgetfulness of pavements; or remark
How very dead the sky is, and how dark—
In passing, with the air of two that pore
On things familiar, having been before.
It is our way of knowing what is near.
This is the time, this is the holy year
We planned for, casting every cable off.
That was a board-creak; that was the horse's cough;
That was no wind, we say; and looking down,
Smile at the wolf-dog, Sam, who dreams of brown
Clipped fields that he will lope in when he wakes.
He dreams, and draws his ankles up, and slakes

192

Imaginary thirsts at frozen pools.
He is the wolf-dog, he is the one that fools
New comers up the yard; for gentler beast
Prowled never to the pantry for a feast.
He is the boys' companion, who at dusk
Ran rings with them tonight, and worried the husk
Of daylight in his teeth, and stood his hair
Wind-upright. Now he sleeps unthinking there,
Companion of the boys, who long ago
Climbed the dark stairs to bed. So we below
Should come there too, we say; and say it again,
And laugh to hear the clock tick out the ten.
We are not sleepy; this is the holy year.
Let it tick on to midnight, and for cheer
Start coffee in the kitchen, while I spread
Bright jam upon the goodness of cut bread.

. . . We were awakened by a double shout:
"Get up, you lazy people, and look out!"
There was a weight of stillness on my eyes;
But in my ears innumerable sighs
Of snowflakes settling groundward past the glass.
I stood and stared, saying for jest "Alas!
My sight fails, I can see the merest dim
Milk-whiteness!" "We must bring it up to him!"
Cried one; and both were going, when I told them:
"Dress!" So now, as breakfast waits, behold them
Marching through a mist of falling specks.
They stop and raise their faces, and it flecks
Their foreheads till they laugh; then treading on,
Leave tracks across the swiftly thickening lawn.
I let them go this morning for the milk—
The car wheels turning softly in a silk
New coverlet as wide as eyes could see.
The chimney smoke was rising, round and free,
From every ridge of shingles: even there
Where Grandmother waved and pointed at the air.
The wolf-dog running with us need not pause,
Tasting the untamed whiteness; for his jaws
Dipped as he loped along, and fiercely entered
Now the far past wherein his mind was centered.

Back at the barn the Shetland ponies wheeled,
Biting each other's manes, their little field
Grown boundless by some fantasy, and fenceless.
They romped like shaggy dogs, and were as senseless,
Fluttering at the gate, as moths, and small.
They waited for the big one in the stall.
She whinnied as we came, and only stopped
When I rose up the ladder and hay dropped.
She will have finished breakfast in an hour.
So we, and through a sudden whirling shower
Shall bring her to the ponies. Then our talk
Will come once more to sleds, and up the walk
I shall again make promises; and keep them,
Thinking of flakes and how a wind can heap them.
This wind is gentle, and the grey sheet sways.
I am no prophet if it falls and stays.

. . . All yesterday it melted, and at night
Was nothing, and the prophecy was right.
But in a play-house corner stand the sleds,
Almost as high as the excited heads
Of two that will be on them when the slopes
Glisten once more. And so the boys have hopes
While I have present pleasure; for the ground
Grows musical wherever I am bound.
The mud was gone as quickly as the snow:
An afternoon of thaw, but then a low
Crisp sunset sound of shrinking, and the crack
Of coldness like a panther coming back.
Tonight the snowless evening and the moon
Kept my late feet contented with a tune
More ancient than the meadows, where the stones
Rise ever up: unburiable bones.
The bareness of the world was like a bell
My feet, accustomed, struck; and striking well,
Let the rung sound be mingled with the dry
Primeval winter moonlight flowing by.
Alone outdoors and late, the resonant lawn
Moved with me as I lagged, and moving on
Bore all my senses fieldward to those bones
Of permanence, the unalterable stones.

There is no such intensity of lasting
Anywhere out of meadows, where the fasting
Grasses worship something in December
Older than any moist root can remember;
Older than age, drier than any drouth;
Something not to be praised by word of mouth.
I did not praise them then, nor shall henceforth;
But shall remind me, so, what change is worth:
Timothy round a rock, and daisies hiding
Something that will be there again—abiding
Longer than hope and stronger than old despair;
Something not to be dated under the air.
I looked at stones; and faces looked at me:
Sidewise, always sidewise, past a tree
Or slanting down some corner, or obliquely
Squinting where the moon fell, and as weakly.
I saw them not but knew them: the tired faces
Of those who may not leave their acred places:
Those of a time long gone that never dies.
You know it by the darkness of their eyes,
And by the way they work to comprehend
Who lives here now beyond a century's end.
Who lives and does not labor, and makes light
Of the grim gods that once were day, were night;
That carved a cheek, bent breasts, and knotted hands.
Not one of them withdraws or understands.
Not one of them but looked at me; and I,
Intruder here, seemed helpless to reply.
Not by their older choosing are we here,
Not by their doom made free of gods and fear.
Was then the better time? I said; and thought
How excellently winter moonshine taught
The shapes of winter trees. That maple there,
How shadeless, how upflowing, and how fair!
Even without their leaves the elm-limbs drooped;
The alders leaned; and birches interlooped
Their lacy, blackened fingers past the pines.
The great dead chestnut where the loud crow dines
Writhed on, its mighty arms unskilled to fall.
The evergreens were solid over all,
And hickories and tulips, few of limb,

Held what they had straight out for time to trim.
Was then the better world, I wondered—daring
Suddenly now an answer from the staring
People of old days, the accusing faces.
But none of us, tree-watching on these places,
Ever will hear a sentence from the source.
Gone is their blood, and spent their bitter force;
They only live to chafe us down the wind
And leave us ever afterward thin-skinned:
Wondering on them, the only-good,
On whom these lighter feet too long intrude.

. . . We have had company of Friday nights.
We have looked out of windows till the lights
Of cars too long in coming dipped and streamed;
Then ended by the door as time had dreamed.
Two late ones from the city, blinking here
In the warm lamplight, with the kittens near—
These have been shown their room, the spare northeast one;
Have laughed and begged a bite: even the least one,
Even a crust to pay them for the ride.
Already coffee bubbled, fit to glide,
As quickly as cups were ready, from the spout.
Already there were cookies placed about;
And soon the supper entered that would keep us
Longer awake than wise, with talk to steep us
In every winter's moment we had missed.
So we unrolled our pleasures, till the list
Grew endless, and the meaning of it fled.
So, as the boys before us, up to bed.
For all of us a lazy breakfast waited,
With coffee and tobacco, brownly mated,
Warming the day to come. We tilted chairs,
Lit pipes, and fingered forks; till unawares
Time bore us half to noon; and looking out,
We argued what the weather was about.
Some said it would be overcast till night,
Settling themselves forever; but the right
Was mostly with the walkers and the curious.
First then the barn, where the black mare was furious,
Tossing as I excused our long delay.

No answer, but the eyes among the hay
Dived languorously and said I was forgiven.
The cutter by the car could not be driven.
I found it years ago and dragged it here
To a dry floor and braced it; but the clear
Curved figure will be never swift again.
Snow or no snow, it is for living men
Another last reminder of the old
Dim people who are dead. A crimson fold
Of lining flaps and braves the window frost.
But all the rest is poor and language-lost:
No bells to shake, no orders to be going
Down a long hill where only time is snowing—
Flake by flake forgotten, till the white
Far past of it is shadowy with night.
We took the road and turned, and crossed the bridge;
Then, needing not to beg the privilege,
Crossed neighbor Allyn's meadow to his row
Of sandknolls; then, as all the cattle go,
Between the roundest couple home to tea.
So Saturday, and night, when we agree
What games shall silence evening, and what talk
Shall bring the ghost whose breast is brittle chalk.
So Sunday, with a visit to the great
Grandfather pine that guards the burial gate.
Neglected there, the town's first graveyard lies
Where once the Hurlburt roadway took the rise,
Bringing a country mourner up to pray.
But year by year the woodchucks have their way,
And higher mounds are there than used to reckon
The small well-buried length of smith or deacon.
So all the week-end over, and the pair
Departed; and a blizzard in the air.

. . . That second snow fulfilled us while it lasted.
But now for two brown weeks the fields have fasted
Under a windless, under a lukewarm sun.
Christmas Eve and New Year's Day are done,
And here we stand expectant, straining dumbly
Toward a long stretch that will not lie so comely:
Three dark, inclement months before the spring.

Or such the hope; we want no softer thing,
No disappointment deepened day by day.
That second snow, dissolving, drained away
Too much of sudden glory, and too much
Of the towered god whose mantle we must touch.
There was no blizzard in it after all.
Only a thickening sky, so slow to fall
That Monday passed, and Tuesday. Then a hush;
Then a faint flick, as if a fox's brush
Had gained the woods in safety, and the hole;
Then steadily, steadily down the winter stole.
All afternoon it hissed among some clump
Of shrubbery, and deepened round the pump;
All afternoon, till time put out the light.
Then the black rustling through the soundless night:
Dark flake on flake colliding where no gaze
Of beast or person followed. Dim the ways
Of snow in great high darkness; strange the sound
Of whiteness come invisible to ground.
And yet the lamps awhile allowed the glance
Of a stray whirl of moth wings blown to dance,
Confused, beyond the four and twenty panes.
Here once we sat and watched the autumn rains
Stitching a wall of water. Now the snow—
A frailer fall, and gentler—came to sew
New raiment for the sun-accustomed sashes.
The upstairs window that a north wind lashes,
Beating the maple on it gust by gust,
Hung silent, like a picture; but it thrust
Pure light on brilliant branches, layered well
With silver that as slowly rose and fell,
No visible lawn beneath it, and no thing,
Round or above, save blackness in a ring:
A prone, suspended skeleton creeping hither,
All knuckle joints and bare bones twigged together.
Next morning then, with Christmas five days off,
What wonder if we called this well enough?
What wonder if the two boys prematurely
Counted upon continuance, and surely
Bragged of a snowy hill for him, the guest:
The expected boy, of all their friends the best,

Due now from deep Virginia on a night;
Their own, to play a week with out of sight?
So off they hurried, pulling the sleds behind them,
To cross the nearest meadow-stretch and find them
Somewhere a perfect slope that they could pack:
The runners for the hundredth time and back
Deep-sinking through the softness, with dragged feet
To finish a rough design and leave it neat.
I watched them for a little from the road,
Then called, and she came with me to the snowed
White forest edge, and over the wall inspected
The prints of birds; or how a deer directed
Leap after leap to gain his inland thicket.
A pine branch sagged to the earth, but I could flick it,
Filling my neck with flakes as up it reared,
Snow-loosened of its many-pointed beard.
Meanwhile the cry of coasters over the hill,
With moment interruptions, clear and still,
That said the feet were staggering up again.
We came, and Sam the wolf-dog joined them then
In a loud, urgent welcome, bark and word.
For he had crossed the field to make a third,
And close-pursued them, snapping at their feet
Now up the slope, now down; then off to meet
Plump Snappy, most companionable cat,
Who, plowing the snow alone, arrived and sat
Like something stone of Egypt, not for play.
He watched us, two by two, slide swift away,
Then turned his head, encouraging the weak one,
Snippy, the little sister, the grey meek one,
Who half from home had squatted in a track;
And wailed until we saved her, walking back.
That was the day, with four days still to come,
We prophesied long whiteness; hearing the hum
Of trees contracted slowly in no wind;
Or watching the clouds a clear sun dipped and thinned.
That was the night the low moon, all but waned,
Came to me once—upstarting at the strained
Hurt sound of something strangled in the woods—
Came to me at the window, over floods
Of waveless shining silence, and I said:

There is a month of coldness dead ahead.
But Thursday of a sudden thawed it all,
And Friday, like a silly thing of fall,
An innocent late-summer thing, declared
Calm days, with every melting meadow bared.
So when they blew their horn and gained the gate—
Those weary three Virginians—only a late
Cool breath of proper evening blew to greet them.
Sam leapt out ahead of us to meet them.
Then the old rejoicing, four and three;
With talk of the north till bedtime, and the tree
We all must bring tomorrow: a picked pine
To anchor in a room with block and twine.
We found it, best of several by a swamp,
And sawed and bore it hither amid the romp
Of boys and tumbling cats, that on warm haunches
Settled to watch us trim the bristling branches;
Looping the ends with silver-studded cord
And lo, with more than patience could afford
Of cranberries and popcorn needled through:
Now red, now white, now one and one, and two.
From every room, when darkness well was down,
Came packages of mystery, in brown
Creased paper if a boy or man were giver;
But if a lady, candle-light would quiver
On multicolored tissue, gold and green.
Then silence, with a glow behind the screen
To point our way to bed, the lamps unlighted.
Then dawn, and stairs acreak, and something sighted
Even beyond the door that we had closed;
Then breakfast, and the mysteries deposed.
No more the ache of waiting; shed the power
Preeminent of any future hour.
That was the height; the rest was going down,
With random walks, or driving into town,
Or sitting after sunfall over tea.
We tidied rooms and set the spangled tree
Midway the snowless lawn, and spiked it there—
Popcorn and berries on it, and a square
Of suet tied with string to tempt the flying
Birds. But there were kittens always spying,

Ready to pounce and punish; and at last
A brief wind laid it over like a mast.
The rest was milder pleasure, suiting well
Our seven tongues that had so much to tell.
We talked. And then the final day was come.
Farewell, you three! And if the end was dumb,
Remember this: there was no charm to say
As down the hill your fenders sloped away.
So Christmas Eve and New Year's Day are done;
And still the lukewarm, still the windless sun
Possesses what it watches: hidden here,
A barn and painted house, from which appear
Four little figures scanning a clear sky.
It doubtless will be clouded by and by,
And doubtless yield each one his small desire.
Now only tracks, minute upon the mire.

. . . O welcome night-wind, crazily arriving,
You had not warned us till we heard you striving,
Here and at every corner of the house—
Now a great beast and now a nibbling mouse—
Striving in every stature to undo us;
There was no rumor of your marching to us,
No swift annunciation; or eight hands
Loud, loud had hailed you, giving you our lands,
Ourselves, and all this valley to unsettle.
We only lay and heard you; heard the rattle
Of shutters, and caught the groan as you went on
Of nails from weather-boarding all but drawn.
We only lay, pulling the covers higher,
Until at dayrise, grouping about the fire,
We greeted a hundred frost-hills on the panes;
Looked through, and saw the still wind-worried lanes
Thrash heavily; and walking out a little,
Said the snapped, hanging branches were wind-spittle.
Nor was the blowing over; still at twelve
High limbs were double-curving, like a helve,
And through the day, beneath white clouds and round ones,
All was a sea, with us the happy drowned ones—
Drifting among the layers of thin cold,
Self-separated. Some, the slow and old,

Slid lazily, floating beyond a world;
But some were childish-violent, and curled
And slapped our willing foreheads as they raced.
Layer upon clear layer built a waste
Of space for minds to work in, high and low.
Then the loud night that bade the softness go,
With iron for morning ground, and every print
Of dog or man foot stamped as in a mint:
All metal, all eternal, if this cold,
High, many-shelving universe could hold.
It held; and laid a film across the pond;
Laid more, and laying others, brought the fond
Brown wolf-dog there to slide beside the boys—
Bewildered, but enchanted by the noise
Of brittle alder-sticks and clapping hands.
So now the ice in hourly thickened bands
Is pressing tight around us, pond and lawn.
One moment, and the mighty gale was gone,
Far-whistling. Then a silence, and the fall
To nothing. Then the crisp iron over all.

. . . Slap, slap, the sound of car chains going by,
With elsewhere only stillness, under dry
Fantastic heaps of white the wind renews.
It reached us evenly, as snowfalls use;
But there were days of fury when the air,
Whirled white as flour, was powdery everywhere;
Till now the finest grains, like desert sand,
Wait upon eddies they will not withstand.
The snow-plows on the highway come and go:
Not vainly, but a devil takes the snow
Some windy times, and then the car lanes fill
Along the leeward side of fence or hill.
The boys are in the snow house we had made
Before this blowing weather overlaid
The first wet fall with something crisp as salt.
Four walls we packed without a single fault
Between a pair of solid shutter forms.
A roof, an eastern door away from storms,
Two windows at the ends—a bread knife cut them,
Neatly, but there was then no way to shut them—

A piece of crate for cushion, and a bag:
This is their windy fortress that a flag
Flies every day in front of, and that Sam
Lies guarding, less the dragon than the lamb.
There was a man with anthracite for eyes,
And pennies for his buttons; but he lies,
Forgotten, uncreated, where he fell.
There was a castle wall beyond the well
With store of snowballs piled against a siege,
And apples for the starving, lord or liege;
But now it too is levelled, and delight
Dwells only in this hovel at the right.
Below the sheds and halfway to the wall
Stands a lean ice house, windowless and tall,
Whose ancient door hung open day by day
Till the last shining cake was stowed away.
When ice was fourteen inches teams were hitched;
Saws buzzed; and like a waterland bewitched
The silver floor divided, line and angle.
Then loaded trucks, with pairs of tongs to dangle,
Teasing the helpful boys until they tried—
Slipped, fell, and were convinced. And so inside
Sleep twice a hundred pieces of the pond,
Preserved against the dog days and beyond.

. . . These are the undistinguishable days.
This is the calm dead center of the maze
Whereinto we have wandered, and in time
Shall wander forth again, and slowly climb
A wall the other side of which is change.
Now everything is like, with nothing strange
To keep our hands aware of what they do.
This is the winter's heart, that must renew
Its steady, steady beating when an embered
Joy is all we have, and thoughts remembered.
Therefore do I listen while I may,
Monotony, to what your whispers say
Of systole, diastole, and the ribbed
Sweet rituals wherein our wills are cribbed.
Therefore shall I count the doings here
Of one full day, and represent the year.

We rise at eight, but I an hour before
Have put the pipeless furnace in a roar;
Descending slow in slippers, robe, and socks
To where, as in some Southern ship that rocks,
Dry cargo-wood inhabits all the hold.
Our destination only the days unfold:
Tier on tier down-sloping to warm weather.
But many a hundred chunks lie yet together,
Snug in their odorous rows. So I inspire
Last evening's spent and barely-breathing fire;
Pull off my gloves; ascend the under-stair;
And smoke a chilly moment in a chair.
Then up again. But they are coming down,
Each head of hair in tangles at the crown;
And suddenly we smell a breakfast waiting:
Bacon and yellow eggs; or, alternating,
Buckwheat cakes with butter for anointing;
Or third-day porridge, grey and disappointing.
Prepared with steaming water and the comb,
We gather about the range—the morning home
Of kittens, too, and Sam the wolf-dog, stretched
Full length behind it while our plates are fetched.
The Irish hands that laid our dining table
Were up in early darkness, whence a fable
Of ghost or saint, night-walking, has its rise.
We listen, masked amusement in our eyes,
And finishing our fare, proceed to measure
Whether this day is planned for work or pleasure.
There is a woodshed faucet where I fill
Two water pails, and through the winter-still
Bound morning beat the music that she loves:
The restless mare whose foretop, smoothed with gloves,
Will hang with hay-stalk in it while she drinks.
She knows my coming footfall, and she thinks
To speed her slave's arrival with a neigh.
I am too proud to hurry; yet the hay
Seems due her, and the water, none the less.
So up to where last summer's grasses press
Their rustling weight on weight; and casting down
High pitchforkfuls, I stuff the slats with brown,

Stiff breakfast which the clever ponies hear.
I listen to their trotting, small and clear,
Round the curved path to where the western door
Stands open night or day, whatever roar
Of winds or pelt of snow drives ruthless in.
They are from northern islands where the din
Of winter never daunts them. Unconfined,
They wander about the paddock till the mined
Mute hayfall wakes their wisdom. Then they race,
Two blown and hairy creatures, into place.
I leave them there, slow-nibbling, eyes astare,
And go to prod the motor in his lair:
Four thousand pounds inert, and chilled so well
Some mornings I can barely solve the spell.
I have been baffled when a weakened spark
Has failed to fire the monster, and the dark
Webbed shadows of the room have missed his roar.
I have discovered drifts against the door,
And shovelled; I have watched a winter's rains
Turn ice, and been in misery with chains:
Now on, now off, now broken and now mended;
I have as often wished a year were ended.
But now the long thing moves, and backing out
Brings Sam, who disobeys my daily shout
And lopes to where the open meadows tempt him.
I could be angry, but his ears exempt him,
Waiting erect and friendly when I come.
My way was longer round; but now the strum
Of pistons will be answered by his feet,
That guide me to the milkhouse, dark, unneat,
Where the day's pail awaits me. Then the mile
Retravelled, past the cemetery stile
That leads among the six-foot frozen mounds.
There have been mornings when I heard the sounds
Of pick and frozen shovel at a grave;
But mostly snow and timeless silence—save
That cries of farmer children ring in the wood,
Where the white Hollow school long years has stood.
Some of them wave and call my distant name;
Then bells, and marching in to serious game;
While I at my own corner mount the hill

Past Bailey's house, and hers, where now a still
White shaft of smoke that bends above the brook
Declares Grandmother up. A pause; a look;
Good morning to her, cheerful at the door;
Then on to where the barn receives the roar
Of cylinders again until they cease.
Now to the restless mare, whom I release—
High stepping, in perpetual surprise—
To where the ponies shake their shaggy eyes.
All day will they be three beyond a gate,
Ground-musical, and free of their estate;
While we that own them, in and out of doors
Must labor at our self-appointed chores.
Now the grey tool house where the chisels hang,
And hammers lie, and saws with sharpened fang
Rest nightly on their nails, invites my skill.
I am no maker, but a floor can fill
With shavings from the least instructed plane.
Or there is wood to split, come snow or rain,
When the black stove grows hungry, and the dry
Deep kitchen box demands a fresh supply.
Ten times the barrow, loaded, piles its pieces
High at the woodshed end, till all the creases
Fold a fair week of darkness, and the dented
Chopping block is with cold wounds contented.
There is one root the garden still can give.
Under the snow, under the stubble, live
Our golden parsnips, planted and forgotten.
Nothing of them is altered or frost-rotten.
The blunt pick thuds in the ground, and up they heave:
A miracle for winter to believe.
I bring them in for dinner on this day;
And while the kettle, boiling their ice away,
Fills half a room with steam I take the road
Once more, to curiosity's abode:
That box where now the mail man will have been.
Arriving slow, I thrust my fingers in;
Draw letters forth, a bundle, or a card;
And out of time abstracted pace the hard
White ground again to where three wait for me.
No ancient courier with a king's decree

Rode ever up a hill and brought so much
As these chilled messages the mind can touch,
Restoring warmth, reviving every word
That yesterday with its own motion stirred.
Meanwhile the boys have had their little school:
Two pupils and a mother, mild of rule,
Who after beds were made and dinner planned,
Called them to where the home-built easels stand
And where the primer waits that one can read.
The younger mind admits a younger need:
Long blocks that tilt together till a boat
Sits sailing; or a castle with a moat;
Or dungeon towers to keep a kitten in—
The almond-eyed four-footed Saracen.
To painting then: tongues out and foreheads glowing,
With bannerets of bright vermilion flowing
Over and up and down; or blues, or blacks,
Full to the very corners past the tacks.
One thing remains: a paragraph to trace
On paper from the blackboard's printed face.
The boy leans long upon the table leaf,
Procrastinating; for the task was brief,
And both of them had still an hour to play.
But there he leans, unwilling, till the day
Brings twelve; and half-past twelve; and brings the white
Sealed letters that are now the noon's delight.
So dinner, and a nap for everyone
Where neither snow may enter nor the sun.
So then the afternoon, that still is short—
Midwinter lags behind the sky's report:
Each day a little longer, but the dark
Comes down before a coaster may remark.
While there is light we seek the genial store,
Off by the covered bridge; or wanting more,
Ride over two east ranges to the town
Of brass that bore the body of John Brown.
Here pavements like a puzzle run and spread;
And here a shop front, gold by gaudy red,
Demands immediate entrance; for a dime
Buys anything, land-born or maritime:
A ball, a wooden car, a masted boat,

An outboard motor that will never float;
A magnet's curve, completed by a bar;
A leaden blue policeman with his star.
So home across the ranges, past the edge
Of evening, till the last high-drifted hedge
Declares the clear necessity of chains.
So out to frosty spokes and windy lanes
Where the snow, blowing, whips the wrist and scatters;
Then upward, while a broken chain-link clatters;
Upward into the barn, the engine dying
Soundless; but the ponies are replying,
Huddled before the big one at the gate.
Scarcely we listen, for we estimate
Two hours this side of supper. Time for tea.
We light the lamps and sip the mystery,
Cup after shadowy cup, with toasted cheese.
There are no country moments like to these;
When afternoon is night, and night belongs
Like a dark heirloom of descended songs
To four that sit in solitude and hear them
Through the fond nothingness that nestles near them.
From the warm circle of the shaded lamp
At last I walk to where the ponies stamp
And the tall guardian mare is loud with thirst.
A boy with lighted lantern sheds the first
Long pair of scantling shadows on the snow;
While I, the water-bearer, dimly go
Through the great backward crescent drawn behind us.
There have been evenings when she would not mind us—
The lurking mare, complacent down the meadow.
But now a clear low whistle cleaves her shadow,
Precipitately arriving. So we lead her,
Plunging, past the corner post; and heed her
Sighing as she nuzzles in the pail.
The lantern from a high and rusty nail
Swings gently, casting circles on the hay.
The kittens somewhere, noiselessly at play,
Keep watch of us, and scan the waiting door.
They love a barn, but love the kitchen more;
And lessons still may linger in each mind
Of the long milkless night they sat confined.

We leave the ponies munching in their room
And blow our lantern black, resolved to come
By starlight home—Orion and the Bears
Low-shining; but aloft upon the stairs,
Bright Castor holding Pollux by the hand.
Now endless evening, like a painted band,
Starts moving, moving past us, and we seize,
Soft-reaching, all that momently can please.
There is an hour for singing, when the book
Lies open, and a rolling eye may look
For prompting at the words of Nelly Gray,
Darby and Joan, The Miller, Old Dog Tray;
Malbrouck that went to war, and Hoosen Johnny;
Or over the ocean, over the sea my bonnie.
The dominoes that once amused us well
Lie in their box and envy bagatelle,
Whose twenty balls, thrust up the tilted board,
Pause and return—click, click—a thousand scored!
With game or song the clock goes round to eight:
Past time for two to sleep, whose laggard gait
We must not hope to hurry up the landing.
Each elder then knows where a book is standing,
Tall on the crowded table; and begins
What may go on until the darkness thins:
Page after page upturned against the light.
For so it was, on such a nipping night,
That Holmes, or Doctor Thorndyke, heard the bell
And raced with lawless death to Camberwell;
Or Watson, in an alley with his master,
Felt the steel fingers as a crutch came faster:
Tapping, tapping, tapping, till the court
Blazed with a sudden pistol's blind report.
This is the hour, and this the placeless room
For smooth concocted tales of lust and doom;
This the remote, the sanctuary year
When the safe soul must fabricate a fear.
Many a milder evening passes, too,
With Royal Casino, Rummy, and a few
Swift-changing hands of High-Low-Jack-and-the-Game.
But then three weeks ago the chess men came;
Since when, no night so busy that it misses

The march of angry Queens, whose scalloped tresses,
Stiffly erected, fly to guard a King.
We are two novices, and rashly fling
Pawns, bishops, knights, and rooks into the fray;
Yet time and blood have taught us wiser play.
There was a gift at Christmas time of Tarot—
Untaught, but we can shuffle them and harrow
A loreless mind with him, the Hanging Man;
So all those numbered mysteries that plan
What future folds the player, and what past
Is carved upon the great Tower overcast,
So every wand and pentacle and sword
Lies curious, unfathomed, on the board.
We have been known, as never back in town,
To idle till the clock weights settled down,
And till the sound of ticking ceased unheard.
We have rejoiced some evenings at the word
Of neighbors driving over; when the names,
Smith, Prentice, Landeck, interrupted games
With something else of equal clear delight.
For there was talking now into the night,
With news of health, and trips away from home,
And how the kitchen beer went all to foam.
Gossip of Hautboy, Dibble, and Great Hill,
Gossip and jest and argument, until:
Goodbye, Smith, Landeck, Prentice; come again;
Goodnight. And so a day is ended then.
Each four and twenty hours, until we rise,
Go thus. And thus the holy winter flies.

. . . February flies, with little summers
Hidden in its beard: unlicensed mummers
Performing April antics for a day.
The sun from the horizon swings away;
The sky melts upward, and a windless hand
Scatters the seeds of warmth along the land.
They will not grow, for ice is underneath,
And every creature tastes it. But a wreath
Lies thrown by playful chance upon the smiling
Meadows that a season is beguiling.

210

Today was so, but we were not deceived;
Though what the wolf-dog and the cats believed
There is no art of knowing. They pursued
Our every venturing step and found it good:
Down the crisp meadows to the aspen grove;
Over the highway, where a salesman drove
Dry wheels on dry macadam; then the neck
Of Harrison's pasture to the Hollenbeck.
We stood, the seven walkers, on a stone
And watched the river, waveless and alone,
Go slipping, slipping under, gravelly clear.
Snippy, a mile from nowhere, crouched to peer
At nothing in the sand; then bolder sat.
Three weeks, we said, and she would be a cat
With fearsome crying kittens of her own.
Ten months with us, no more, and nearly grown!
So Snappy, arriving plump and solemn there,
Good-natured sat, the guardian of the pair.
There was a barn foundation to explore,
Ancient of fields beyond. The rotting floor
Forewarned us, and we did not enter in;
But strolled, and where tall timothy had been
Lay half an hour on stubble under the sun;
While Sam, excited by a scent, must run
Low-whining up the fences; till a voice
Recalled him, and we made the hapless choice
Of eastward marshy meadows for return.
The hummocks mired us, but a cat could learn
The causeway's secret truth; and what we lost
Came back to us at home with tea and toast.

. . . Since yesterday a hundred years have gone.
The fore-and-after season, living on,
Rouses itself and finds its bitter breath.
This wind holds on to winter as to death.
There is no end, we say, and sauntering out,
Northwestward lean till we are whirled about,
Mute neck and shoulders stinging with the snow;
Or on this Sunday morning think to go,
Foot-heavy, where the giant maples spread
Their smooth enormous branches, long since dead.
Still in this waste of wind they do not fall;

But stiffen, like old serpents sent to crawl
On dense, on layered air; until the charm
Is lifted, and descending out of harm,
They lie leaf-covered, rigid in decay
Until the last small worm has turned away.
Here in the woodland clearings they patrol,
The wind drives steadily upon its goal.
But yonder where the hemlocks lace together
There is a sudden calm, a death of weather.
The shade is black, as once in late July
When here we walked escaping yellow sky.
The shade is black and even, and the snow
Comes filtered to the open cones below:
Slowly, slowly, slowly; strange the hush,
Here in this darkened desert of the thrush.
No hermits now; yet bands of chickadees
Tread fearless of us, chirping in the trees.
The ferns of June are withered on the rocks
Midway the icy stream that bends and locks
This needled promontory where we stand.
Oh, happy time! when nothing makes demand;
When all the earth, surrendering its strength,
Regains a taller potency at length;
Sleeps on in purest might of nothing done
Till summer heaves on high the exacting sun.

. . . Ice everywhere, a comic inch of it.
Four veteran walkers of a sudden sit
Wide-sprawling; but the cat that went so sure
Waits in the shed, distrustful and demure.
On this one day the dark mare, left inside,
Stands munching while the startled ponies slide—
Their path a river, and the river frozen—
Until a barn's captivity is chosen.
Ice everywhere; but over Goshen way
Ice on the mountains: murderous display.
Down the wild road to where the lanes were dry
We crept on crunching chains; then letting fly,
Passed houses till we gained the known plateau.
Yet now no more familiar, for the glow
Of crystals, like an ocean, blinded eyes

Untutored in the way a forest dies:
Slim birch and maple, sycamore and larch
Bent low before the mysteries of March;
Bent glassy-low, or splintered to a heap
Of glittering fragments that the sunrays sweep—
The sun, ironic, heartless, come to glance
At death and beauty shivering in a dance.

. . . I have been absent through the ending days
Of March beyond the mountains, where the ways
Of all the world drive onward as before.
I have been absent from the windy door;
Have gazed on travel-mornings out of flying
Windows at a distant winter dying.
But not our own, I said; and still believe
There will be news at home of its reprieve.
Nothing of that can change. And yet the doubt
Creeps into me as I look homesick out
On farms that are reminding me of one
Not distant now, beneath the selfsame sun.
A further valley, and a further range,
And I shall see if anything be strange.
Another dozen stations, and the three
I have been absent from will run to me,
And tell me if they know. At which the tears
Come premature, and stillness stops my ears.

. . . That very Wednesday, going to Great Hill,
The ruts all melted and the road was swill;
The hub caps foundered, and a number plate
Rose out of mire to recognize the spate.
All underground was overflowing for us,
Helpless until a wakened workhorse bore us,
Backward, absurd, to dry macadam land.
So April, with a wild unwelcome hand,
Showers proof upon us here of winter gone.
Our visitors on Friday night are wan:
Town-tired, and do not know it till we tell them.
The stripling cats, until we thought to bell them,
Havocked among the juncos, dropped to feed
On what the lawn still held of husk or seed.

213

A hundred misty bellies and blue backs
Move unmolested northward, leaving tracks
On certain darker mornings when a flurry
Satins the ground—not deep enough to worry
Those busy bills that, helped by hopping feet,
Find out the fruit of barberries and eat.
The apple barrels, picked over, have revealed
How many Baldwins never will be peeled;
The fungus spreads, and spots of deathly white
Show where the teeth of time have been to bite.
The wolf-dog has abandoned us by day;
He is in love across the scented way.
Nothing can keep him when the wind arrives;
He chews his chain, or alternately strives
Till the round collar slips and he goes running.
The ponies' noses have as old a cunning.
There is no forage yet, but they can smell
Green tropics creeping hither, and will fell
Each night a length of fence for dumb escape;
Then stumble back at breakfast time and gape,
Wit-withered, at the breach they cannot solve.
So, as the weeks implacably revolve
Of early, windy April, come the sprays
Of wood viburnum in the pathless ways
Where rocks and bent witch-hazel boughs declare
Once more their truce, awakening to air.
So, as the world turned sunward, Snippy died.
In the dim middle of a night she cried,
Desperate upon the steps; and lived a day.
But we have laid her slenderly away.
Her young within her she was not to bear;
So Snappy sits disconsolately there,
Under the branching crabtree; faced about,
Fixed on the clods, as if to stare her out.

. . . Spring is not yet; though how can this be long:
This crush of silence, this untimely-wrong,
Wide, cruel weight of whiteness, wing-descended
Even as we declared the winter ended?
Last night it happened. Everything, unwarned,
Suffered the soundless swoop of him the Horned,

The Universal Owl, whose ruthless plumes
Settled like death, distributing our dooms;
No feather heavy, but the sum of all
Seemed ultimate: earth's sepulchre and pall.
Not a flake settled on the flimsiest twig
But stayed; until this morning all were big
With monstrous moveless worms, that in the sun
Drip swiftly; but the evil has been done.
How fair it was last evening, when our lamp
Shone out on fleecy lilacs; yet the damp,
The clammy hand of this last dying snow—
How terrible to touch, and inly know:
This is the breaking end. So now at noon,
Divided, we behold the orchard strewn
With murdered buds and down-demolished branches.
So, by the graveyard, death upon its haunches
Sits in the form of great-grandfather-pine's
Chiefest of giant limbs, whose blackened lines
Trace there a new design of death across
Bare stones for whom no novelty of loss,
No morning news of woe can tell them more
Than that another winter shuts the door.
Divided thus—admiring, yet appalled—
We watch the season, poor, unfuneralled,
Pass with no mourners on; and recognize
What most we loved here impotent to rise.
If any sight could soften us to spring,
It is this melted, this emaciate thing.

. . . So April's plumefall was the last one, leaving
Nothing behind save midmonth warmth, and heaving
Roots, rain-drenched on many a sodden day.
Now even the rain is gone, that kept us grey;
Even the rain, preserving darkness too.
After the flood dry weather, hot and blue,
Washed every stain of winter off, and brightly
Gave us this world, so changeable and sightly:
Grass upon the mountains; smokeless-green
May fire that will not languish till the lean,
Brown, bitten earth, monotonous with stone,
Hides under hotness, leafy and alone;

Shade everywhere—as here beneath the crab,
Where Snippy lies, and rumors of Queen Mab
Bring bees to set the blossoms in a roar
While marvelling children pace the petalled floor;
Shade then for her, the borrowed Tabby, lying
With three new kittens, curious and crying:
The summer's offspring, not to be confused
With those somehow more brave that March misused.
Now the sleek mare is shod again, and trots
Each day beneath her mistress, over lots
Green-rising, or along a sandy road:
Each of them glad, the bearer and the load;
But I that walk to meet them down the lawn
Remember lazy mornings lost and gone:
Remember the cold, remember the lantern, hanging
There by her nose at night, and blizzards banging
Somewhere a shabby door; and my decision
Goes to the old, the February vision.
How old it is now, only a rake and spade;
Only a wolf-dog, panting in the shade;
Only a coatless, an oblivious pair
Of boys for whom all days to come are fair;
Only her warm hand, patting down the seed
Where sunlight lingers and the frost is freed;
Only the hay-land, live again with snakes;
Only these things can say what memory aches—
Oh, vainly—to recapture; only such
Can tell of the holy time our blood will touch—
Oh, never again, and never; only June,
That sings of something over deathly soon.
Already the mind's forgetfulness has blended
Music with music; and the months are ended.

SONNETS

I

I said: It will not blow this way again;
The branches of my life too soon are old;
The wind is kind to early-withered men
Lest they remember and confess the cold.
I said, and scarcely knew that it was I,
Hanging my leaves there in the springless year.
I said; and did not listen to a high,
Loud sound of March that filled the woods with fear.
Then it was all around me, till at last
Love like a hurricane of hate was blowing,
Bruising me everywhere. Yet I was fast,
And stood among the ruins of his going.
   Only the after stillness came and showed
   These blossoms on me everywhere, like blood.

II

No wonder-deed done in the oldest time
Whose whiteness burns oblivion away,
No miracle of grass, whose muted rhyme
Outsings the dawn and silences the jay,
No fiend's invention, no good man's endeavor,
No other tale of love is so untrue
As this one of my heart, that empties never,
But fills even as you take, and still is new.
It cannot be there is more love to come;
Yet, coming on, love tells me I have lied.
So I must learn to listen and grow dumb,
Believing in a heart that never died:
   Believing then in you, who like a dream
   Draw out of me this ever waking stream.

III

You may grow tired of my incessant tongue,
That loves perhaps too well the work of praise.
You may turn otherwhere, and search among
All men for one who keeps the wordless ways.
This you may do, and I admit the fault
Of loving you too wakefully to cease.
Oh, I have tried to mend me, but the salt
Of silence never brought these lips release.
Still must they harken to the thoughts behind
That form and flow to utter your perfection.
Still must they move before a driven mind
Marching to death in your unchanged direction.
    Therefore at least I bind them with one thong,
    This reticence that wraps a formal song.

IV

As if there lay one other sky beyond
This sky that was enough for any man;
As if the midnight bloomed, and frond on frond
Of blackness waved across Aldebaran;
Or the bent miser, opening his box,
Found double gold; or some most comely youth,
Walking at noon, caught light among his locks,
And the sun paled, impoverished of truth;
So is the love that fills me an excess,
Unlacked before, unwaited till it came;
Unneeded now—but, oh, the mind's distress
If it should lose one letter of your name!
    If nature strolled with her proportioning knife
    And pruned this farthest limb that is my life!

V

No throat had ever told me what I know,
And knowing now so well, pity a lover's
Silence; for the voice of love is low;
It cannot rise to what the heart discovers.

218

It cannot sing as high as love's own mind,
Which, truant among birds, flies daily back
With a wide restlessness, and looks behind
At everything the darkened house will lack.
Therefore I hold these words inside my heart,
Therefore I tie each thought that would ascend.
They languish, but it is the better part,
And there is sweeter music in the end—
    Unheard by even you, on whom the sound
    Gathers like dew upon the senseless ground.

V I

Chasten your fears, I have not been destroyed,
All that was in me once is living still;
Only I know there was this slender void,
This threading vein through an unconscious hill.
Empty of you, it nourished every part
With nothingness, and I was none the worse.
Filled with you suddenly, it is the start
Of older riches than I can rehearse:
Joy like a hidden river that no stone
Ever is worn away by where it runs;
Peace in the darkest passages of bone,
And buried light as from a hundred suns;
    With tolerance, that sweetens as it flows
    This blood whose red remembers late the rose.

V I I

That you were there to see before I saw,
Midway the range of old day-lighted things,
That you were there, and so by vision's law
The truth of you went off in widened rings;
That you lived ever in such early time
Is past my understanding, save that now,
This evening, I have seen the day-stars climb
Down step by step of darkness; and I vow,

No more than you they needed night between,
No more than you they watched the world away—
As here upon no earth I stand and lean,
Loving your light that is the end of day;
  With no beginning after, for the dawn
  Was grey, and I am glad that it is gone.

VIII

When I am called by Love to give account
Of the one thing that holds me unto you,
I will obey him to the strict amount;
One nameless thing I know, and it must do.
I will tell Love how first you looked at me:
Head down, and something level in your eyes;
How still you stood and looked; and I could see
Half-risen modesty, to rule surprise;
How then you spoke, and how your voice was low,
And how your arms hung perfectly await.
I will ask Love himself to pause and go,
And look, and understand my changeless state:
  Rooted again within your level gaze,
  Eternal now across the evening ways.

IX

All of the steps that our slow love has taken
Were your own steps at last, who led the way.
I was too fixed—or like an oak was shaken
That has been marked to fall yet never may.
Never unless you taught me had I known it:
Love must be advancing or it dies.
You found each resting-place, but had outgrown it
Before I too was ready to arise.
Love is a journey to no end, except
One traveller, halting, cannot journey more.
When I awoke you had as wisely stepped
As the sole fox across a forest floor;
  So I would always follow you; and will
  To the last hedge upon the highest hill.

X

The time not spent in kissing you is chaff
Gone windily away; is desert bones;
Is the lost acorn; the discarded half
Of ore from which were plucked the golden stones;
Is air beyond our breathing; is the dust
That rings another world, nor brings it rain;
Is worse than nothing had: the final crust
Was there, and it was fatal to refrain.
So have I said, yet it was never true.
Poor talk, you had your uses all the while.
Slow words, between your pauses hung the two
Far eyes I had forgotten, and the smile.
    Not that I had forgotten; but the heart
    Grows blind if it too seldom holds apart.

XI

Where is the wit that I could sometimes wield?
And yours, for you were happier than I?
Where is the hand that held the tapered shield,
Daring the sharpest arrows to let fly?
My wrists are down, I am without defense,
And what is worse, incompetent to wound;
My regiments are sleeping in their tents;
My talk at last is gentle and untuned.
And yours, for you were readier to strike,
And sat upon the swifter-coming horse—
Now do you understand what love is like?
I think he cannot even feel remorse,
    This mischievous small killer in the dark
    Who cuts two living tongues out for a lark.

XII

I disagreed, and you misunderstood,
And the sick moments dragged their wings along.
What matters, though, one worm within the wood,
What matters one rude note within the song?

221

There still is all of time, wherein this hour
Will sweeten as it ages and be relished.
Love is no love that lacks the bitter power
With its own ugliness to be embellished.
There still is all of song, that will enclose
These wounded wings and heal them till they lift,
And the worm sleep, and the musician doze—
Swooning to hear a melody so swift
    That no one there can guess the happy hand,
    Save you and me, who both will understand.

XIII

Come with me, Love, and listen all the while,
And warn me if I say too much again.
She cannot see that I am bare of guile,
Or that there grow as many loves as men.
She cannot estimate my love is me.
She takes me as I am, but it should alter.
It should be tentative, observe degree,
And in a kind of greenness never falter.
So come with me and watch my ripened tongue,
For I am willing now that she be suited;
Let her believe that I am only hung
With blossoms that so heavily am fruited.
    Then in good time she may accept my words;
    Unless the worms have had them, and the birds.

XIV

I was confused; I cannot promise more
This morning than to keep these miles between us.
I can do that, although the heart grow sore
And the night weep for ever having seen us.
I can do that; but I will not engage
To come and slay this love before your eyes.
Let it die here, without the extra wage
Of torture that would shame us everywise.

Let me come afterward, however long,
And say to you I love you none the less.
Nor will I speak of any righted wrong.
Let it be dead, and let us both confess
    With laughter how we fasted forty days
    In the kind wilderness of time's delays.

XV

Should this end now it were the end of light,
That would no longer reach an earth receded;
And the grey death of odor; and a blight
On taste and touch, with every sound unheeded.
I could no longer count the falling days,
Nor weigh an ounce of sorrow out to pain;
It were the end of knowledge when the ways
Of feeling are as reason to the brain.
Should it end suddenly—but I am wrong.
Nothing so invisible can shatter.
Our love is not an object, like the long
Cold hand of time, that is the purest matter.
    But that is something different, and slow,
    And closes gradually, as the senses go.

XVI

Leave me not overlong at this remove;
In the half-darkness, Love, I see too well
My shortness when some measurement shall prove
How far below her hope I always fell.
Keep me no longer, Love, for there is that;
And this, which is more dreadful to attest:
Out of the dusk I have been staring at
Her face is gone that was my only rest.
My dwelling-place, her eyes, cannot be found;
I look, but see as little, coming home,
As the long voyager whose only sound
Is sighing when he finds the ocean foam

Still hung to make a curtain high and dim
Between the house of his true life and him.

XVII

When I came back to your unlifted eyes,
And spoke to you, inquiring how we did,
And you looked up without the least surmise—
Then the old music, that so long was hid,
Sounded; and I knew it was to pour
Forever while we lived, with no abating.
The unskilled players were unskilled no more,
And every string had sweetened by its waiting.
There will be nothing now but one clear tone,
Of which we shall not tire; and when it pauses
We shall exist upon love's faith alone,
That knows all silence to its deepest causes;
    And comprehends the ever devious ways
    I still must follow as I sing your praise.

XVIII

I would dislike you if you used an art
To make me love you more than this, the most;
For it is only downward that the heart
Could move from such an eminence. Poor boast!
Each day I am confounded, for you give
Each day the wheel of love a little turn;
And I go headlong with it, lest I live
Henceforth one arc behind; and never learn
There is no going downward in our love;
I could not fall and lose you if I tried.
There is no under here, and no above,
But round and round; and distances have died.
    Nor am I ever giddy, for love's air,
    Like this of earth, turns with it everywhere.

224

XIX

How can I prove that I have undersung,
Like you, the written air of our affection?
You do not sing at all, but keep among
Dark words that tell of love by indirection.
And have I sung too high? It is not so.
I rose, but it was never to be reached—
This simplest note that any reed could blow;
Yet not my voice, however it beseeched
Bird, sky, and grass to lend their happy skill,
And every buried lover all his art.
They laughed; and he advised my stubborn will
To cease within the silence of your heart;
    Which I would have it do were I as wise
    As one who had not listened to your eyes.

XX

Let it be always secret what we say;
And where we meet, be that our world alone.
Nor think us ever guilty, since our day
Is one on which no shadow-bands have shown.
Shame is a shadow that will never fall
On us who have cut down the trees of pride.
Let the world darken past the garden wall;
The space within is conscienceless and wide.
Nor think us ever weary, or in need
Of company to bring the night at last.
Love is a lonely and contented deed,
Done in a desert that is sweet and vast;
    Where neither of us turns a timeless head
    To see the world behind us that is dead.

XXI

As the blue fringes of this flower desire
Comparison; yet even this old glass,
Wherein some workman hid the sky afire,
Is not the same; and so the mind must pass,

And look along the world, and never come
To the pure hue repeated—thus I range
Through the live chronicles that tell the sum
Of love's known history; and each is strange.
No love is like our love beyond the start;
Two look upon each other, then we lose them.
They whisper to each other, but apart,
In a wild shade, and we can never use them;
 Likening ourselves to nothing more
 Than two late comers as the long day wore.

XXII

Sometimes I fear that I too soon was mastered.
Sometimes I think that you would have me still
Untaken—not like any crippled dastard,
Here with my hands up and my useless will.
Yet I must run the risk of being sure.
I tell you I am captive, every inch;
And was so long ago that I am pure
Even of the memory that pride could flinch,
And look away, and dream of being free.
I tell you this, and ask you then to know,
Nothing so well could prove my high degree,
Nothing so well declare the worthy foe.
 I am no more ashamed to kiss the rod
 Than the king was, acknowledging the god.

XXIII

What golden spider warmed himself and spun
This web that is the flesh upon your bones;
Warming himself beneath a spicy sun
That caught the winds and let their little moans,
Like woven music, enter every place
To hide until love's fingers should be near?
What artisan was singing at your face?
Who wrapped the rest, that too will disappear?

For time, that made the spinner, lets him die.
He will be long in leaving, yet he must;
So every moistened thread of you will dry:
At first to lace; but then a little dust.
   And I— Oh, time will take my desolate hand
   And sift it on you, letting it be sand.

XXIV

I carry in me always, since you live,
The devil of an uncontrolled delight.
He is my hidden master, whom you give
No heed, for he has seldom come in sight.
No passer-by may know I am possessed,
And even you will never learn his power.
The host himself is helpless when the guest
Sits on and on, and, smiling hour by hour,
Spreads darkest joy that round him ever flows
Like a sweet, bitter poison. So I keep
This fellow of the smile, and no one knows;
And so it only seems to be asleep—
   My laughter, that the world forever misses;
   Yet here it is, like sun upon our kisses.

XXV

Oh, I could talk forever, and as smoothly
As angels, were I farther from the fire.
I am the coal, and so I say uncouthly
Less than I mean, and more than you require.
Or if the distance widens on some days,
And I am for the moment swift of tongue,
A sudden sword will stop me on the phrase,
And every sentence after be unstrung.
Or if I once again am well contained,
And cool, as though I grew in watered ground,
The green with which my branches have been veined
Runs red, and I am rooted in the sound

Of blooming under earth, and blowing cold.
There is no single way it can be told.

XXVI

My fancy is less cruel than it is kind,
Though cruel it is to bring your spirit here,
Letting it seem your body; for I bind
No arms within these arms when you appear.
They know, and my eyes know, you have been standing
Most of a summer's day beyond the door.
But they have not the magic for commanding
One solid proof: a shadow on the floor.
Your lack of so impalpable a thing
Convinces me at last you never came,
And stood, and looked upon your underling;
Or if you did, my reason was to blame:
    Refusing then to recognize in you
    What such an afternoon might filter through.

XXVII

The earth is full of spirits once again.
Maidens in the marshes, bearing light,
Laugh the old ones up, the little men;
The ground remembers goblins day and night.
For every standing tree there is a face
That, somewhere hidden, soon must flicker home;
Each mountain side is rippled with the race
Of night-returning devil-face and gnome.
The thought of you is everywhere. It rises
Sometimes like a fiend and stares at me.
I am the helpless savage who devises
Charms; and knows he never will be free.
    Never shall I walk another wood
    Than this of your fixed eyes and pointed hood.

XXVIII

Never to be renewed or to increase,
And never to be changed from what it was:
The love that was the maker of this lease
Was love-upon-first-sight, whom all the laws
Of happiness obey, and kingdoms coming
Choose to be the glory of their thrones.
He is the oldest love, he is the humming
Of these incessant bees among my bones;
He is the senses' king; my youngest thought
He molds before I know it has been born;
He is the flesh's despot; the inwrought,
Deep joy; or in my side the sudden thorn.
   Oh, strange that on that day I was so strong,
   Bearing him all at once; and now so long!

XXIX

This book declares my love is a condition,
Determined in the tissue; but it lies.
I banish the impertinent physician;
I must refuse to credit one so wise.
Or if there must be fables, let them tell
Of wounds that were inflicted from the flank;
How once we faced each other, and there fell
Swift arrows out of nothing, and they drank
My blood, and put a poison in its place;
My courage, and refilled me with desire;
How then the tincture spread, till into grace
I stumbled, and the punishment of fire—
   Unending, for no heart in all that heaven
   Recovers from a wound the god has given.

XXX

The longest hour is swifter than I thought.
It is more cruel, having a sharper end.
So time is my close foe; yet I am taught
Some safety by this fear that is my friend:

229

This fear of eyes that if they ever used
Their utmost power would then I think destroy me;
This awe of something not to be abused,
Lest the world break, and love no more employ me.
For such a fear it is withholds my hands
At the last greedy instant; there I wait,
Lowly, as the shaded hunter stands
And lets the shining pheasant pass in state—
  Something that is too beautiful to miss;
  Yet the dream holds me while the sickles hiss.

XXXI

These things I say, no one of them can reach
The roundness of the sphere that is your truth.
They are but lonely segments, they beseech
Environment and complement. Time's tooth
Devours even while I write; though did it starve,
I still would stand too far from either pole.
Had I eternity, I could but carve
Inscriptions that were partial to the whole.
Not even all together would declare
This roundness, that more swift than words can follow,
Grows, until the mind is thin as air,
And what is most compendious most hollow.
  Better that I should cease, and so re-enter
  Love's little room, revolving at the center.

XXXII

Not pride it was that made me say so much
Bearing on my own mind in these, your songs.
Intended for your praise, they did but touch
Idea, where your beauty best belongs,
And straightway thought was active, bringing proof,
Here in my heart's possession, of your power.
These but effects; the cause remains aloof;
There is no certain entrance to the tower.

If any gate were open I would climb,
Life-long, and reach your verity at last;
And sing— Oh, I can hear the happy rhyme
Break upward, I can see the overcast
   Part swiftly, and can lose the final sound.
   Alas! I never heard it from this ground.

XXXIII

My only need—you ask me, and I tell you—
Is that henceforth forever you exist.
You are not mine; I may not ever bell you
Like an owned animal for night and mist.
My only need, whatever darkness take me,
Whatever tears close now my separate eyes,
Is that you live, and let the knowledge make me
Immortal as the day that never dies—
That, swift and even, turns into the sun,
As turns the after-shadow down to death.
Let neither then my night, my day be done;
Let them both swing in silence, with no breath
   To call you from the distances you keep.
   Would they were little; would that my love could sleep.

THE EYES

Turn where he would that autumn, when the time
Was evening, and there was no wind at all;
Turn where he would he saw them, and he said:
"I am grown old, it is my ending fall;
These are my visitation." Then he smiled.
"They have not seen that I am reconciled.

"They cannot tell me what I first had known.
I learned it long ago, and made surrender.
My bones are at the mercy of the years,
That, coming on, will find as my defender
Nothing but this smile. It cannot harm them,
Though it may shine and for a day disarm them."

As lightly then as this he bore the eyes
That out of every evening stared at him.
Turn where he would they found him; past the door,
Past trees and down the lawn, or through the dim
Road light that bound him in, a noiseless river.
So lightly could he look, so little shiver.

So little did he fear those changeless eyes
That he could fail to see the person changed.
It never was the same tall body there,
Nor the same hair, so carefully arranged:
So perfect and so parted, with a white
Down-line that was indelible by night.

It seemed a woman's hair, and then a man's;
But always it was drawn upon with fire:
Cold fire; and cold the eyes, whatever bones
Held the spare flesh as on a frame of wire—
Dangled, inconstant; but the staring three,
The eyes and that one line, would always be.

Would always be, he said. It was October,
And the last leaf had settled to the lawn.
So the last night was there that he would turn,
Expecting them in silence to have gone.
Would always be. He said it, half aloud,
And trembled; for the rigid one had bowed.

Only an instant, but it seemed enough:
The eyes gone swiftly out, the line erect.
Then the head vanished, and the shoulders flowed
Like a mist backward, till the dusk was specked
With lingerings of terror. So they faded;
And there he stood, implacably invaded.

Turn where he would the face must follow now;
Sleep as he might, his lids come cool together,
Something more cold than peace would enter, slowly,
Like a mist inward, till the mind's calm weather
Ceased, and a shouldered figure gathered form
Out of pressed distance and the soundless storm.

Nor would the eyes that watched him, and the hair—
Unblown, for all was windless there and wild,
Unblinking, for there was no rain to fall
Though the fog drifted and the sky was piled—
Nor would the triple watcher then unfold
Merely the tale of time and growing old.

Something more terrible, for him alone,
Something without a name until he said it.
Yet so far he was tongueless—asking now
What old forgotten guilt had lain and bred it.
Ruthless on the couch of what lost deed.
What wound, that so long afterward could bleed.

What evil? But he ever had been blameless;
He had been praised too sweetly not to know.
There was no saint more mannerly of conscience;
He had stopped short and let the others go:
Stumbling into errors he could see
Too clearly not to shun them. He was free,

And knew it—could remember, could remember
Multitudes of gentlenesses done:
Angers turned away until they withered,
Challenges unpampered, and the one
Deep lust that is the darkener of eyes—
Oh, love had been the better thing, and wise!

With this for past he could outstare the present.
Whatever face it was, he would come smiling,
Tomorrow, after sunset, and implore it
Fiercely to speak. He would himself—beguiling,
With memory at his back—demand the charge;
Then, listening, explain; and be at large.

He was not waited for. The room he lay in—
Stiffened there, with lids too dry to close—
Tilted at some moment after midnight,
Standing him halfway up; so he arose;
Took step; and like a walker in his sleep
Found the whole firmament with eyes acreep.

233

They moved as if at random, round and round,
And slowly, till he tried to look away;
When, suddenly assembling, they transfixed him
With a cold, single stare, that he must stay
Forever now beneath; as if his life
Lay victim to some never falling knife.

"It will not fall," he said, "it will not fall.
This face will never utter what it knows.
The words I have awaited will deny me
Even a malediction at the close.
The final and the sacrificial jest
Is silence and those eyes along the west.

"Two eyes, and only two, with parted hair
On high to make their mockery more sleek;
More sure my cold confusion, lest I breed
Some courage from that gaze, and stand and speak.
If now I should address that shining sneer,
It will not hear," he said; "it will not hear.

"This mind will never open to my words.
I was convicted easily and well.
Too late for pleading now." And yet he started;
And the black sky became a listening shell,
Contracted in an instant to the size
Of a thin voice beseeching. "Awful eyes—

"More awful that you never yet have closed,
More terrible than any sightless end—
Let down your weight of malice, slowly, swiftly;
Make it in thunder, make it in ice descend,
Make it in mist befoul me, cry me lost;
Spend, spend yourself, although I be the cost!

"I will go under gladly, so I know
One moment of my enemy's close breath.
I can be parted happily from night—
This night—if I but catch the look of death.
Be hideous and torture me, be slow;
Only begin, and let the levers go.

234

"What engine are you, stealthily devised?
What hand is there, what purpose past the dark?
I beg an instant's vision of the power
So hidden that a world may not remark
How strangely I am visited, how long
I linger in suspension for no wrong.

"No wrong unless you name it, for I say
That I have loathed the bright way and the cruel.
I have seen bodies burning, but the match
Never was mine, and never was I the fuel.
Never have I been thievish after pleasure.
I have kept home, I have respected measure.

"I have not been that plunderer of joy
Who drinks our brother's blood and creeps away;
Letting it dry within him till the rust,
Like a fine crafty poison, spreads decay:
At first a potent hatred, but grey time
Enfeebles it and whitens it to lime.

"I have been bravely diffident, like love;
I have been lawful, keeping our sister's peace.
No lamb has ever huddled to its mother,
Fearing my steps; inviolate the fleece.
Lust ages, but love steadily is younger;
I have been patient, I have not hurried hunger.

"I have not sped the day, oh, terrible eyes.
Nor shall I now boast longer. I have ended.
Nor was it boasting, Gazer; it was truth,
With pride and with a little anger blended.
If you have heard me, even the anger goes.
I was exhausted, waiting." He arose,

Still like a walking sleeper, and still waiting;
But no word came for answer from the eyes.
Only they glittered lazily, and gathered
Fragments of mist, gathered them magnet wise,
And wreathed them into smiles, and slowly slept;
While in his weak astonishment he wept.

235

They would not even trouble to undo him.
Time was long, with evenings still to come.
He looked again; they dozed and were complacent.
He tried to call again, but he was dumb.
It was no world for words, his feet were saying,
Leading him in at last; nor one for praying.

"I will outmock them then," he lay and whispered.
"Tomorrow must I seem indifferent too.
Tomorrow when they waken they must find me
Difficult, unreachable, and new.
I shall not even wonder if they still
Keep station there, wishing me endless ill."

But never has there been the strength in man
To move all heaven, putting it out of thought.
And so he must remember and look upward—
At nothingness all day; but evening brought
Dead stillness like a cannon at his heart:
The stillness of a battle timed to start.

Strain as he would to flee it, when the hour
Came suddenly with trumpets, he was waiting.
He looked, and they were there, and they were ready.
The toying time was over, and the baiting.
At last they were full weaponed, shaft and pike.
They were too cold and close now not to strike.

It seemed a woman's face and then a man's,
Swift-altering, swift-clearing; but the eyes
Changed never; they were fixed upon his trembling;
They stared beyond all pity and despise;
They waited without feeling, like the hands
Of judges when the nameless prisoner stands.

They waited, and he waited; then a voice
Broke heavily through stillness like a wave;
Far off, but heaving inland, and pursued
Uncountably by others, till the brave
High shore of his new courage shook and crumbled;
Then he was ready, then for all time was humbled.

"You will not be destroyed," he heard them saying;
Thickly rolled the waters, deep the waves;
"Nor comforted"—oh, hoarsely came their laughter;
"The final word is not the word that saves.
It is the merest verity, and men
Never may lose the sound of it again.

"This night will bring the end of us—the eyes—
And soon the hair you hated will be clouds
Parted with summer lightning; so our words,
Remembered, will resume their ancient shrouds,
Deep in the pit of time." But now they reared—
Armed waves of unrelenting war—and speared.

"We are the changeless person you denied.
We are the men and women you have slain.
Escaping after death, we wandered hither—
Home—and shall remain; and shall remain.
There is no such eternity for you.
The whole of you must perish as it grew:

"Quietly and palely, out of hearing,
With every dreadful gentleness confessed;
Nothing into nothing will go swiftly,
Passing us then whom you have not possessed.
We shall not know the moment, or inquire;
Forgetting you forever by this fire.

"The death of you is nothing, for you never
In all of time were implement to anguish.
We waited for the terror and the iron;
You softened them to love and let us languish.
Love? But it was feebleness and fear.
Pity? It was judgment and a sneer.

"We should have been invaded, as the sun
Drops suddenly, a serpent, into shade.
We needed to be threatened, as the knife
Flies—and there is blood along the blade.
There should have been an ambush and a foe,
With after-wounds, remembering that woe.

"There should have come against us in the dark
Hard hands, with sharp desire upon a cheek.
The eagle does no honor to the lamb
By kindness and the folding of his beak.
Our food was never danger: not a taste
Of fury, not a tempest hot with haste.

"These, these you must refuse us like a god.
You condescended to us, and we died:
Witnesses that you had been the savior:
Meek, meek! but swollen inwardly with pride.
Safe, safe—it was not worth the dying for.
We should have perished otherwise, by war.

"Or should, surviving battles all the way,
Have ripened to the center, and been warmed
By love that is the after-core of pain,
By pity that wounded wisdom has informed.
We should have lived or died—for it is one—
Full in the wind, full in the burning sun.

"For too much shadow, pale one, and excess
Of caring, we condemn you now to know:
The end of you, the all of you, is nothing.
Cold, cold the coming daylight and the snow.
Cold, cold! And so farewell, uncruel-kind,,
Unborn, existless monster of the mind!"

When he could lift his face the sky was empty:
Soundless, like eternity, and white.
Dead white the falling dome; but where the ground was,
Greyness, as of ashes fresh and light.
But round his feet a darkness; and no day
Ever would burn the least of it away.

Tomorrow, and then always, it was round him,
A field of perfect darkness that he paced.
Not stumbling, for that wilderness is stoneless,
And over it hangs still the whitened waste.
No dawn or evening now beyond his eyes.
No alteration ever till he dies.

238

THE TOWER

GROWING A LITTLE OLDER

Growing a little older is suddenly
Standing a little still;
Then forward again, with something learned
Of the slow skill
Of skies,
Where motion dies.

Growing a little older is holding
One day a question back;
Then letting it go, with something seen
Of the faint crack
To crawl
Twixt nothing and all.

Growing a little older is hiding
Shivers of sudden fear;
Then letting them work, with something guessed
Of the deep spear
Of joy,
That too will destroy.

WHY, LORD

Why, Lord, must something in us
    Yearly die?
And our most true remembrance of it
    Lie?
Until the pure forgetting
    By and by.

Why then must something other
  Come and grow?
Renewing us for nothing, save the
  Slow
Upbuilding of this bed
  Of needles, so.

Why is the soil not bitter
  Where we stand?
Whose, Lord, upon our roots
  The sweetening hand?
For so it is: we love
  No shallower land.

JOY CANNOT BE CONTAINED

Joy cannot be contained.
I know, for I have seen
The stricken eyes; and strained
To hear the blood's machine;

Have watched awhile and listened:
Terrible the stillness!
Then the eyes have glistened,
As from illness;

Then the heart has sounded,
Breaking in the dark;
As if the seas, impounded,
Had set again to work.

FATE COMES UNSWERVING

Fate comes unswerving like a frightened horse
Sky-maddened on a white mid-afternoon.
Fate comes unseeing, and the blinded hooves
Drum a shrill thunder to a noteless tune
That dies into the forest, where an owl
Returns it to the midnight and the moon.

Lean neither way, for nothing can escape.
No walker in a field knows whence it comes.
Only there is an instant when the dust
Whirls upward and the round horizon hums.
Then the feet loudest, and the final leap.
With afterward no dream of any drums.

WIT

Wit is the only wall
Between us and the dark.
Wit is perpetual daybreak
And skylark
Springing off the unshaken stone
Of man's blood and the mind's bone.

Wit is the only breath
That keeps our eyelids warm,
Facing the driven ice
Of an old storm
That blows as ever it has blown
Against imperishable stone.

Wit is the lighted house
Of our triumphant talk,
Where only weakly comes now
The slow walk
Of outer creatures past the stone,
Moving in a tongueless moan.

PRAISE

Praise is no crust of snow
That fell long since and formed,
And now one day will enter the shut earth:
Stale wine, and warmed.

Praise is directest rain
That comes when it is needed:
Cool in its newness, and descending where
Desire has seeded.

Praise is merest water:
Nothing, but enough.
Nor makes it any choice of how it feeds
Smooth ground or rough.

Praise falls on both alike,
And is at once beloved.
There is no good that is not prospered then;
Nor evil proved.

PITY

Pity is a naked sin,
   And a stripped weakness.
It does not wear the long clothes,
   The proud clothes of meekness.

Pity drops as suddenly,
   And is as frightening,
Entering the white breast,
   As streakèd lightning.

Pity comes, pity goes
   With a great rudeness,
Having not anything to do
   With love or goodness.

MEEKNESS AFTER WRATH

Of all perfected things,
Man-made or devil-god-made; yea, or both;
Nothing so undefective is, and fine,
As thundered wrath.

Nothing! save this mute
That follows like a lamb beside the udder,
Gesturing, when the mind—except it burst—
Cannot grow madder.

Nothing so pure as this:
The after-meekness, lacking any tongue;
Nor anything so powerful, though it lives,
Poor child, not long.

THE TOWER

The greater world is water,
The lesser world is land.
Out of moving vastness
Promontories stand.
Out of undulation
Heaves the firm sand.

The flood of moments, flowing,
Bears desire away;
Returning unto wideness
Distributable clay.
But not the hill of reason,
The mind's high play.

The greater world is water;
This little world is rock.
Beneath it subterranean
Sinews interlock;
And round it, silent, silent,
Wheels the invisible flock.

HOW CAN MAN HIS STATURE KNOW

How can man his stature know,
    And so far grow?
How be incapable of less,
    Or of excess?
How can man the image find
That shall be matter to his mind?

How can man be like the least
   Clear herb or beast?
How be faithful, cold or warm,
   To his own form?
How can man as plainly be
As the sure mole, nor ask to see?

How can man contrive to borrow
   No more sorrow?
How return what he has taken?
   Nor be shaken,
When he wears the world no longer,
By the simplicity of hunger?

NEVER TO ASK

Happy the mind alone,
Dissecting the body's mesh;
Happy, until the bone
Is there in a flash.
Happy this thing of knives
Until it arrives.

Better that it divide
Waves, and the ruly winds;
Let it go deep and wide
In the alien lands.
Let a plow quit the loam
When it comes home.

The moving whole, and the heat,
And the nine-day fever, love;
How the cracked heart can beat,
And eagle turn dove—
Let it be wisdom's task
Never to ask.

THE CONFINEMENT

Whence, whence this heat of the brain?
I know, I know, he said:
The sleeplessness of continents and stars,
Rivers, and oily pavements, and old wars
Across too small a bed.

Whence, whence this fever-sight,
This still inflamed research?
I know. It is the press of the last sphere
To shrink its mighty pride and enter here:
All heaven in a church.

Whence, whence this burning bone,
This furnace in a skull?
Listen! I have heard the chafed complaint
Of thrice too large a cargo, hot and faint
Within too weak a hull.

Whence, whence this little fire
Whereon no fuel is put?
But it is fed with Africa's great groans,
And wrinkle-deep Aldebaran's live moans,
Recessed within a nut.

RETURN TO RITUAL

AS FROM ARABIAN ASHES

As from Arabian ashes
A dustless bird arose;
And still the purple body
In a vast spiral goes,
   Envying the sun,
   The unrenewing one;

As from this waste of changes
There is a mind can fly,
And sail beyond confusion
In a fixed sky;
   But still it will remember
   Maytime and December;

So I, that now am starting,
And am so faithful-sworn,
Almost repent the voyage,
Almost am unreborn,
   Foreseeing, over the foam,
   The phoenix circling home.

THE BYSTANDERS

Who is this host of folk this fair spread day?
And who these few that stand and do not run:
Watching the others only, in the way
Of the dark stars outside the circled sun?
Strange, but the less are greater; only they
Have number; here the many are the one.

Strange, but the host is single, like a beam
Of noon that folds its particles inside.
Strange, but the few are many. Yet they dream
Of darkness, and of standing unespied,
Watching the rabble current—envied stream!
One river! though it is both deep and wide.

Here on the shore, in an imagined night,
They stand and wrap their arms; but on each face
Falls the dead flush of a reflected light
That fringes their aloofness as with lace:
The memory of a multitude's sweet might;
The flowing, and the union, and the grace.

The greyness all around them is old mist
Engendered by the chill of their contempt.
These were the few that labored to resist,
And the flood set them, separate and exempt,
Here on the windless shore. But now they twist
With a new longing, and the frail attempt,

Returning, to go smoothly once again
Down the sole river where the lashes close
And the eyes, sinking, dream of dancing men.
Yet here they stand in their uneven rows,
Superior forever—until when
Death lifts a hollow socket-bone and blows.

WHY SING AT ALL

Why sing at all when the parched
Throat gives forth, unwillingly, dry sounds,
Wing-withered, that ascend
And rustle between the skull's deserted bounds?

The dim bone valleys there
Lie long and are unvisited by rain.
This dust, this music, rising,
Deepens the grey ground-cover, spreads the stain.

Why sing? But the tongue's attempt
May startle the chambered silence, and awake
Some spring whence joy, thin-flowing,
Trickles awhile; then rivers; and then a lake;

Then green, then sunny waters;
Then grass, and a bird-live forest moist with shade.
Why sing at all? But a sound
May serve, and a hopeless wasteland be unmade.

Oh, the long, toneless drouth!
Oh, the sunk pathways, shrivelled of their gladness!
Somehow the end arrives:
Drouth's end, with intermittency and madness.

Oh, the sweet run of rain!
Oh, the fresh floods, how carelessly they fall!
So will they have their end.
Yet sing! Or they will not come, not come at all.

RETURN TO RITUAL

The mother of life indulges all our wandering
Down the lone paths that narrow into peace.
She knows too well the gradual discovery
And the slow turning round until we cease:
Resolved upon the wide road once again
Whose dust hangs over day and mantles men.

Here is the drumming phalanx, here is the multitude;
Listen, and let us watch them over the stile.
We that remember clean moss ways and the tamaracks,
Let us be timorous now and shudder awhile.
We shall be early enough, no matter when,
Mother of dust, O mother of dust and men.

How time passes, here by the wall of eternity!
Even so soon we summon her; we are prepared.
Already these feet are lifting in a wild sympathy;
Who can remember the cool of a day unshared?
Mother of marches, mother, receive us then.
Listen! The dust is humming a song to the men.

NOW THIS JOY

What was that life I led?
Answer, dumb wit that out of darkness clambers.
More yesterdays than now this joy remembers
Had I a liar's heart, pretending glad?

How could I think deception when the seated
Circle of old and young ones knew me wrong?
The multitude was hopeful of my tongue.
Was I the fool, and waited?

Was I the vain one, wanting
All a loud world to marvel upon my truth?
I do remember now, I heard them both:
My own still voice and that one, hoarsely chanting.

Was it too rough for rightness?
Answer, my new-found wit, and bid me know
Every wild tune by night, without one flaw,
And whether I lose by lateness.

ANOTHER MUSIC

The harmony of morning, and a thrush's
Throat among the sleep-deserted boughs;
Expiring mists that murmur all the day
Of a clear dusk, with music at the close;
Wind harp, rain song, night madrigal and round:
There is no word melodious as those.

Rage of the viol whose deep and shady room
Is sounded to a tempest by the strings;
Sweet keys depressed, swift rise upon a note
Whence all the narrow soul of music hangs;
The lifted flute, the reed, and horns agreeing:
Words in the wake of these are scrannel gongs.

249

In them another music, half of sound
And half of something taciturn between;
In them another ringing, not for ears,
Not loud; but in the chambers of a brain
Are bells that clap an answer when the words
Move orderly, with truth among the train.

IT IS A MOVELESS MOMENT

It is a moveless moment, with no wings,
No feet to bring it flying. There it stays,
And there it would be always, like the dead,
But that we turn and find it on some days.
The merest turn; the neck would hardly know;
Then the sky dips, and all the landmarks go.

So is the world contracted to our eyes,
That, lacking any room for more, for less,
See all of it together, fine and small,
With no mark on it of our nothingness.
The littleness is lost that we could measure—
Knowing not then of this compacter treasure.

It is the moment when we understand,
Relaxing every effort to be wise.
It is the moment of our boundary's fall:
Proud stone, that we had armed against surprise.
It is the merest moment. Then again
We turn and are distinguishable men.

THIS AMBER SUNSTREAM

This amber sunstream, with an hour to live,
Flows carelessly, and does not save itself;
Nor recognizes any entered room—
This room; nor hears the clock upon a shelf,
Declaring the lone hour; for where it goes
All space in a great silence ever flows.

No living man may know it till this hour,
When the clear sunstream, thickening to amber,
Moves like a sea, and the sunk hulls of houses
Let it come slowly through, as divers clamber,
Feeling for gold. So now into this room
Peer the large eyes, unopen to their doom.

Another hour and nothing will be here.
Even upon themselves the eyes will close.
Nor will this bulk, withdrawing, die outdoors
In night, that from another silence flows.
No living man in any western room
But sits at amber sunset round a tomb.

ON SUCH A DAY AS THIS ONE

On such a day as this one, time and sky
Flow round our shoulders mingled past division;
Past asking which, past hearing, for on high
One silence broods: the ultimate elision.

Such a day as this one lifts the seas
And loses them in air—as blue, as thin.
Yet not the seas; there is no current moving;
Not anything translucent, wave or fin.

Such a day as this one is the end;
Or would be if there were no shoulders listening.
Nothing but their question saves the world;
And that high sun, upon the silence glistening.

PHENOMENA

He thought some things were not to be compared.
They sprang from their own seed, that once had dared,
Dropping from several stars, to sow by night
One half of earth with unexplained delight.
Then morning came upon her equal feet,
And levelling her voice denied the sweet,

Sharp difference; she was not to be confused
By novelty of names, and form abused.
So noon and afternoon saw nothing strange.
Only at twilight did unreason range,
And only now by night is wisdom had
In a spun world of which the name is mad;
Only through darkness will the meaning shine
Of things that are but planets fallen fine;
Only the black meridian declares
That old descent from big and little Bears.

LABORATORY STILL LIFE

This apple now, and this smooth block of wood
That long ago forgot the watery tree—
The round red thing remembers in its wet heart,
The patient cube is mindless and immortal—
Set them on the table and declare
Their density, position, form, and mass.
Bring the slim brain that walks on calipers—
The little bow legs caper while you wait—
Bring the ruled retina, and pads of paper,
And take the sharpened pencil from its sheath.
Now weigh them well, the apple and the wood;
Let the mind's least antennae touch and write,
And writing, not remember what they touched.
There will be only figures at the finish,
Bodiless worms that if you stoop and peer
Cross-edgewise of the chart you will not find.
It is a flight of moths from skull to paper,
And back to the bone again, the hollow room.

Whereas the deep eye innocent of numbers,
Moist eye moving in a world of shapes,
Warm eye wonderful in child or man,
Sees only a bright apple and a cube.
The deep eye looks, and there is nothing more
Than a red apple with a watery heart,
Than a blank face of wood that has forgotten.

The deep eye looks, and not a word comes forth.
Nothing is here for counting or dividing,
Nothing to understand; nothing to add.
Only the red round face grows redder, rounder,
And the six flattened cheeks widen a little,
Complacent of their enduringness indoors.

TIME AND WATER

The humped back of the beaver, and the four
Curved teeth that bring the poplar splashing down—
There in the lake it lies, and the silver branches
Turn, in the day, in the night, to a watery brown—
The upthrust and pond-dividing whiskers
Say that the world is wet, and seasons drown.

Swimming in darkness, nearing his willow dam,
Pausing before he climbs to the dripping sticks,
He is eternally far from hills and deserts,
Roads, and the odorous barns, and the drying ricks;
The beaver is only credulous of meadows
A rising river enters and moistly licks.

Diving in darkness, down to the lily roots,
Turning and paddling off and rising slow,
The beaver descends again and finds his burrow,
Rises again and is home, and he says: I know.
Water is endless, time is an undulation,
Water is all there is, and seasons flow.

SPREAD, SPREAD

Spread, spread, November rain;
Sleep-bringing river, widen so
That every meadow takes the stain
Of rising death's first overflow.

Instruct the trees that are adorned
Too bravely now, and drown their blood.
Leave not a sunwise slope unwarned
Against the white, the final flood.

Invisibly the banks of time
Give way; the unseen river reaches.
The mist of change begins to climb
And slide along the grassy beaches:

Sliding until no further drop
Of dryness lives in any vein;
When even change will, flowing, stop,
And stumps no more remember rain.

THE OTHER HOUSE

The leafless road midwinters by itself,
And the slat gate, wired open, never swings.
Should the loop rust, and weaken in the wind,
Two posts will join that now are separate things;
Forgetful how they guarded the little space
One entering coat could fill, one entering face.

We spoke of strangers happening to pass,
And wondered if such openness were wise.
But the posts know; they have not felt each other
Since the high sun was shaded from their eyes.
We spoke of footprints; but a sparrow's track
Is all that diverges in and circles back.

Even a look from us so distant here,
Even a sigh might leave its line on snow:
Up the still road and in, then round and round;
Then stopping, for we must no further go.
Let the line pause mid-yard; there let it end,
Lest the sad chimneys smile, and smoke pretend.

SHE IS THE YOUNGEST

She is the youngest of the wood,
Yet is there many a newer thing.
The hemlock with the ragged hood
Droops in everlasting spring.

Above the snow, or when the leaves
Lie well around her, safe and dead,
Not a wind but lowly weaves
The delicate spine; deflects the head;

Picks up the green and greyish cape
That all but flowed into the earth.
Grave, grave the maiden shape,
Out of love awhile with mirth.

Sad, sad, but it is well:
How she looks upon the ground
Cures the melancholy spell
Of age and coldness all around.

Sad, sad, but what she means
Is that the world is old and strong;
Indulgent still to one that leans
On youthful sorrow overlong.

SOMEWHAT MORE SLOWLY

Somewhat more slowly, lengthener of days—
Oh, you that pull the crusted nails of winter—
Somewhat more slowly work. Within is lying
One who would not hear too soon the splinter
Of wrapping-boards; nor see too soon your light
Enter and like a thief put out the night.

Lay down your hammer somewhere in the snow,
Deep snow and dark, and drop your chisel after.
Sleep there upon the wind, as far away
As April, and be deaf to this my laughter:

Muffled in the linen of a box
Upon whose lid Time comes, Time comes and knocks.

But comes not yet if you lie long and dream,
And, wakened on a morning, doubt your eyes.
Look then for those you lost—you will upturn them,
Cold beneath the snow—and slowly rise,
And slowly make approach. I shall be rested;
Nor is death then unwillingly molested.

THE STORY-TELLER

WHAT IS THE HOUR

What is the hour, how loud the clock,
When the heart knows itself for rock?
Or is it ignorant? Does the rose
More silently than centuries close?
Perhaps no man so long ahead
Predicts the flint, proclaims the dead.

There was the year it opened wide
And tore a hole in his calm side.
Strange the petals' hingèd strength,
Staining, staining all his length
With wasted blood; until they shut,
And he forgot the flesh's cut.

There was the day it stirred again
And straightway stopped; and chilled him then.
There was the fear his pain had ceased.
But it returned, and it increased;
There was a rose within him said
He must be happy while it bled.

Is there no rose inside him now?
Is there no vein to disavow
This rocky stillness? So he stands,
Exploring silence with his hands;
Wonders, waits; and leans to hear
That valvèd sound of yesteryear.

HE WAS NOT WISE

He was not wise to dally with the curves
Of earth and set his fancy continent-free.
The game at first was merry, and he smiled;
He was at home with aliens, land and sea:
Stoking a fire with bullies west by south
In the same hour that Persia curled her mouth.

He felt the flame, he tapped the pearly teeth;
He blessed himself and nestled to his kind.
But then he scudded further, and beheld
Tall men of China chatting as they dined;
Flew on, and by an island strange of name
Struck sail; for now the terror of it came.

One porch too many, folding in its shade
Some brow unseen, some lip, destroyed the count.
Here was the death of number, the abstract
Mute reckoning—how dim the pure amount!
How far desire, how close the little space
Encircling every watched and silent face.

THE ESCAPE

Going from us at last,
He gave himself forever
Unto the mudded nest,
Unto the dog and the beaver.

Sick of the way we stood,
He pondered upon flying,
Or envied the triple thud
Of horses' hooves; whose neighing

Came to him sweeter than talk,
Whereof he too was tired.
No silences now he broke,
No emptiness he explored.

Going from us, he never
Sent one syllable home.
We called him wild; but the plover
Watched him, and was tame.

THE HERMIT

On a grey hill above the talk of streams,
Where not a risen rock repeats the wind
And no tree groans with standing, and no grass
Rustles upon itself, the still feet stay.

Here no hidden deity, bespoken,
Utters a thunderous answer ill or good.
Only the feet are here, and these straight hands,
And one pale mind, sending its column up

Of silence. It is silence that he says
Will wash the earth below him of its pain.
Words are but fire we pour into old wounds
That long ago wove blood into the sky.

So the white column, rising, spreads and comes
Down softly midst our sounds, and we are soothed.
He says the sky is healing, too; and hears
Some day the whole world dreaming under snow.

MEMORIAL

If nothing else let this poor paper say,
Outwhitening time and those subduing voices,
How once a black-eyed doctor drove away,
After she died, behind his dappled horses.

This shall not be memorial for her,
Nor him, the black-eyed man, nor for the dappled
Shadow upon two breasts; but as they were
That morning, let each word of them be tripled.

Within a room she lay, and they were going—
The bright defeated man and those long faces
Slanted upon the wind—and time was snowing
Forgetfulness already, as he uses.

And still he would, had not this paper power,
Holding the four together, to remember.
These hungry hooves will not outstep the hour,
Nor the dark eyes come ever home to slumber.

GOING HOME

His thought of it was like a button pressed.
Far away the figures started going;
A silver watch ticked in a sleepy vest,
And on the porch an apron string was blowing.

His thought again was like a fly-wheel cranked,
And circular machinery set gliding.
The little town turned truly, as the banked
Brown houses followed in and out of hiding.

His travel, once he went, was like the troop
Of farmers in an autumn to the fair.
All year the field was flat, but now the coop
Of turkeys and the horses would be there;

People moving everywhere and nodding,
Little boys with birds and yellow whips;
A person at a counter would be wadding
Rifles, and the girls would hold their hips.

His coming near was like the soft arrival
Of gods around a thing that they have made;
And will again forget; but long survival
Saves it, once again the trance is laid.

HIGHWAY GHOST

The gravelly road is gone.
Old people, whirled behind a windy wheel,
Huddle their coats about them and remember
How they went proudly once;

How the eight ringing feet
Flung gritty pebbles into the grass,
And how the four high iron tires
Sang in the sand.

Old men, silently borne
Where now the way goes black and wide
And smoothly like a river into the wood,
Old men, saying nothing,

See a white horse come curving,
Swinging an empty buggy round the hill.
The white feet fall without a noise, approaching,
And thin wheels lightly follow.

Spokes flicker by,
And grey heads, nodding at each other, turn
To see between the curtains what is there.
Nothing at all is there.

The gravelly road is gone,
And dim eyes, drawn around a bend forever,
Have in them only history, and the fall
Of a slow shadow.

OLD TUNE

The words of this old woeful song
Float so merrily along,
Out of ages that they sweeten
Though the hearts of men were eaten.
This old tale of souls that brake
Falls softly on us, flake by flake.

He raised the knife;
She spread her gown
And begged for life;
But only a frown
Got ever that wife;
Got ever that wife,
Hey derrikin down.

This tune that came so long a road
Has shed the sorrow of its load.

Though its burden will endure
The air is merciful and pure.
This bitter tale of one that died
Leaves only honey in our side.

> The knife it fell;
> She spread her coat
> And made a well
> Of that white throat.
> She made a well
> For him in hell,
> High dollikin dote.
> So merrily float
> With him in hell,
> High dollikin dote.

THE STORY-TELLER

He talked, and as he talked
Wallpaper came alive;
Suddenly ghosts walked,
And four doors were five;

Calendars ran backward,
And maps had mouths;
Ships went tackward
In a great drowse;

Trains climbed trees,
And soon dripped down
Like honey of bees
On the cold brick town.

He had wakened a worm
In the world's brain,
And nothing stood firm
Until day again.

262

RECOGNITION SCENE

From many a mile the son,
From a third of the earth the father;
Each of them bearing his sign
Of kinship high as a feather.
Dusky the hour, and late;
What shall we do that wait?

We shall not quit the grove,
We shall not rise and scatter.
Something deep as the grave
Holds every heart in a flutter.
Dewy the night. No bird—
There! Who trembled? Who heard?

Who spied him, tall in the west?
Old is the night, and bitter.
Far in the eastern waste
Who caught a faint hoof and a clatter?
Now closer—now here—he draws—
Oh, insupportable pause!

TO A FRIEND
HESITATING BEFORE CHANGE

Shatter the moldy glass
Wherein you look too long.
The arm of time is ready,
And trembles at the gong.
Nod and let it fall,
And stand outside the wall.

Such suddenness of sound
Will loosen every tree,
And though your house is broken
The mountains will run free
With frosty colors, new and fine,
Set upon each curvèd line.

263

Or else—and who can say?—
Darkness will be there,
With danger at its heart,
And teeth about to tear.
Even then I tell you change;
So it be strange.

THE FRIENDSHIP

It was so mild a thing to see,
People saw it silently.
Such peace was in it people said
It would not alter with them dead.

None knew the difficult design
They worked to follow, line by line,
Nor in the sending of a glance
How much was art, how little chance;

Nor how that courtesy was kept
Wherethrough no step was overstepped.
There was no hazard in these hands
That wove a set of silken bands

Binding honor unto praise,
And tying tenderness, that lays
No single burden on a friend
As far as to the tethered end.

Not a disagreeing word
Between the two was ever heard.
But when it ended with them dead,
Buried bones got up and bled.

THE UNWANTED LONELY

Make way for them, who nothing see
Beyond the shadow of their eyes.
Make way for that—the sharpened cone
That shoots before them now as flies

The pointing night of an eclipse,
Wherein a day's triangle dies.

Make way for them; they lost their hope
Longer ago than faith can heal.
They walk condemned, yet think to find
Some face perhaps that still can feel.
But let them pass you; be not one
Transfixèd willingly with steel.

Make way for them, and turn your head
Perhaps with pity; yet be strong.
What they can penetrate you with
Is thin and poor; but it is long,
And will not break. It is the fear
Of light's dislike; and is not wrong.

LAUGH NOT TOO LOUDLY

He said that we must thank the gods
For vanity, which like a wheel
Whirls a man or woman now and then
Till the soul bulges, and a giddy heel
Is pivotal to something oversized.
He said the vain were vases under seal.

"Opened, though, there's nothing there."
Admitting this, he only smiled.
"As barren, top and bottom, as a tomb;
Not even filled with future, like a child."
He said this too was true; but must insist
That vacancy not always be reviled.

"They are the sacrifice," he said,
"So that a miracle can be.
The soul, that is invisible, becomes
A something then which anyone may see.
Laugh not too loudly, for the gods translate
Only the brave, the wild. The rest go free."

THE PHILANDERER

It was the very innocence of love;
Though words were whispered that have toppled walls
And taken sleeping lives, he was a dove
Nesting in little gables, whither his calls
Brought momentary mates to share the dim,
Sweet dawn along the eaves, and strut with him.

The nearness of the morning was what saved him.
He never would have dared the naked night;
And they were such as never would have braved him
In the true dark. It was a pretty fright,
A flutter of alarm beside a door;
Then the sun came, and there was nothing more.

It was delicious doom to be suspended
Thus between having and not having them.
What never had begun was never ended,
Save that some tried a deeper stratagem
And flew to him at midnight. Then he ran,
Lest now he be possessed as proper man.

He ran, and they were glad that it was so.
It was their doom to play at the surrender.
Having themselves again, they still could go
Remembering the eyes of this pretender;
Leaving a lonely portion of them there,
Under the soft eaves beyond the stair.

ANTIPATHIES

Item, the man by whom he was reminded
Of the dead calfish days before the rope
Broke, and he ran till he was tired of running;
This fellow, staring here and snorting hope,
Dangled the ancient tether past a wall.
Right there it was. Had he come thence at all?

Item, another one who knew too well
The paths that he had come by, if he came;
Who shrank the middle distance till it sat,
A small divided desert, full of tame

Four-footed memories, that by day remarked
His face with little coyote eyes and barked.

Item, the newly known one with the brow
That wore a different wisdom from his own.
What loss in that, he wondered? Yet he saw
How each comes only once, and comes alone;
And asked the wind if many wandered off
In a sheep's night, missing the wether's cough.

MODERN SINNER

He was of an old mind,
And so would have preferred
Consciences less kind
Around him when he erred:
Darker wires to bind
The scarcely cagèd bird.

Such wings as now he wore
Delivered him in vain
Without a narrow door
To take him in again,
And shut, and hide the sore
No probing would explain.

For still he could be healed
And try another flight.
Now all was sunny field,
With never a stroke of night.
So wearily he wheeled
Into the endless white.

THE BORE

He was not helped by knowing well
How cold he made us, and how weary.
He must have told himself at last
He was not saved by being sorry.

Better than anyone he saw
The stealthy turn, the trained escape,
Or if he came too soon for these,
How frantic courtesy could wrap

Desire to fly with skill to stay—
A twitching wing beneath the feather;
How within a greying eye
The kindest agony can gather.

And did he witness this too well?
Was then the knowledge but the cause?
Long time we looked, but could not find
A way of learning why he was.

PARTITIONS

She fled into herself before the sun.
When the wind rose her thoughts became a thicket,
Drawing her in, while firmly one by one
Thin leaves behind her laced the final wicket.
None of our voices ever got so far
As to the trembling center of that maze.
We found the margin easy, but a bar
Of shadows lay across the deeper ways.
Sometimes we waited; then a face would peer
Half woman through the laurel, and half deer.

She was afraid of openness and act.
A deed would tear the bravest barrier down.
She loved the lone partitions where she tracked
Green fancies never trampled into brown.
We called to her, extending our still hands;
She only stared and smiled, and we could see
No meaning in that brow, or in the bands
Of fear that tightened, tightened quietly.
Safe in her lanes she wandered. Was she wise?
The answer is dead leaves upon the eyes.

THE PHOTOGRAPHS

The person on the sidewalk is possessed
Of a loud secret, capable of crying.
This haster among the many holds himself
Like a mute man that presently is dying.
And yet there is old age for him—and those
In the pressed parcel he would be untying.

His children's faces, wrapped against the sun,
Sing low between the still sleeve and the heart.
This holder of his tongue sends more than breath
Invisibly ahead of him: sends part,
Sends all of him, advancing as he goes
To a frail music, soundless at the start.

He hears it there and hardly may contain
His joy that Time can sing so young a song.
He follows it, prophetical of days
When the grown burden suddenly is strong.
Thereafter—but his smiling is confined
To the live moment, mercifully long.

IT SHOULD BE EASY

It should be easy, letting the small feet go;
Quick should it turn, the necessary knob;
Empty this porch of any following eye
Fixed upon waves wherein a head shall bob
Now up, now down forever; till it rises,
And floats and disappears among the mob.

We should be sure the shoulders will return,
And the hands reach and click the lock again.
We should be thoughtless, occupying days
With a new ritual modified to men.
We should be proud and let a trumpet say
How close the waters welter about the den.

269

And solitude would soothe us, were it not
For the slow sound of breakers near the door:
Reminders of the many farther out,
Of the lost many, nameless evermore,
That young with pride set seaward long ago,
Leaving the grey alone, the mother shore.

It would be easy, letting the cap depart,
And the small face that never looks around;
But the firm coast line—suddenly it bends;
Suddenly it follows, and the sound
Of hopeless cries is heard; until the waves
Wash once again on straight and silent ground.

THE MONUMENT

Swift cruelties to children are a pyramid
Built of soft stones that harden under time.
They were not quarried, they were not shapened craftily,
They were unconscious then of granite or lime.
They were not planned at all. But they have altitude;
They are too high for memory to climb.

When memory is merciless, and labors,
Gaining the topmost cube, and lingers there,
The view is of an undivided wasteland
Down from the breather's height through darkened air;
Nothing familiar now except the still voice
Bidding him measure deserts if he dare.

Better the climb untaken, and the guilt
Forgotten, could the mind go clear around.
But the long way is endless, and the stones
Are numberless; immovable the mound.
It is our own memorial, and stands
In front of us wherever we are bound.

SIMPLE BEAST

With rope, knife, gun, brass knucks, and bloody laws
Earth everywhere is noisy; not with paws
Of leopards silent, not with saber-toothed
Long tigers paced all year upon and smoothed.
That was the age of hunger, when the taken
Fourfoot with a moment's dread was shaken;
Then the slow-closing eyes; then over stones
Time's scattering of the picked, the cleanly bones.
This is the age of anger, when the hail
Beats corn and rose alike, and leaves a trail
More sluttish that it tells man's appetite.
This is the age of gluttony and spite.
With lash and bomb, blue fire and bayonet
Earth everywhere is littered. Earth is wet
With blood not drained for drinking, earth is loud
With sounds not made for hearing, earth is plowed
By steel that will not reap it. Earth is least
Like what earth was when beast was simple beast.

STRIKE THEN THE RUSTED STRINGS

Strike then the rusted strings.
Pound, pound the sluggard voice.
And bid deposèd kings
With our poor selves rejoice.

Hang branches from the rafters;
But where the doors have been,
Hang thorns to prick the laughter
Of lost ones coming in.

Pour liquor that will widen
The skull's already smile.
The darkness we have died in,
Let it be red awhile.

Let it be white, and burn us
Unto the finest ash.
Let music be the furnace.
Let every fiddle flash.

Ha! and now we gather.
Ho! and now we part.
Let every bone be lather,
Next to the fiery heart.

Let every arm, upswinging,
Be melted as it goes.
So, to such a singing,
The stoniest sadness flows.

Be still! for they are letting
The last poor devil in.
Now shut the door! forgetting
Whatever deaths have been.

Ha! and now we gather.
Ho! and now we part.
The last one dances rather
Stiffly at the start.

EPITAPHS

For Two Men

When these were idle shouting boys
Their mouths could make an equal noise.

When these were young and earnest men
One managed all the talking then.

When he grew famous he forgot
The other one that here doth rot.

But which is now the louder dust
The eyeless worms have not discussed.

For One Unburied

Stranger, do not think to find
The banter here of parting bones;
We let the desert wind unbind
His flesh, and scatter it like stones.

He was impatient with the jest
Of eyes enlarging underground.
So his are open to the west,
And day diminishing around.

There all the pieces of him lie,
Too far apart to understand
The comedy of ribs awry
And sockets filling up with sand.

For a Maiden

This girl was not to go
Until two shoulders cast
Shadow upon her snow,
And melted it at last.

The warmth she had within
Still waited to be found.
The coverlet is thin.
Be curious, cold ground.

Exploring with your frost,
Go down as deep, as deep,
As linen; then be lost
In thaw, and a long sleep.

For a Fickle Man

Two women had these words engraved:
The first and last of whom he tired.
One told the other, while they lived,
The thing between them he desired.

What now it is they do not know,
Or where he seeks it round the sun.
They only ask the wind to blow,
And that his will be ever done.

273

For a Jester

The things he used to do, and laugh,
Are blown along with other chaff.

Never to rustle and arise,
Here the kernel of him lies,

The solid portion of the man.
And this we count; but feel the fan,

And lift a sudden far-off look
At what the wind of harvest took.

For Two Brothers

Let no man say that either mind
Heard willingly the scythe behind.

The edge was on them ere they knew,
With that undone which words could do;

And now is done upon a stone
That time has not come back and mown.

Until it tumbles, brother and brother
Understand they loved each other.

REPORT OF ANGELS

THERE IS NO LANGUAGE

There is no language that the heart learns wholly.
One thing it fails at, though it deeply tries.
It cannot ask a question; it is only
Skilful in surrenders and replies.

Most eagerly it answers, and most softly
It gives the needy asker surest proof.
But when itself is doubtful comes the dumbness.
What most is meant remains the most aloof.

The heart is never childlike, though it stammers,
And half the words it weeps for are refused.
The ancient one can do no more than answer;
It cannot beg, as once the young one used.

REPORT OF ANGELS

"Nothing for envy there"—
Folding their dustless wings—
"Nothing, beyond this pair
Of impossible things:

"Love, wherein their limbs,
Trembling, desire to die;
And sleep, that darkly swims,
Drowning each brain and eye.

"Nothing is there for us,
Who may not cease to know;
But heaven was merciless,
Fixing our eyelids so;

275

"Whereon no tide may run,
Rolling its night ahead;
Where love is a labor done,
And death long since was dead."

ALWAYS EVENING

You eyes, forever west of afternoon,
And, oh, you setting-sun-descended hair,
Make every day of absence die more soon
Than minutes, that it may be evening there
Forever, shadeless eyes,
Wherein all distance dies.

Forever be the hour that is the end,
The hour that blackens daytime and the grass.
O eyes, it is the moment when you send
Hither most heat, as through a burning-glass;
Hither excessive light,
Love's lie against the night.

Be always spicy evening, my love's mind,
Contracting to yourself the deaths of roses.
Gather into an instant every kind
Of fragrance that the waste of time encloses,
Letting the long world shrink
Into one drop; and drink.

HIS LADY LACKS NOT ANYTHING

His lady lacks not anything
Save a beholder:
Wiser born than was the king,
Yet noway older;
Young and wise, and fit to sing
What none has told her.

Say it quickly to the queen:
How she dissembles,
Letting only that be seen
Which time resembles;
How at the rest, the ageless green—
How my verse trembles.

Tell her nevertheless I know;
And am suspended
Here between an ancient woe
And one unended.
Music fails, as long ago;
Nor can be mended.

THEY WERE GOOD FORTUNE'S

They were good fortune's maid and man;
The gift of love between them passed
As lightly as the snow comes,
And silent to the last.

They talked, but not of what was given;
There it hung, by chance descended;
Each but held a hand out,
And exchange was ended.

So colorless, so soft a thing,
So free—they would not name it love;
It was but whitened wind-fall,
Slanting from above.

So painless, it was not themselves.
They never knew that flesh can tear,
Suddenly, as boughs break
Upon snow-heavy air.

THE WILLINGNESS

The willingness that Lucy wears
Becomes her like a fitted gown;
Nor is there any seam to see
Until the thing is down:
The whole of it, as if a lone
Young tree had cast its crown.

Those leaves that make so loose a ring
Will never again be hung together.
The flying bird does not regain
A single drifted feather.
So Lucy stands forever now
Unlaced against the weather.

The willingness that Lucy wore
Was nothing to this naked side.
And yet the truth of her is both;
The raiment never lied.
Desire without, desire within:
So is love simplified.

THE FIRST BLOW

Embrace it, though it be
A salt new inland sea;
Make the most of such a pain
As never now can come again.

It is the first, and quenches
Even what it drenches;
Heart, too soon you will outgrow
This unremembered overflow.

You will grow wise, and lose
Black honey from a bruise;
Anticipate this weeping while
The drained, inevitable smile.

LET NOT YOUR STRICTNESS VARY

Let not your strictness vary;
Be less, be less than just;
In a mild January
We miss the frost.

I have a store of wood in;
The windows well are stopped;
I sleep a sleep that sudden
August would interrupt.

Let not your coldness, going,
Leave too well prepared
One whom years of snowing
Have into virtue snared.

Let every May-fly slumber,
And in deep holes the fox.
Nor will I lie and number
Centuries to equinox.

THE DIFFERENCE

Day after day, for her, the sun
Drew semicircles smooth and high.
A week was seven domes across a desert,
And any afternoon took long to die:
Rounding the great curve downward not too fast,
Not falling; not a shadow ran awry.

His day was two thin lightning lines
Pitched here one instant like a tent;
Then night; and there was neither afternoon
Nor evening to be witness how they went.
His day was but a burning at the top;
Then the steep fall, and every spark was spent.

They lived together only thus:
One tick of noon their common day;
And many a noon, so meeting, each would ask:
What found the other past the middle way?

279

But neither he whose leap was like a star
Nor she who curved and swung could ever say.

SHE SAID TOO LITTLE

She said too little, he too much.
She drooped; he could not droop enough.
Between a sigh, between a song,
Simplicity defeated both.

He was importunate with proof,
But undervalued then the pause.
She was judge of something else,
Something silent in the blood,

Something destined to be loud
If only words could fail and wait.
She never heard it; or explained
What sound is deeper than the throat.

They were not different save in this:
He paused too little, she too long.
But each was farther at the close
Than all northwest, and spreading storms.

FIRST ALARM

Nothing could be stranger
Than this silence was.
There never had been danger
Until the sharpened saws
Of pride cut in and in,
Unbuilding what had been.

Nothing was the matter,
Except they barely talked.
The end had come of chatter.
They whipped it, but it balked
At climbing the two hills
Of their awakened wills.

There was a time, perhaps,
When they would do with stillness;
But now it seemed relapse
Into a worse illness
Than any mending lover
Ever got up and over.

I PASSED THE SLEEPY RIDGES

I passed the sleepy ridges
Whereon my love had looked.
Her house was by the bridges
Where the slow rivers crooked.

Many and many a morning,
As the white sun would rise,
The darkness, at her warning,
Flowed down upon her eyes,

That took it in and saved it;
Oh! there was room and more.
With her own tears she laved it,
There by the turning shore.

There were two crooked streams there.
Heavily went they round.
Now darkness only seems there;
And dewless is the ground.

BY THEIR OWN IGNORANCE

By their own ignorance I knew them,
And the tall way they stood;
Denying she had ever wandered through them,
Entering that wood.

By their indifference I proved them,
Those high old border trees;
Pretending that no thunderbolt had grooved them:
Each heart at ease.

No lesser lie could they be brooding:
A footfall had not died.
The truth, I said, was weaker praise; intruding
No more upon that pride.

HERE THEN HE LAY

In Memoriam
C.L.V.D.
1857-1933

Where mild men gathered he was half at home,
Though all of him was treasured for his eyes.
The other half, dark-ranging, never paused;
And still it goes, and still the curving skies
Contain the soundless footfalls of a man
Whose moving part our obsequies outran.

Here then he lay, and stationary flowers
Were like the words of good men come to see:
All pure, all nodding whiteness; final proof
Of wonder—save the last, the far degree.
Already, while the compliments uncurled,
He gathered with the dark ones of the world;

Came noiseless up, and shed the afternoon
Like a thin shoe behind him; so he stands
Eternally in twilight, and the rest
Acknowledge nothing alien in his hands,
That hour by hour acknowledge nothing there
Save the full dusk and the sufficient air.

It was the eyes that brought him; so he stays
Despite the something different in his walk.
Round, round he moves among them, and each one
Is different: more the panther, more the hawk,
More the slow-treading dove; yet no disguise
May alter their unburiable eyes.

Both sun and shade are in them, pair by pair,
Both everlasting day and boundless dark.
This is the field to which the few have come;
These are the visions death could never mark.
There was no way to deepen such a gaze
Save with this dusk, abstracted from all days.

There now his feet fall silently, and now
He is both old and young, his hope the same:
Ranging the mild world, sowing it with pride,
And leaving not a meadow of it tame;
Praising all men that have the quenchless eye;
Yet loving the unlustred who will die.

There was a pride within him that refused,
As the sun does, to scorn the lesser thing;
And there was winter wildness, blowing up
The smallest out-of-mind leaf-underling,
That, looked upon, came quick to life; but then
With his warm night he covered it again.

We praised him for the kindness of his talk,
And a meek heart mortality had kissed.
We might have sung the justice of a glance
Wherein not even littleness was missed.
Then, then we should have added his desire
For the great few and the unburning fire.

We told a tale of charity, and hands
Long practiced in the banishment of pain.
We knew his mind's ambition, and his tongue's
Swift temper, and his wisdom to refrain.
We should have known how nothing held him back
From the great dusk and from the trodden track.

He treads it now, and he is never tired.
There where he goes, intensity is ease.
No strict requirement but of old was met;
The world at last is single that he sees.
All one, the world is round him that he saw
When he looked past us, innocent of awe.

THE LAST LOOK AND
OTHER POEMS

1937

To
Scott Buchanan

I

AXLE SONG

That any thing should be—
Place, time, earth, error—
And a round eye in man to see:
That was the terror.

And a true mind to try
Cube, sphere, deep, short, and long:
That was the burden of the sky's
Hoarse axle song.

Improbable the stoat,
The mouse, toad, worm, wolf, tiger;
Unthinkable the stallion's trot,
Behemoth's swagger.

Unspeakable; yet worse—
Name, look, feel, memory, and number:
Man there with his perverse
Power not to slumber.

Let things created sleep:
Rock, beast, rain, sand, and sliding river.
So growled the earth's revolving heap;
And will forever.

THE ECSTASY

For he so loved the world today
That he fell down like dead, and lay,
His left arm dangled at the sofa's side,
Smiling inanely.

287

You would have said he searched the rug
For signature of pin, of bug,
Of sunbeam. But the silence of his eyesight:
That explained him.

That was the symptom: nothing seen,
Yet a whole world washed dark and clean
By his acceptance—oh, a mile away
Horses were grateful;

Curveted, and clipped the ground
While here, relaxing from all sound,
He let the mohair heft him: light as wheatstraw,
Harvested lately.

INARTICULATE

The morning flashed like mica,
And the tendrils stretched
Like dawnrays: every leaf a little sun.
A wind flowered out of nowhere,
And the birds inwove
Bright walls of air with streaks of curving song.

The horses fed like angels,
And the pasture spread
Like tidegrass: greenness foaming over all.
The fencewire dripped with dewdrops,
And the rabbits sat
High-eared across the never parching ground.

He wandered, he the lost one,
And his tongueless joy
Made gestures: bending rib and dancing bone.
Felicity is limbless,
But an inward joint
Grows flexible, and hidden liquors flow.

He would have sung the season,
And his fiery joy

288

Flung upward: towers of tune, and bannered words.
He would have hymned the wholeness;
But he paused and heard
Part after part thin-piping in its place,

And knew the day concerted;
For his ranging joy
Still counted, adding choristers to these.
So he discovered dumbness,
And his humble eye
Found duty, and he glittered, tall with tears.

NO FAITH

What held the bones together? Not belief,
Not anything he could probe, no ligament god.
Why was the world so one for him yet many,
So woman and yet so speechless? Then the odd,
The furtive, ashamed security. We wondered.
But there was no faith in him that sang or thundered.

There was no understanding in this man
Of his own simplest secret: of the way
Earth's air kept warm for him, and how there shone
Always another light outdoors of day.
He would have chosen darkness; he denied
What was so strange, so palpable, inside;

He said he could be unhappy. But we knew.
There was this sweet continuum, this flesh;
There were these bones, articulated so:
A web they were, with music up the mesh,
A frame of hidden wires too deep for tone,
A skeleton wholeness, humming to him alone.

He must have heard the harmony, but he swore
Time talked to him in separated sounds.
He took them as they came and loved them singly:
Each one, he parried, perfect within its bounds.
As for the burden's end, the tune's direction—
He smiled; he was content with disconnection.

Yet who could smile and mean it? Who could rest,
As this man did, midway the million things?
Who else could be serene at truth's circumference
When only the known center of it sings?
Who else but he?—submissive to each part
Till it became the all, the homeless heart.

THE GOOD FATES

I see the dun, low western house,
I see the propless porch,
I see the grass and cherry-leaves
That a June sun would scorch;

While flies buzzed through the broken screen—
I hear one in the room,
I hear one settle on the plush
Past the piano's gloom.

Then silence in this forward part;
But there are doors and doors,
And deviously the clatter comes
Of middle summer's chores;

Of deep pots simmering on the fire,
Of strainers dropping juice;
Of knives; though most of all I hear
Three tongues upon the loose:

My aunt and her warm daughters there,
My cousins, whom I stand
Long years away and listen to
Across a changing land.

There is no sound has sung to me
Since then so rich a song;
So reticent of injury,
And yet so laughing strong;

So stopless; for the afternoon
Hangs high above us; waits
While their lost voices hum to me
Across these seven States;

Hum busily above the pans,
Unconscious how I hear
What he and she and Charlie did
In that fine cherry year.

THE CORNETIST

When the last freight, dusk-musical, had gone,
Groaning along the dark rails to St. Louis,
When the warm night, complete across the cornfields,
Said there was nothing now, no motion left,
No possible sound, we heard him:
Rocked on the silent porch and heard the low notes

Leave on their level errand like the last sound
Ever to be man-blown about the earth.
Like the last man this sentry of the switches
Blew, and the mournful notes, transcending cinders,
Floated above the corn leaves:
Floated above the silks, until arriving,

Arriving, they invaded our warm darkness,
Deep in the still veranda, and we laughed:
"Why, there he is, that pitiful lone devil;
There is the Frisco nightingale again,
There is our mocking-bird-man"—
Laughed, and said these things, and went to bed.

And slept; but there are nights now when I waken,
After these years, and all these miles away,
When I sit up and listen for the last sound
Man will have made alive; and doubt a little
Whether we should have laughed;
Whether we should have pitied that poor soul.

You were too sure of being there forever,
And I too soon was leaving to be wise.
Not that his horn had wisdom; but at nighttime
Man has a need of man, and he was there,
Always; the horn was there
Always; and joy, I think, was why we laughed.

And slept; for there is many an hour of drearness,
Many an hour unloud with lips or brass,
When I lie still and listen for the last note
Ever some lung has blown; and am self-envious,
Thinking I once could laugh;
Thinking I once could pity that poor soul.

AT LAST INCLEMENT WEATHER

At last inclement weather.
After a month of death—
Of holding it and staring—
Day grins; blows out its breath;

Grimaces; and, deep-growling,
Furies the bated air;
Of which the lack-love atoms
Had fainted pair by pair.

Now in the wind's excitement
They dance a tumbled round:
Their first and only madness,
Their single rage of sound.

Invisible the clashing;
Unheard the little cries;
Save that in us they echo;
Our particles uprise—

Dimensionless, dark pieces,
Yet are they fiery strong—
And sting us with their whirling,
And lift us high and long;

And threaten us with flying
Like cannon balls apart;
Save that the skin is thinner,
And tougher next to the heart.

ANIMAL-WORSHIP

Once on this ancient plain there fell the shade
Of a great loping hare who hid the sun;
Who darkened the high sky; and has not made
Another unearthly visit since that one.

Even that day is dead; no solemn eyes
Remain of those that watched him down the North;
Or those that feasted yearly, Indian wise,
On the small furless copies he sent forth:

The timorous rabbits, ancient on this plain,
Who now no more bring messages of cold;
Sons of the great mild hare whose dozing brain
At the world's upper edge grows dimly old.

In a sunk nest of snow he lies and dreams;
Down a grey depth he slumbers, long from here;
While the plowed plain forgets him, and the teams
Trample, and fatherless rabbits shake with fear.

No longer does their blood remember time,
No longer do they feel their far descent;
As the loud valley crows cry out and climb,
Sky-highward, where the one great raven went,

So long ago, so darkly through these hills,
That the last man is buried who was told;
That the last wing is mildewed, and the bills
Of once deep-knowing birds are green with mould.

So the loud western crow wings flap and lift,
And sagely now the beaks consider corn;
But none of them remembers here the swift
Vast body whence their images were born.

Past a blue mountain, westernmost of all,
He floats among the mist-pools, round and round;
And meeting the Hawk, floats on; no feathers fall;
For they go by, those gods, without a sound.

There is no beast or bird too delicate now
For man's vain understanding; no shod feet
Veer shyly from their pathways; no heads bow
Benignly when a man and serpent meet.

No creature upon four paws, in field or wood,
By rivers or by runways, stares and wins:
His muteness meaning wisdom, and his hood
Some heraldry of old where birth begins,

Where truth, where secret might, where sun and moon,
Where song and words of song, and what to pray.
There was a time when foxes set the tune;
And tigers; but it is another day.

It is the beasts' oblivion, when they run
Uncounted unto cover; when they shrink,
Denying their tall origin; when one
Trots lonely in the dew that he will drink;

When two by two they wander, with no word
Between them of the Hawk, the burrowed Hare;
The Raven, or the Bullock, or the herd
Of tempest-laughing Stallions, or the Bear.

One only of earth's animals is proud;
One only of its movers can be still.
Man only sits at rest and sees the crowd
File curving by, deflective to his will;

Sits on and sees, with nothing spread above,
No weird ancestral wing, no hovering mane;
Sits loftily, too certain of self-love
Ever to see a world upon the wane:

His world and theirs, the strangers whom he knows
Forgetfully, from their own selves disguised.
Man is time's fool, who withers the wild rose
Of that young day when gods were recognized.

MILLENNIUM

The dream of this new man upon the earth
Was not of angels walking, their bright hair
Day-dusty, and their feet a little slowed,
Their litheness dimmed a little in dense air.

Nor was it of wild hunters strayed away
From an interior forest, the gold hides
Sun-tarnished, and the flying leopard-tails
Wind-ravelled, and a shadow up their sides.

Nor men in rusty mail, nor passion-struck
Lean lovers, nor the tall ones in a grove,
Bare-shouldered, who dispute the evening down;
Nor saints in cells; nor loafers round the stove;

Nor farmers in the field; nor clever eyes
Pale-squinting into clefts of a machine.
The dream of this new man upon the earth
Was new of its own self. No brain had seen

What he saw when he scanned the coming day.
Square-headed then the heroes; high-oblong
The faces, and the ankles stiff with strength;
Heels hobbed; the insteps braided with a thong;

Caps eagle-beaked, and sooty overalls
Steam-blown as, pouring forth in swarthy pairs,
Their shoulders like Leviathan, their hands
Good-humored, like the idle paws of bears

Down-hanging, thumb-and-fingerless, they strode,
One giant by the other, up the world.
And over them the angular steel tubes
Joined smoke to smoke, and jagged sparks were hurled;

And lines as straight as lightning led the way
To a foretold horizon, whither stamped,
Unending, file on file; and tireless sang
One song; and shook the mountains as they tramped.

THE LAST LOOK

The great eyes died around this room;
Died everywhere; no matter what wall's blankness,
He printed a pair of circles on it; filled
All four of them; surviving with a rankness

Terrible now to us, the livers-on;
The more so that we loved him for his quiet.
He was a man most delicate: not loud
Like this, like these round eyes; like this gaunt riot

Of spent, unsmiling gazes; for at the last,
Trying to smile farewell to us, he could not.
So it appeared that day, I mean. We now
Think otherwise. He looked at us and would not.

Why? But if we knew this, we had known
The other man, the man before the illness.
Now that he is a stranger—studying back,
We were unjust, loving him for his stillness.

That was the least of him. The great eyes prove it,
Lingering on these walls, and hanging fire
With the same truth we buried in the box—
Subdued then to the sermon and the choir,

Yet louder; for the concert here of walls
Is music's self, the sound of someone staring
Utterly, at all things, till they spoke.
This man alone was capable of sharing

Ultimate name and number. This is where—
Yes, this is where he lay, and where the ceiling
Said his last word for him; and where his eyes
Still wander past us, listening and feeling.

II

PRIVATE WORSHIP

She lay there in the stone folds of his life
Like a blue flower in granite. This he knew;
And knew how now inextricably the petals
Clung to the rock; recessed beyond his hand-thrust;
More deeply in, past more forgotten windings
Than his rude tongue could utter, praising her.

He praised her with his eyes, beholding oddly
Not what another saw, but what she added,
Thinning today and shattering with a slow smile,
To the small flower within, to the saved secret.
She was not his to have; except that something,
Always like petals falling, entered him.

She was not his to keep—except the brightness,
Flowing from her, that lived in him like dew;
And the kind flesh he could remember touching,
And the unconscious lips, and both her eyes:
These lay in him like leaves, beyond the last turn
Breathing the rocky darkness till it bloomed.

It was not large, this chamber of the blue flower,
Nor could the scent escape; nor the least color
Ebb from that place and stain the outer stone.
Nothing upon his grey sides told the fable,
Nothing of love or lightness, nothing of song;
Nothing of her at all. Yet he could fancy—

Oh, he could feel where petals spread their softness,
Gathered from windfalls of her when she smiled;
Growing some days, he thought, as if to burst him—
Oh, he could see the split halves, and the torn flower
Fluttering in sudden sun; and see the great stain—
Oh, he could see what tears had done to stone.

WINTER TRYST

When the Atlantic upsloped itself
Like roofs of higher and higher houses,
To the great ridge, the foaming shelf
Whereon no dolphin ever browses;

When the wild grey broke into white,
And ships rose endward, crushing mountains;
When it was thus, and icy light
Poured up from phosphorescent fountains:

When it was thus, at winter's crest,
A vessel arrived; and the annual ocean,
Faithfully setting her down in the west,
Repented awhile of its furious motion;

Subsided; but only until that prow
Was pointed again, and a passenger, waving,
Wept in the channel, reminded now
Of eleven months, and the duty of braving

A spring and a summer, and longer fall
Till the month of the year that was set for returning;
Then the grey slopes; and the port, and the tall
Still lover—O time! O bitter adjourning!

When the Atlantic upheaved its whole
And the bottomless world dared keels to try it:
Then was the season; this poor soul
Only that month kept longing quiet.

Only that month: most difficult,
Most dark. Most loveless, and most unable.
Yet it was hers. And time's result
Is love's most fair, most speechless fable.

THE LETTER

You will not doubt I loved her,
You are too wise, and know
Too well that love is little,
Too well that love is low.

Or may be. Mine was groundward.
Confession is content.
How could there be idea
Where all was accident?

I mean I loved her forearm
Just as it lay to see.
What she was least aware of
Is what she was to me.

I mean there was a tired way
Her ankles crossed the floor.
And there were sleep and sweetness
In the slant cape she wore.

I mean that I remember,
Now she is gone awhile,
Nothing about her forehead
Save that the hair could smile;

Nothing about her bosom
Save that it could be still;
Her very breath was patient,
Climbing that slender hill.

Intelligent her waist was,
As though both heart and brain
Lived there along with silence,
And with them love had lain

So long ago I learned it
Almost too late, I fear.
At least I do remember
These things, and you must hear.

299

THE WHISPERER

Be extra careful by this door,
No least, least sound, she said.
It is my brother Oliver's,
And he would strike you dead.

Come on. It is the top step now,
And carpet all the way.
But wide enough for only one,
Unless you carry me.

I love your face as hot as this.
Put me down, though, and creep.
My father! He would strangle you,
I think, like any sheep.

Now take me up again, again;
We're at the landing post.
You hear her saying Hush, and Hush?
It is my mother's ghost.

She would have loved you, loving me.
She had a voice as fine—
I love you more for such a kiss,
And here is mine, is mine.

And one for her— Oh, quick, the door!
I cannot bear it so.
The vestibule, and out; for now
Who passes that would know?

Here we could stand all night and let
Strange people smile and stare.
But you must go, and I must lie
Alone up there, up there.

Remember? But I understand.
More with a kiss is said.
And do not mind it if I cry,
Passing my mother's bed.

HOW SUCH A LADY

She waits in a grey high house, this lady, and waits;
Morning upon loud morning no one ascends.
Daytime is cobble-clamorous down by the gates;
Daytime or nighttime, nobody comes to her hands.

She does not keep them folded across her knees;
She is not sitting and waiting, or even saying:
I am alone in a grey high mansion, and these
Are the sign of my pride and patience who am dying.

She lives by an endless labor of going and turning
And losing the count of corners, and measuring walls;
Or sits, in a gilded chair not made for mourning,
Mending the ancient lace with the mouse's holes.

How such a lady can keep her wristbands flying
Never a man may guess. No man is there.
Yet it is true she waits. Her hands are praying
Suddenly to be his, and quiet as air.

PROPER CLAY

Their little room grew light with cries;
He woke and heard them thread the dark,
He woke and felt them like the rays
Of some unlawful dawn at work:

Some random sunrise, lost and small,
That found the room's heart, vein by vein.
But she was whispering to the wall,
And he must see what she had seen.

He asked her gently, and she wept.
"Oh, I have dreamed the ancient dream.
My time was on me, and I slept;
And I grew greater than I am;

"And lay like dead; but when I lived,
Three wingèd midwives wrapped the child.
It was a god that I had loved,
It was a hero I had held.

301

"Stretch out your mortal hands, I beg.
Say common sentences to me.
Lie cold and still, that I may brag
How close I am to proper clay.

"Let this within me hear the truth.
Speak loud to it." He stopped her lips.
He smoothed the covers over both.
It was a dream perhaps, perhaps,

Yet why this radiance round the room,
And why this trembling at her waist?
And then he smiled. It was the same
Undoubted flesh that he had kissed;

She lay unchanged from what she was,
She cried as ever woman cried.
Yet why this light along his brows?
And whence the music no one made?

NEIGHBOR GIRL

You do not know me then, she said.
Well, it is what you asked.
I went away ten thousand miles,
And altered me, and masked.

Your son has never been so safe
As when I heard you cry:
Rather than he be country wed,
Oh, I would see him die!

And has he lived, and has it gone
Forgetful-well with him?
And have you found another face,
And is my own so dim?

But listen! It is doubly gone.
I came to bring you word
How both of you are safe from me,
And if there be a third,

She too may smile and slip to bed
And never glance around;
I am so changed from what I was
I make no earthly sound;

I do not stare like that great girl
Who foddered her father's sheep.
I am more thin than thread—and look!
How listlessly I creep;

Yet not too slowly, going hence,
For if you laid a hand
Like this, like this upon me there,
You scarce would understand.

You do not know how far I've been,
Nor why this patch of white
Like frost upon my forehead grows.
Good father-in-law, goodnight.

IS THIS THE MAN

Is this the man who multiplied,
Divided, added, and was quick
As any wizard to subtract,
As any conjurer to trick
Love's innocent numbers, love's eleven,
Love's unswift arithmetic?

Is this the man who hung the air
With spangled syllables all day?
And was indifferent if wind
Bore every word like webs away?
For there was more that he could spin;
Such love was infinite to say?

Is this the man who carried fire
And left a radiance all night?
Undid the shadows and released
Some old incarcerated light?
Some moldy beam that lived and spread
And was to love as second sight?

303

Is this the man? For it is dusk,
And he is standing dark and still.
For there is silence; not a sound
Weaves out of him against his will.
For he is awkward; he has lost
Even the memory of skill.

Even the memory of love—
Oh, inarticulate, betrayed!
Oh, this the man for whom the world
Was honor-bright and cleanly made.
Yet here he stands, as darkly dumb
As love's first guiltless renegade.

SOMETHING ACRID

Giving him up, she kept the art
Still to engreen his desert part;
His conscience's high inner hill—
She saved the strength, she nursed the skill
To climb and climb and in that clay
Plant what never can blow away.

The top was sandy to desire;
Knew only wind, loved only fire;
Would have been barren of a shoot
But that she found the ancient root:
Felt moisture out, and creeping thence
Created meadows far and dense.

So memory covered him, and killed
What still were healthy had she willed.
He could have withered into friend
Had she accepted verdure's end.
He now is enemy: the spoil
Of something acrid in the soil.

A DIFFERENT AVARICE

It is a different avarice
From any a shadow hides.
Ambitionless in daylight
And without craft he rides.

He is another miser
Than night's old closet knows.
Inhabitant of highways,
Nodding, he comes and goes.

He is a man still grieving
For his small house's heart.
Never again to beat there,
She was the muffled part,

She was the sum not counted,
That now he goes to find
In a wide world and friendly,
In a deep world and kind.

She was the breathing total
That now these numbers build:
People in other houses,
Morning and evening filled—

Oh, numerous, oh, nothing,
Oh, dry and soundless days,
That only set him weeping,
Remembering her ways,

And how their mingled rhythm
Beat time and love in one.
What no one measured, living,
Is infinitely gone.

THE COCKEREL

You are my grandson's bride, she said,
And a dark stranger here.
Sit close, for now my cloudy head
Is by some magic clear.

What I forgot more years ago
Than you have had those eyes—
Sit still awhile! He is below,
And his fox ears are wise.

He is a fox of eighty years,
And turns as quick as then:
As the bright day his pointed ears
Heard me, the helpless hen;

Heard me, that had no sound to make,
Save that I cried awhile,
As each of us stood up to take
The other, well or vile.

It has been well with him and me;
I heard him tell you so.
And grin. Nor do I disagree;
Only, before you go,

Sit close, and hear me say the name
Of one that walked the world
More beautiful than he; but tame—
Oh, tame, with feathers curled;

With plumes that never stood again
After I went and wed.
Nor have I missed him in my den,
Making a fox's bed.

I have been thoughtless; yet this day
Turns me a moment home;
To the green lawn, and to the way
The sun gilded his comb.

BEYOND COMPARE

All he can hope for is that hills and children
In a sky-eyed conspiracy will say:
"There he goes now, the old one; but the young one—
Ah, she was lifelike; she will not waste away.

"She is as fair as then; and it is years now
Since anyone saw her forehead under a cap.
There never was such another worn by woman:
One of the signs and secrets, like her lap.

"When she was in a low chair, tired of talking,
Something about her there denied the rest.
Something about her sitting was not weary,
Something in her was motionless and blest.

"Yet she could move, and then all things went with her:
Neither too swift a harmony nor slow.
Children upon the highway will remember.
All of these hills were there, and they should know.

"This is the bare beginning; she was endless.
There is no number named that would enclose
Each of her clear particulars; abstraction
Dies in the deed, as language in a rose.

"There was the way she had of answering questions:
Not with her lips alone; the shoulders tried;
And the dropped hands succeeded. But how tell it?
Truth is a deep oblivion, and a wide.

"Let her not live in sentences. She merits
Memory, and is anterior to sound.
Let us forget these lines that we have spoken,
Lest they be steel and bind her to the ground.

"Let her be what she was, unpaired, unequalled;
Centered within the circle of her kind.
She is alone there"—patiently he listens,
Hopeful of death when light shall be defined.

III

THE BUNDLE

He was too tightly bound—
The faggots pressed like one together—
For the bright wire to be unwound
And he be loosened to the weather.

There was a kind of day,
The air almost dissolving bones,
When he could wish the knot away,
And he distributed like stones:

Keeping their hardness still,
So they be scattered soft apart;
Space between them like a hill,
And time discovering his heart.

There was a kind of eye—
His children's, tethered at the rim—
Oh, he could even wish to die
If death could make them free of him.

Oh, he could be dispersed,
And the lean sticks grow fat with ease.
But he was fearful of the worst—
And panic then was his disease—

Lest the first break be last:
The wire a serpent in the air;
Fragments of him flying past;
Then all at once a nothing there.

Many the milder ways.
He scoured the world and counted, so.
But not for him the vagrant gaze
And the light-minded letting go.

Not for him the field—
Though he could watch across the wall—
Where the bones danced, and children wheeled,
And songs ascended at nightfall.

THE INVASION

Know thy good self, he said,
But if it be
Permissible, physician,
Know not me.

You have been swift enough,
And tramped as far
Already as to my sentries:
Sons of war.

Know thyself and them:
Count up those fears;
Lead off those joys—lifelong
My prisoners,

My dwarves of thought, fair slaves
By me deformed.
Then rest; there is a room
Not to be stormed.

I shall breed other watchers
For the walls.
Take these and march. Minute
Be their footfalls.

THE RUNAWAYS

Upon a summer Sunday: sweet the sound
Of noon's high warmness flowing to the ground;

Upon a summer Sunday: wide the song
Of strengthless wings that bore the sky along;

Upon a summer Sunday: strange the power,
Inaudible, that opened every flower;

On Sunday, in the summer, through the white
Mid-world they wandered, meditating flight.

With every boundary melted, still they ran,
Still looked for where the end of earth began;

Still truant; but, dissolving far ahead,
The edge of day as effortlessly fled,

As innocently distanced all they were
Of quick-eared dog and fat philosopher.

On Sunday, in the summer, down a field,
Leader and led, alternately they wheeled

Till the great grass possessed them, and the sky
No longer was a map to measure by;

Till round and round they floated, lost and small,
Like butterflies that afterward will fall

But now between the great sky and the ground,
Sun-tethered, dance all morning meadow-bound.

Upon a summer Sunday, when the light
Of perfect noon was everywhere and white—

Pure death of place and color—then the pair
Grew sudden-silent, hungry for home's air;

Paused, turned; remembered shadows in a yard;
And had again their own high wall and hard.

THE ONLY THING

He was not waiting for us, he was not
Standing at any window. He was
Busy in some one room, we said,
Holding the rest of them in his head.

He could do that; he liked it better
Than waiting, than wanting us with him; he was
The only thing then for States around;
Not even a star, not even a sound.

Wherever he was, we said, the ceiling
Had opened to let him through; and the walls
Upstairs—they had folded behind and followed:
Partitionless now the house, and hollowed.

Then even the house was gone; as if
The center had eaten the circle; as though
The egg of the world devoured its shell.
And so, arriving, we jerked the bell;

Listened, and heard him coming, and wondered
Whether he knew we knew. "Hello!"
Adding across the distance only:
"It hasn't been the least bit lonely."

THE LITTLE DOCTOR

The little doctor with the black
Ambitious eyes had giant horses;
High the reins and loud the splash
Along those muddy country courses.

Black the harness, black the eyes,
And black the phaeton's new fringes.
Dappled, though, the necks and flanks,
And foaming white the fetlocks' plunges—

On and on, a winter's day;
Warm the sudden south-wind thawing;
On and on the doctor watched
Rut after rut with water flowing;

Guided the eight, the silver feet
Proud into pools; and heard the utter
Puddle and plash; received the sound
Most deep, most eloquent to flatter;

Loosened the reins, allowed the hocks
Through flooded grooves to speak his greatness;
Whence the black ambitious eyes
Saw now in everything a fitness;

Saw the hide of dappled rumps,
How it cross-wrinkled with the straining;
How the great backs forward sloped;
How in the manes the wind was moaning.

Yet the straps outsang the wind,
And yet the hoof-spray drowned the grasses.
So in that lost, that country time
The little doctor ever presses.

On and on, a dateless day,
Down sunken roads where death has prospered,
Black-eyed breezes still can blow,
And private glories still be whispered.

THE MUSIC-BOX

When they were almost there his skinny fingers
Tightened upon some secret, and he said:
"You are deceived, there will be no more silence
Than ever;" and licked a knuckle and knocked his head.

"This tilted, motionless bone above my shoulders,
This seedless gourd, this tomb whereon your locks
Shall click—it is a maker of far noises,
A many-times-removed loud music-box.

"Not loud to you, though; so it scarcely matters.
Save that you are deceived. There will be sound.
It is my mind that makes it, as it rushes
Like a fresh wind across the risen ground.

"Like a small animal parting the tops of grasses,
Like a bright face with feelers, so it goes.
It is my mind at work remembering objects;
It is the earth remembering what it knows.

312

"Till then each piece of matter, each grey sliver,
Sleeps; until I arrive; then upward springs!
Oh, the wide cry, the crackling! Oh, the music!
As my still thought runs rustling over things.

"It is more swift, more audible than sunrise,
Than day's advancing limit, whispered light.
Half of my sleepers waken unto darkness;
But half are heaven-blinded, noon for night.

"My earth is one imaginable moment,
A whirl of whiteness spindled with pure black.
There only is an instant's breath of stillness;
A dream of nothing; then I am drumming back!"

When they were there, relaxing his long fingers
He smiled upon them, fastening the door.
"Peace on you then," he said; "but on your planet
There never will be silence any more."

THE MEETING

It was no intercourse of palms;
Or foreheads, mutual-bowed;
Or tongues, returning courtesies;
It was so far from loud
That one of the two hears only now
The rustle of a shroud;

Hears only now, by thinking back,
And pressing fact before,
A corridor's white vacancy;
The darkness of a door;
And how the other, secret there,
Looked out; and looks no more.

The eyes of illness make for sound
The scratching of a pen—
Oh, every inch of pallid wall
Is traced again, again;
Unceasing; but a deeper sound
Looks out of dying men.

313

So on that night, unknown to him,
So in that thoughtless hall,
So round him clung a whispering
Half hoarse, half musical.
So round him rang the silence's
Mute break, and shadow's fall.

He hears it only now, and knows
How tight the vision drew;
How longingly the other looked;
And how he merely threw
His cape across his back; tripped down,
And whistled over dew.

TANTRUM WINGS

Rather than ups and downs,
Now here, now high,
Rather than tantrum wings he would have known
No skill to fly.

Rather than lightning joy—
His will and theirs
Sky-wedded—he would lubberly have moved;
Been caved with bears;

Been lame upon a ledge;
Refused the top:
So evenness be in him, and cool blood,
And motion stop.

Rather than he be else,
Be juster, though,
They took him as he was—they loved him more
For high, for low;

For doubtfulness all day,
For noon, for night.
The average of this man was burning cloud,
Was thrashed sunlight.

EXAGGERATOR

The truth for him was like a tree,
Was like a funnel; like a fan;
Like any point from which a cone
Spreads upside down until the span
From base to base across the top
Cannot be guessed by any man.

The truth for him was not the seed,
Was not the apex, handle, spout;
Was not the particle or germ,
Or what grew thence so wild and stout;
Was not the great, the upper end.
It was the joy of starting out:

Of feeling something in him rise
And widen instantly; and swell,
As if the wind and he were one,
And blew upon each other well;
As if the sky and he were single:
Clapper there and flangèd bell.

The truth for him was hearing quick
The cordage whistle, and the whine
Of wakened metal; something bronze;
Something moaning thin and fine,
Something low; until it burst,
And all was plangent with word-shine.

The truth for him was leaving earth
Between two beams that sloped and rose;
And never joined—the angle's bound
Was all of distance at the close;
Whence he descended, narrowing down
And resting gently where he chose.

MIMIC

Summing him, we subtracted
The men he acted.
Yet he was not contained
In what remained.
Still must he overflow
Lest numbers know.

All that ourselves could be
Is what you see.
Starved, unchangeable stuff
Was task enough.
But not for him, whose feigning
Was girth and gaining.

Wit-wonderful, he discolored
Himself to dullard;
Ceased, and as soon began
More god than man;
Descended, and was the least
Articulate beast.

Nor have we yet divined
The one behind;
Save that the many have told
Of water and gold;
And how such clear excess
Is lastingness.

WIND-CURE

Coming up here to mend, she picked this window,
The big east one, the clear one, so that lying,
Our sister, like a broken lily stem—
Twice broken, waist and breast—
Her careful eyes could feed upon the low lawn,
The trees, and over walls a mile of meadow.

With the still house behind her as she watched,
And the dark west, that waited at the corners,
The whole west, that never spoke a word—
But waited there, and swelled—
She lay upon her soft side, expectant,
Trusting the loved east, the planned October.

Then round it rushed, that devil there behind her,
Both ways, and put the sun out like a breath.
It only was the third of her sweet mornings—
One, two, three's a charm—
When half the world came warlike round both angles,
When there was wind from nowhere, so that stone walls

Wimpled, and the maddened grasses pulled,
Insane of root, their forelocks everywhichway
Diving, and the maple trees, leaf-wounded—
The first high leaves to fall—
Bent sudden-double, dazed, as up the roadway
One dust-whirl met another whirl descending.

Or then the gales agreed, so that a music,
Single but heaven-harsh, whined overhead
Straight onward, stretching hours upon a note—
Hours, evenings, days—
Till each of us grew fearful, and went tiptoe
Thinking to find her mad. But she lay smiling,

On her soft side lay smiling, turning upward
No longer a tired eye, no longer strengthless.
Beyond the glass she listened to that fury—
Gazed at it, wild again—
Then whispered to us, bending for the low words,
"Oh, you and I, wind, you and I forever!"

THE BREATHING SPELL

The black share-cropper, grizzled in his prime,
Night's face grown frosty-grey with terror's noises—
Six children on the floor pretend to sleep
While white men prowl outdoors in dark disguises;

Level their guns, and laugh; and then the pause
Till crack! two holes high up, and plaster flying;
He does not duck, the croucher by the stove,
He does not catch what this new sound is saying—

The black share-cropper, deafened long ago
To the discord of misery, half-dozes;
Hears no more hunger now; ignores the banged,
The dispossessing door; drowns all those noises,

Dreaming. He is bent beneath a dream
Sky-tall and windless-wide, with rivers running
Waveless, and the smoke above a train
Cloud-stationary, distant, over fanning

Elm trees that he counts along the line:
One, two, and dipping three, and arched eleven.
It is a mile of quiet he has found,
It is a township's peace that he is given.

He moves among the low weeds, mute as they.
The wrappings of his feet are gauze on gravel.
And when the white, the black men pass him, slow,
The greeting of each eye is round and civil.

Even the moment's battle, and the storm,
And the down pitch of timbers—even the falling
Forest is no roar against his ears,
Time-tempered, and the wounded are not wailing:

Stout bodies that collided as in mist,
Rock-hearted trees descending there like feathers.
By the cold stove he drowses, safe from sound,
While midnight clears its throat and morning gathers.

INCORRIGIBLE

We never could see it wound him, the tipped weakness
That flew, oh, deadly often, while a twang
Like music with a plume of malice in it,
Like sorrow's rawhide, sounded in his ears.
But not in ours. We only heard, harmonious,
The outer song, the one he wrapped it with.

He never could believe they were immortal:
The bowstring there behind him, and the sprung
White wand that let the feathered arrow fly.
He had lost count of subtlety's directions;
Supposed the compass rounded. But his back
Somehow was always magnet, for it came.

Meanwhile he faced us, hopeful of his cure.
If that was all the poison, he was well.
He had outstared the circle; so he faced us,
Smiling, and we could envy such a man:
So wise against his weakness, and so ready.
So ready until tomorrow wheeled around!

His very hope exposed him; and his effort
Never again to doubt of proving good;
And his long list of victories—it wanted
Only one more, the next. But he would win.
And that was when we missed him: when he lay there
With the last barb—he knew it—through his spine.

He knew it, and a month of song succeeded.
Now he had finished mending, now was whole.
The quiver had been dropped where moths, inside it,
Measured the print of arrows; while green leaves
Fell calmly and were drifted to the mouth;
And while he sang, flesh-innocent, his song.

It was a song of moths and sleeping needles.
Under some glass an arrow never swung.
All of the norths were numbered; the wind rested;
Under some cloth a heart beat still and clear.
Under some song—oh, then it was the earth shook,
Shifting an inch, and feathers flew and flew.

FORECLOSURE

So he sat down and slowly, slowly
Worked at his Christian name;
Watching the gold and halfway smiling
As the last letter came;
Till the whole sound was there, and shouted,
Suddenly, his shame.

Between this word then and the other—
His and his father's too—
He stared at the pen as if its handle
Were a great horn, and blew;
Then lowered the point and quietly labored
Till the last ink was through.

So he got up, and through the wide silence
Wandered; and song began.
Not the old tune, for that was buried
Where the slow writing ran;
But remnants, hung in the wind awhile,
And impotent to scan.

There was the bell that once had brought him,
Frightened, across the field;
There was the mad white shepherd's barking,
And the hurt child, unhealed;
There was a hen whose brood came piping
To the red worm revealed.

There was quick trampling on a stairway,
Until doors sealed the sound.
There were the drums of winter booming
When the lame boy was drowned.
So his lost land went with him, pulling
Its tatters close around.

ORDEAL

Sir Eglamour has limped a mile
And left his blood on forest leaves.
Here he must rest himself awhile;
Looks round the hut; undoes his greaves;
Falls down like death, and cannot smile
At thought of plumes or banded sleeves;

Cannot remember now the wine,
The lances glittering in the hall,
The goblets lifted at a sign,
The ceiling dusky over all,
The waiting trumpets, and the nine
Young nervous minstrels by the wall.

Sir Eglamour is not to die,
Though blood is dropping from him still.
It is to cease; for in this sty
There waits another test of will.
Strength conquers wounds, but straw may try
How much of knighthood it can kill.

This dampened heap whereon he lies,
These rafters, songless and obscure,
These rotted shingles, and the flies
Whose country buzz he must endure:
What thing among them knows him wise,
Who now will name him bold and pure?

Without a lady by his side,
Without the proclamation's din—
And then a door is opened wide,
For now the king is coming in—
Without their praises, how can pride
Feed on itself and not grow thin?

Sir Eglamour, how can your fire
Feed on itself and never cool?
How will you pray when this poor mire
In its indifference thinks you fool?
So far from pomp is there desire?
Can flesh remember every rule?

OLD LANDSCAPE

There was some kind of safety in the feathery
Forest rising leftward from the lake—
The lake no more a mirror, and the shadows
Deepened in a frame of time, of dust,
Of slumber—there was safety in the ageless
Trees a hand once painted, plume by plume.

Across the tarnished waters, on a level
Waste, a blackened lawn, the castle towered,
Its windows morning-darkened, like an ogre's
Eyes that have been dreamless year on year;
Its moat no longer glittering, and the country
Carts all mired with time, the fetlocks fouled.

But there was safety leftward, by a faded
Bridge that in the foreground leapt the stream—
The stream no longer lustrous where the timbers
Fell on it like shadows. There his eye
Found comfort, and his feet imagined movement,
And he entered, and he mounted toward the grove.

And there was safety for him in the shaggy
Ceiling of dusk leaves, of lofty down
A brush had swiftly painted—thinking only
Of sloped masses, maybe; yet the hand
Might well have fancied feathers, and the under
Breast of what great nameless brooding bird.

So anyhow for him, who now in safety
Glided through the silence, and who heard
Soft beatings overhead as of a heartstroke
Muffled from the world, and from the carters
Struggling at the moat, and from the lake
Whose poisoned waters glittered under change.

IV

YOUNG WOMAN AT A WINDOW

Who so valiant to decide?
Who so prompt and proper-active?
Yet each muscle in her brain
Relaxes now; is unrestrictive;
Lets her lean upon this dark
November night wind; lets it work—

Oh, lets it ask her if she thinks,
Oh, lets it whisper if she knows
How much of time is like a stream
Down which her headless body flows;
How many answers, proudly made,
Will be like minnows overlaid

With inch on inch of glossy black,
With depth on depth of sliding water;
Lets it dare her to predict
Those floods of silence coming later;
Till she melts, and leaning long
Is only conscious of wind-song.

Who so valorous of voice?
Who so staunch upon the ground?
But wind-and-water-song at work
Stops both her ears against the sound
Of someone here she used to know;
Of someone saying: It is so.

She leans and loses every word.
Her loudest wisdom well is gone.
But still the current of the night
Comes with its foaming on and on;
Pours round the sill; dissolves the hands;
And still the dreamless body stands.

Young man of many sorrows, do you know
How narrow the sweet night is, and how soon
This hemisphere above you will be split,
Letting light in, the monster; letting clear waves
Shatter the scented cloud? Do you, the feaster,
Know the great air as tasteless on the tongue?

You cannot measure smallness; you believe
Still in the darkened stature, you are rounded
Still with all color's thickness, you can count
More sorrows than the night was numbered for.
You groan. But what of sunrise, and the white time
Coming? What of the voice lost round the sky?

Do not so much as listen to me asking.
Keep to your little dome, whereof the sound grows
Nightly: throat and dusky metal joined.
Keep to your little darkness, where the rose thorns
Pierce the rich heart of odor, and the eye
Is opened upon soft shapes, and sorrows flow.

Never look up, anticipating night's end.
So near the limit is, so low the ceiling,
Almost a glance would lift you. Or the mind would.
Let it keep home awhile, and miss the high
Wide-swinging waves, the coolness, the great clearness.
They are another joy, not spread for now.

Through the great oneness over you—so high there,
So far, so all around, that even earth shrinks,
Even the world is one dropped poppy seed—
Through the glass-white immensity go flashing
Ages of light criss cross; the soundless beacons
Wheel, and the great air sparkles, blind with time.

Young man of the dense sorrows, you will rise there;
You will cast off, delectable, this load.
You will be wind and sky-ray, you will thin there
To the pure beam, transparent, self-denied.
Yet will your tongue not taste; nor will that presence
Sing in your ears, like this one, all day long.

YOUNG BLOOD

After so many blushes,
And stoppings at the heart,
How it recovers—rushes—
Stings every part—
And pauses; for these lovers
Are sluggish movers.

Experiment of fingers,
Faint breathing in and out—
Enough of something lingers
Lest passion doubt;
And flames; for in these children
Is flint and cauldron.

Yet there is time for burning,
And many an ashen place.
Let them be; they are learning
Fear's courteous face.
Perceive. The hands of these lovers
Are delicate rovers.

CHANGELING

This woman is bewildered,
This mother of a son
Cries out upon imposture:
He's not the one,
He's not the hunger-helpless,
The clamorous one.

325

Where is the other hidden?
And if he still is fed,
Why has he grown ungrateful?
Is famine dead?
Is foolishness? No answer;
No curl of head.

She nourishes a stranger,
And knows it by his wish
For anything but dainties.
Untouched the dish.
Unshatterable the silence.
Undone the leash.

THE WIDOWER

The little fellow—partly fool—
Remembers perfectly his mother.
Nobody better understands
There never will be such another.

His pretty sisters, said the man,
Are not so wise with all their wit.
For them already she is saint,
So they improve her as they sit,

Recalling only she was cool,
Remarking always how she smiled.
And this is rare and touching-fine;
But truth is with the coarser child.

He has not ceased, when he is wrong,
To hear the angry volume close,
And tapping step: to him the thorns
Are real as petals down the rose.

The flower is firm; gone slow to bed,
He gazes suddenly and grins;
Pulls bare his neck for her caress;
Recites the goat's, the parrot's sins.

But then tomorrow he will run
Like any thief to miss the wrath
Of someone coming tall and red:
It is herself upon the path.

It is herself, and nowise changed
As late with them, the weeping pair.
They have the spirit, he the flesh.
And either sight is sad to bear.

THE VIGIL

Young Walter keeps all winter
In a high land and cold.
Nor has he any fortune,
Save that his blood is gold;
Save that his eyes have riches,
Deep-woven, damask-old.

I hear that round his house there
The mountains crack like ice;
But he has bread, with buckwheat
Honey upon each slice;
And cats that range the kitchen,
Killing the famished mice.

I hear there is a woodlot,
And that he daily tramps
With birch and alder cuttings,
And heaps the hearth, and stamps;
And by their flicker nightly
Reads late, disdaining lamps.

I hear that farmer people,
Who lived here once and died,
Left rows of witless volumes,
And that young Walter cried:
"They will be buckram coaches
Wherein my fancies ride!"

I hear that he goes through them;
Blows off the dust and lint;
Finishes every chapter;
Is faithful to the stint;
And that his mind has gilded
Some tales as in a mint.

Young Walter is not coming
Like other heroes home.
His wars are solitary,
His shield the honeycomb;
His hostages the fire-log,
The tabby cat, the tome.

THIS IS THE BOY

This is the boy that rode nine hundred
Miles. And did the porter,
Bowing to you, feign and find you
Seventeen or older?

Was there a lady down the aisle
Looked up and smiled; decided
It were a pity if a child—
So were you then invaded?

Or was the double seat and bag;
The narrow glass, the bell;
The polished berth above you—boy,
Were these your own and all?

Whence if you turned a quiet head
You saw the country spin,
Nearby more swift, far off more slow,
And humorless horses run?

Whence if you leaned you saw the pillows
Propped in a slumbrous row?
And the shut eyes? And did you shiver,
Suddenly? And sway,

Ecstatic, lonely, on the plush,
To such a rhythm, rising,
As only flange and rail produce,
Past copying, past praising?

Exploring forward, did you pause
In the loud gale and clank
Of vestibules? And spell the names—
Plum Valley, Onderdonck,

Septentrion, Minervaville,
Darius—did you walk
Through Glendon to the dining car?
And did you careless take

That leather seat, high, single there,
And blink in silvershine
As now the sun poured in to please
The veteran of the train?

NOISY CHINA

The forty acre oatfield,
The hedge fence, the raincrow,
The silence—the boy said:
Sound, sound? it lies so
Forever, sweet and dead;

Forever with its head down,
Sleepily and sidewise,
Cheek upon the warm grain,
Dreamily, and dove's cries
Never leave a stain;

Never may corrupt this,
The silence, the sweet sun,
The low breath—the boy leaned,
Guarding his horizon
Against the loud fiend.

329

Half around the bent world,
Even then, in Peking,
Even then a boy said:
Sound? it is a fierce wing
Forever overhead;

Another wing, a thousand more,
A swift flock—the quills whirr,
The feathers beat, and gabble falls
Like droppings where the dews were,
Like hail along the walls.

Sound? it is a cracked voice;
The pigeon men will never die:
The starlings, ravens, jackdaws.
The little maid that used to lie—
What is she now but crow's caws?

SPECTRAL BOY

I told you I would come, he said,
I told you with these very eyes.
Be not ashamed. The grave is deep,
And terror in it dies.

If in these circles that you see
There is the old, the child's alarm,
It does not live to startle you,
Or work the pulse's harm.

It was not gathered underground,
It was not freed upon a day,
Except that something might come home
Of the whipped soul, and stay.

Except the fever, all is here.
My deathless part, my fear, returns.
Be not ashamed. The grave is cold.
Nothing in it burns.

330

I have not suffered since I died,
Though I have lain with eyes as round
As when you fixed them; but enlarged,
Some days, from lack of sound.

And so there fell to me an hour
Of utter quiet; then I rose,
And am revisiting old Time,
Before his close.

Was I not washed and buried well?
Why this desire, why this research
For time and wrath? Be still, I beg!
What now? This twitch and lurch—

You would escape me, but I swear
I was not sent to punish you.
I came alone, that fear might form
Once more on me like dew.

No longer groan and hide your hands.
This thing I seek is chill and sweet.
Be not ashamed. The grave is pure.
No horror now. No heat.

SIN OF OMISSION

He will remember this; the cunning Fates,
Seeing all seventy years laid flat ahead—
The spring-tight coil of days unrolls for them,
Their little and deep long eyes forewatch the dead—
The mouse-eyed Fates can number the known times
He will remember this, the thing unsaid.

Only to say it now would soothe that man,
His father, come to sound him in his room;
Most friendly, but the stairs are still acreak,
And the boy, deafened to another doom,
Says nothing; he is guilty of desire
For the mind's silence, waiting to resume.

What it was filled with, he the least of all
In a far day will know; remembering then—
So the Fates reckon—how he ran and called,
Hoping to bring the shoulders up again;
But only called half-loudly in his pride,
And in the pride of him the best of men.

He will remember this, and loathe the hour
When his fair tongue, malingering, stood still.
He will rehearse the sentences not said;
Pretending that he climbed the lonely hill;
Pretending that he met him at the top,
Articulate, and cured him of his ill:

His need to know, so innocent, how sons
Read in their rooms the dark, the dear-bought books;
How in his own good flesh the strange thing grew,
Thought's inward river, nourishing deep nooks,
Dyeing them different-green. The boy will feign,
Concealing his long sighs, his backward looks—

Will fabricate warm deeds and laughing words,
His hand upon a chair, his cheeks alive;
Instead of this cool waiting, and this gloom
Wherein no starting syllable can thrive.
He will remember even as he runs.
The Fates run too, and rapider arrive.

BOY DRESSING

There lies the shoe, picked up a minute past
And dropped when something struck him, and he paused,
Eye-rigid, fixing daylight on the door:
Thin daylight, that a careless clock has caused

And windows have conspired with. So his hands,
Conscious of nothing leather, float to work
At buttons on his breast, and at the tie—
He fumbles round it; finishes with a jerk;

Stops dead again, his hair in timeless tangles,
Obedient to a moment that will end—
Bang! Doors downstairs have doomed it. But the shoe.
Remembering, his back begins to bend,

His knee comes up, his fingers at the instep
Play with the knotted laces. Leave him there.
Be tolerant of trances. For he feeds
On time, and drinks the milk of mother air.

HOME FROM SCHOOL

Here they come, the paired brief-cases
Cutting, port and starboard, the waved street;
Their thought all smoke, their laughter the white whistle
Of steam as two slim funnels tilt and meet.

One vessel these, the minds well mingled
And the gay hull oblivious where it goes:
Set homeward, but the helmsman is a dummy,
Drifting them safe whatever folly blows.

One purpose theirs, that no one listens
Down the long tide and faintly overhears.
The sidewalk only billows, and the indifferent
Spray of their footsteps floats and disappears.

At four o'clock arriving, and slowing
Suddenly round and down, the satchels swing.
While the waves wash, and lap at them a little,
The serious white heads together cling.

Then a quick puff—their scheme escapes them,
Splitting aloft and thinning into air.
Divided now the vessel, as each portion
Enters a separate house and climbs a stair.

Only tomorrow, clean and early,
Will they be one again and sail away;
Their end almost forgotten; but no matter;
Innumerable the islands down the bay.

LIKE SON

Your stillness here at evening, with the shade
Wide up and both your hands beneath your head—
I see. It is the same as when I lay,
Just so, and watched the window-people tread:

Our neighbors, at their little squares of glass
Come suddenly to eye, then off again;
Extinguished in the frame until that boy,
That watcher, worked his magic on them then:

Stared, hummed, and brought the dressing gown, the sleeve,
Brought folded arms and faces, brought the smile.
But not for him. For no one. This he knew,
And knows it now with you a whispering while.

See? Neither of us here can be imagined.
They stand as if alone; and how they seem
Is how the planets find them: row on row,
Night-blown, and candle-brief as in a dream.

NO MORE DIFFERENT

The random eye mismates them,
So bearish is the man,
So like a tender goatling
The boy is—and ran

Like this, beside his father,
As long ago as earth,
As long ago as evening,
As bird time, as mirth;

As any mountain old one
Moved with a leafy cry
For music to his loudness,
And with a palm to lie

Like this one in the cavern
Of his too granite hand.
But they are no more different
Than hour-glass and sand;

Requiring so each other
That one gives up his rage,
And one gives up his sweetness.
Divine the average.

MEN AND CHILDREN

What moon presides when mosses grow,
What sun when celandine, may know
The courteous name of one dark star
That comes where men and children are,
But comes most rarely. For it rules
Dusk-suddenly, and none but fools
Foretell it. None but fathers' eyes
Look for it round the evening skies.
Let them not look. They cannot bring
What makes identity to sing
In man, in child—in them as two
Drops of the selfsame merry dew.
They shine together for a while;
Too wise for speech, too clear for smile;
Too unremembering for doubt,
Too blissful. Then the star dims out.
Too single were they to endure,
Too indivisible and pure;
As water may not water be
Longer than there is light to see.

V

THE MOMENTS HE REMEMBERS

The moments he remembers? They are those
In the dog part of him, the sleeping nose,

The animal awakened in him once—
Decrepit the old hound, yet how he hunts

Through the moist lands of youth! Or then he did—
Remembering what time almost has hid:

The hour at sunset when the ball and glove,
Hot with the play, exhaled a leather love,

And his left hand, withdrawn to wipe his eyes,
Sweetened the whole air with musk surprise:

The sweat of horses, tempered with his own,
And the rubbed oil that lingered on alone.

The animal, awakening once more,
Almost can live; except his bones are sore,

And the sunk valleys of his mind can save
Only a few more moments from the grave:

As when the boy, in January wind,
Ran till his face was nipped and scarlet-skinned;

Then stopped, and all of winter like a bell
Rang in his nostrils, soundless. Or the spell—

He can remember, suddenly, his trance
When feet upon the lawn had ceased to dance,

And his small cheeks, enamored of the bruise,
Lay pressed in grass the way sky-witches use,

Straining upon earth's arc, to enter in.
He entered it, the odor—now so thin,

So struggling now, so faint across the ground,
To the old man and the near-sighted hound.

UNCLE ROGER

When he was eighteen autumns old,
With Indian hair and wiry waist,
He says America was a map
Whereon a boy and engine raced.

It was a field of moving fires—
The sparks uprushing, and the red
Of open boilers; and the green
Of signals floating far ahead;

Or else a wild, a lonely plain,
A waiting desert, where the howl
Of locomotives miles away
Was ghosts awalk and beasts aprowl.

What all it was he will not say;
How beautiful he cannot tell.
Yet in his chair I know he hears
The cry of steam, the starting bell.

I know he sees himself asleep
In prairie clover, while the clank
Of couplings on the Danville freight
Is music to him, sweet and rank.

So stretching many a cooler day
On gravelly weeds beside a grade,
He hears the whine of coming wheels,
With desolate whistles overlaid;

337

But feels the rumble in his bones
Before the loud, the nearer sound;
And all the history of a line
Reads out of rumors in the ground.

He can remember a wet dawn,
He can remember a stopped train
In Pennsylvania, and the hoarse,
High notes—again, again—

That tore the mountain walls apart,
That split the cold, the dripping oaks;
And still he hears the lean yell,
And still the dewy engine smokes.

Far in the west a water tower
Leaks in the sun and dampens sand:
The only circle that is dark
In many a mile of desert land.

Yet by the Gulf an endless swamp
Gurgles beneath the trestled ties;
And he has waited on a bluff
To watch the Mississippi rise;

And crawled behind the going flood
And tested bridges, beam on beam,
Until a signal waved ahead
Brought the great wheels, and swish of steam.

He loiters in the branching yards;
He climbs a cabin red with rust.
Those polished engines puffing by
Are doomed like this one unto dust.

He tries the throttle; it is fast;
Corroded gauges cloud his eye.
So this is growing old and old,
So this is what it is to die.

Then Uncle Roger, coming to,
Sits in his chair and nods and smiles;
And clicks his lips through seven years,
And lives again ten thousand miles.

TWO OF YOU

I know you after sixty years;
They have not changed, she said:
Those incombustible black stones
High in your ashen head;
Those coals that, as our passion blew,
Outlasted my poor dread.

Those eyes that I so lowly feared
For their unstopping gaze—
I may not fancy even now
That on my snow it stays;
This level whiteness of my life;
These warm, forgotten ways.

I have come back to look at you,
I have come back to find
The incorruptible straight stalk,
The rod within the rind.
And I can wonder if time erred,
Proving so rigid-kind.

He has made two of you, I say.
Does either of them hear?
That dark one rising inwardly?
This other one—this sere,
This whiter one that snows have singed,
Piling the faggot year?

But not the first, the ageless man.
I see him where he stands,
Stiff prisoner inside the glass,
Contented with smooth hands;
Condemned, erect, and total-deaf
To the sweet run of sands.

339

From the swift song of change, my love,
You long ago were locked;
A young man in an old man's hide,
And both of them are mocked;
Unless you listened, one of you,
When my crisp knuckles knocked.

BAILEY'S HANDS

The right one that he gave me—
I could have shut my eyes
And heard all seventy summers
Rasping at their scythes.

The left one that he lifted,
Tightening his hat—
I could have seen the cut groves
Lie fallen, green and flat;

Or seen a row of handles,
Ash-white and knuckle-worn,
Run back as far as boyhood
And the first field of thorn:

The two-edged axe and sickle,
The pick, the bar, the spade,
The adze, and the long shovel—
Their heads in order laid,

Extending many an autumn
And whitening into bone,
As if the past were marching,
Stone after stone.

So by his hands' old hardness,
And the slow way they waved,
I understood the story:
Snath-written, helve-engraved.

The high heap that now and then,
When the wind thumps it, settles—
The breathing space decreases for the grass
Beneath it, and the nettles—
Will lie, when April thrashes,
Compacted ashes.

Not here, not like this mountain, tossed
From the saw's teeth all fall;
Not here, but humbly leeward of the house,
And ghostly small.
Nothing, after this winter,
Of sap or splinter.

There will be nothing of the difference,
When grass grows again,
Nothing between the big and little mountains
Save two unfrozen men:
The blood in them still running,
Lukewarm and cunning.

For such as them this pyramid
Must pass, becoming flame—
All but a little powder on the ground there
That no lit match could tame.
Lest their poor lives be finished,
Bulk is diminished:

Shrinking until a room expands
To summer under the snow;
Melting away though earth is solid iron,
And ice-flakes blow.
Perhaps itself should stay.
Yet who can say?

Only when he was old enough, and silent:
Not breaking-old; time-coated; that was it;
Only when he was dry enough: but seasoned;
Time-guarded against all weather-warp and split;
Time-roughened, with years of ridges down his bark:
Then only grew he worthy of their remark.

They did not move; but watched him as he came,
Man-tired, and paused and peered among their shade.
No magical advancing; each emerged
Only as slow acquaintance thus was made:
The oaks and he confronted, that was all;
Save that his leaves of ignorance could fall.

They fell, and filled the temperate aging air
With a crisp rustle, flake on flake descending;
Till in some month it ceased, and trunk on trunk
Acknowledged him, in rows without an ending.
The lesser with the greater shadows wove:
He there with them, companions of the grove.

The ash was proud to show him in its side
How narrowly and coldly time had cut:
A flank of iron; and how its sharpened leaves
Stood out too stiff for any wind to shut:
Stubborn; yet some antiquity of grace
Still kept it king, still proved the priestly face.

That maple there, the old man of the wood:
Shaggy, with clefts of shadow in its rind;
Like a deep-bearded deity, becloaked,
Shed down upon him, slowly, what of its mind
Went floating: lightly, lightly; though of late
Time pressed it under centuries of weight.

He touched them all, and moved among their shapes
Like a blind child whom giants might despise.
Yet he was their true copy; so they leaned,
Indulgent to his autumn; met his eyes;
And uttered as much, responding to his hands,
As ever a second childhood understands.

OLD WHITEY

Old Whitey is not met with any more.
There is no farmer left has heard the tale.
No word of him runs swiftly round the store,
Past tea and twine, past lard and candy-pail.

It is not long, not many men have died,
Since the last dodderer insisted here:
"I saw him! Not a dapple on his hide.
Pure white he was, and clean from rump to ear.

"It must have been at midnight; that's his hour,
And never has he come a hair behind.
There suddenly he trotted, pale as flour;
And silent as a paddock in the mind.

"But he was there, not here"—he tapped his head—
"I saw him in the darkness, making three.
I saw the fetlocks falling, and a dread
Of so much softness falling seized on me.

"I whipped my two, I kneeled against the dash;
I did not look, if looking were the cause.
He only trotted faster, and the splash
Of eight feet grew to twelve without a pause;

"Except his hooves were noiseless—that I knew;
And clean; he watched the others, dark with mud.
He had come here from pastures dripped with dew,
On weightless feet that, falling, tried to thud.

"Oh, then it was I pitied him, and looked.
But he was proud, Old Whitey; he had gone."
It is not long, with finger stiffly crooked,
Since the last bent reporter babbled on.

Yet time enough to prove him doubly dead,
This horse that once was flesh and then was cloud.
Now nothing. Even pity for him fled
When the last man remembered he was proud.

THE DISMISSAL

I have not found it strange, she said,
Though it took strength to bear,
That you came back to me so young,
Even to curly hair.

Even to pouting: you whose years
Lengthened to stoic grace.
Something is less impossible, then,
Momently to face.

Momently I listen now
For the stiff alien stride
Of him that was my second rock,
After your father died.

He would not see you if he could,
Nor would I yield a part
Of this that has come back to me
Out of my earliest heart.

You must be ready, my small son,
You must be quick to go;
As when—but it is forty years
Since I stood frowning, so,

And opened the unwelcome door,
And pushed your shoulders out.
You must obey me, now as then,
Whatever the slow doubt.

It will be easier, pale boy.
A word from me, and walls—
Oh, these unlit and noiseless ones
Will swallow your footfalls.

Three backward steps to match those three
That brought you where I lay—
Oh, it is hard that company comes,
And that you must away.

THERE WAS A WIDOW

There was a widow had six sons,
Door-high and gone away;
Not one, returning, but must duck,
Must laugh to hear her say:
"Come in, come in, the room is long;
Lie down, and sleep, and stay.

"Lie down, my tall one, and pretend
Time still is young and clever:
Can make you think, as once you did,
This is your house forever;
No silver key to let you out,
Never, never, never.

"Sleep here, my high one, and observe
How slow the ceiling moves:
Time's meadow, turning round and round;
Invisible the grooves;
Inaudible the engine; dim
The chickadees, the doves.

"Lie still and let their minute-notes
Weave hours and months and years.
It is a net so loud and fine
I will unstop my ears;
Though I have heard the tearing sound
Of one that disappears.

"Time's meadow, tall one, even now
Whirls rapider—is rent!
Were you my own son coming home,
Dear ghost, or demon-sent?"
Then silence; and not one of them
Was laughing when he went.

NO GHOSTS

The sorrows of this old woman taper
And come to a pitiless, come to a sharpened
Unbearable point. Her dead, her lost ones,
Susan and Jasper—oh, she has harkened
Many a midnight, many a morning,
Many a moon's hour, when the darkened

Barnway and goatshed dropped blue shadows—
Oh, she has watched, this woman has listened,
But neither of those two dead and gone ones
Ever will haunt her. Oh, she has fastened
Shutters and windows, and nailed the doors,
And then she has combed her hair, and hastened

And jumped in bed, in the middle chamber
Safest from thieves. But not from spirits.
For they are wilful, and one that flouts them
Never is certain. Down from garrets,
Up from cellars, or through some crack
They may come anyway, like ferrets,

Growing to something great and slender—
A friendly son, a pale-haired daughter—
Growing for hours. But, oh, not Susan,
Oh, not Jasper. They besought her
Never and never to forget.
But time runs by like clearest water,

Cloudless, childless, and she moans
Because of all her deathly losses
This one, this one must be last;
Because of all night's ancient uses
This one, this one long is withered.
So she wipes three kitchen glasses,

And she sets them by her bed
For three to drink if throats be dry;
Half believes herself asleep;
Never opens hand or eye;
Prepares to tremble. But the twain
Are too considerate still, and shy.

THE VISITOR

Something about her hair among these low hills,
These small, odd mountains she never had looked upon,
Something about her hair I say was strange;
For the pure whiteness suddenly was gone.

What in its place was there I scarcely know.
Not grey, not gold, not anything fresh or younger.
Something the other side of whiteness, maybe,
Matching an old thought, minding an ancient hunger.

She had come, she said, contemptuous of mountains;
She was born in a level land—and let her eyes
Go following the valley to its limit;
Then steeply among the ridges let them rise.

Now in an alien moment she made out
A people once all moulded to these shapes.
Her people, too; all moulded; and returning
To the hunched land this side the misty capes.

Without our help she knew which way to look
For the grey range that hid the working ocean.
With her white head she gazed, until the sky
Closed, and the valley sides were soft with motion;

And the hills heaved, and mothers called their children
In a slow, wandering voice to come and sleep.
She had grown doubly old remembering mountains,
And all dead time dropped round her in a heap.

Nothing but death could do it,
After the world had tried.
We living ones were powerless,
Knowing that pride.

Knowing the stiffness in her,
And dreading such a tongue,
We grew immediate greybeards;
Never were young;

Never, until she altered,
Knew wanting or delight.
Then it was death that taught her
Something of appetite.

Then it was friends and husband,
Ceasing where they had been,
Made her so ancient-gentle;
Let mercy in;

Spun white upon her forehead
Where the dark rays had run;
Till of us all she glittered
The luminous one.

Nothing but death so doubly
Could have been winner thus;
Leaving her sometimes pensive,
Pitying us;

Leaving us low and helpless,
Robbed of our proper prime;
Nothing but death the gambler,
And two-faced time.

WE WERE NOT OLD

When the whole valley whitened and the wind split,
Tearing both ways, demolishing direction;
When snow blew up the mountains—but confusion
Tumbled it down again, and whirled its whiteness,
Blinding each dizzy looker—then the dark house
Vanished across the meadows, then the old man
Danced in our minds, a mote, and we could see:

Each of us here could pierce the windy distance,
Each of us here could pity him, surviving
Ages of days for this; all time for now.
He should have died, we said, some pretty summer,
He should have lain down gently in June's lap.
Why should the old back bend another cold inch?
Why should a blizzard whip him who was tame?

Each of us here could think this, and be wrong.
We could not see for snow; and something darker.
We were not old. We had not loved the winter;
Loving its meanness, too, and taking lashes
Hot from the hangman's hand. We were not ancient.
We had not loved, we had not lived with anger.
We had not learned to measure life by blows.

We could not see him smile at all this fury.
We could not see him welcome one more wind—
Sticking his head out secretly and saying:
"Ho!" and drawing it in again, and going
And writing another year down in some book.
Those needles in his brain showed where the page was,
That pricking at the hair roots—that was time.

So while the valley whitened and the sky cracked,
Letting the twofold gale in, and the fourfold
Slither of tossing snow, and the icy voices,
We in our warm bay window pitied the old one.
This was too much, we said. We did not know.
We could not see him crouch beneath the nine-tails,
Grinning and counting the strokes, and crying "Ha!"

AFTER DISORDER

In the clear land he went to after noon,
After disorder, after the growing stopped—
The live root is reluctant, and some soil
Still with scorched leaves is littered where he cropped—
In the cool barren land there were two curtains:
Two days a year oblivion down-dropped.

And lest he choose between them each was all,
Each was enamelled glass on everything.
One hour it was pure autumn, and he smiled;
But then that other suddenness, the spring—
Each was entire, betraying nothing under
Of the veiled bone; of time's remitted sting.

To him the fall said nothing of spent sap;
It was no three-month husking, no high-piled
Good harvest; it was color, and it fell
As if the sun's own shadow, gold and wild,
As if the sky's old wine had dripped and spread,
Painting the round-cheeked earth a russet child.

Not even May was younger. Both were born,
There in that shining land, without true cause;
Both without use or warning; save that history
Slept the long sleep, and time was free to pause
Twice yearly, with a pack upon his back
From which then grandly spilled these bright gewgaws.

YOUTH'S COUNTRY

The little god sat bright across the board:
Man, you could almost see him: and both played—
Oh, both of you in moving swept the files,
Both took and lost, both laughed and were dismayed.
The rooks in place, the pawns upon their meadows—
Old man, it was clear evening when you played.

350

The country of your dotage was clean lit;
Walls ran both ways; time-sharpened were the squares.
It was a pretty land, a promised garden,
With no hot wind to whirl your snowy hairs.
You could forget the lightning and the rain,
And how your feet once pressed among the tares.

You could forget the mistiness, the danger,
And how at sunset horses rubbed the dusk.
But that was long ago, another country,
Of the wild weeds, the fetlock and the tusk;
Of the uncertain fences, and the way
Thickets at night exhaled a threat of musk.

That was another contest, and the odds
Were huge against you; beautiful the loss—
Oh, beautiful your smallness and your stillness,
Waiting upon the thunder of a toss;
Beautiful your eyes, that could not read then
Even the print of day, the riddle's gloss.

Even at noon the board was big as earth is,
With the far trees like islands tilting past.
You did not sit and smile, you did not measure
Meadows that still were shapeless; and the vast
King's voice, you never knew it as a chuckle—
"Check!"—with someone mated at the last.

THE END

I sing of ghosts and people under ground,
Or if they live, absented from green sound.
Not that I dote on death or being still;
But what men would is seldom what they will,
And there is farthest meaning in an end
Past the wild power of any word to mend.
The telltale stalk, and silence at the close,
Is most that may be read of man or rose.
Death is our outline, and a stillness seals
Even the living heart that loudest feels.

351

I am in love with joy, but find it wrapped
In a queer earth, at languages unapt;
With shadows sprinkled over, and no mind
To speak for them and prove they are designed.
I sing of men and shadows, and the light
That none the less shines under them by night.
Then lest I be dog enemy of day,
I add old women talking by the way;
And, not to grow insensible to noise,
Add gossip girls and western-throated boys.

AMERICA'S MYTHOLOGY
1938

AMERICA'S MYTHOLOGY

America's great gods live down the lane;
Or up the next block blend their bulk with stone;
Or stand upon the ploughed hills in the rain;
Or watch a mountain cabin left alone.

Gigantic on the path, they never speak.
Unwitnessed, they are walked through every hour.
They have an older errand; or they seek
New sweets beyond the bound of mortal sour;

Or love the living instant, and so minded,
Bestride the lesser lookers—who can say?
There is no man has seen them but was blinded;
And none has ever found them far away.

America's tall gods are veteran here:
Too close for view, like eagles in the eye;
Like day itself, impalpable and clear;
Like absolute noon's air, unflowing by.

They are the first of all. Before the grey,
Before the copper-colored, they were moving
Green-brown among the deep trees: deep as they,
As curious of the wind, as tempest-loving;

As shaggy dressed, as head-proud; and in summer,
As lazy. So they lived. And so they still
Live everywhere, unknown to the newcomer,
Whom genially they watch. And so they will

To earth's end, feeding on their ancient grain,
Wild wheat tips, and barbed rice tops, and the meat
Of mast wherever richest leaves have lain;
Although they pick the tame fields too, and eat

With fathers at the heads of merry tables;
And sleep on beds for change, and sit with talkers.
Whence all their lore; for man's least deeds are fables
To these old-natured gods, these ancient walkers.

PORCH GOD

And there is one with somewhat pointed ears
And new-moon-whitened eyes, and a thin grin;
Which, widening, is witness that he steers
The rocker talk of wives and takes it in.

All afternoon, past the wisteria sprays,
He listens while they tip and tilt and fan:
Their minds the turning mill from which a haze
Of dust drifts over goddess, maid, and man.

It is the dust delights him, thickening so
The air on which his memory travels back
To the first courtship, and a lofty row
Of eyelids arching high for the attack.

It is the past arrives for him; or now,
With sunset gone and midnight in the vine,
It is the clockless moment when his brow
Deep-wrinkles while young secret fingers twine

And two warm heads come closer. Not a word.
No thought of ear-tips here, or sickle smile.
It only was eternity that stirred;
Only a leather cheek that winced awhile.

DRIVEWAY GOD

Where the two mows divide and green hay hangs
Like hired man's hair, wind-parted in the middle,
He sits and listens while a wet door bangs,
And is to them as fingers to a fiddle:

Playing upon their plough-wit while the rain
Drums gustily on grey boards; drowns the chicks;
Puddles in holes, and drips upon the mane
Of the wild workhorse, hobbled against her tricks.

Shower-livened, hear them laugh: the men and boys
Who all a sultry morning mewed their tongues.
Now elbow-loose they loll, that outer noise
Sweet music to their ears; while brains and lungs

Breathe lustily the tune the jester calls.
His body fills the driveway, beam to beam.
His heart among their heartbeats lifts and falls.
Yet none will know him, even in a dream.

Even when they doze he will be nameless,
This antique cider-mind of gods and men.
Shower-drunken, see him sway and pour the tameless
Liquor into Bill, Dave, Mack, and Ben.

STRANGE TOWN GOD

He is the one that meets us where the first
Small houses, dark and poor, lead into light;
And tells us how the features, best and worst,
Make something like a face in country night.

He is the only townsman who would know.
For the lean rest it is familiar chaos.
His love is older; is a breath to blow
Strict lines from curb to roof till patterns stay us:

Till pausing by the dusk hotel, we count
Street lamps, store fronts, red jail; and farther on,
The first white house again, where the maples mount
That high east hill our road goes up—has gone

Each night like this since who knows when? Who'll say?
The sprawled god never answers in his pride.
The question is enough. And shows the way
To hot hamburgers, coffee, and thin fried.

357

CHERRY LEAF GOD

A dark sky, the wind waiting;
Ladders motionless, and heels
Of pickers vanishing, house-high, among the leaves;

Pails dangled, cherries dropping;
Twigs snapped; and there a limb
Bent low to breaking as a boy, too bold, forgets.

So seems it from the ground; so goes it
Here in the long grass whither he,
Never descending, peers between the green, the red:

The hanging leaves, the dripping hearts
He flutters while he swings beyond—
Huge picker, yet he lies, more light than robin's leg;

Lies; leans over Johnny there;
Swings over Nell; and topmost now,
Swings up and out, heigh ho, as seven pickers climb.

SICKBED GOD

His body wreathes the room like draughts
Of air, of tender air, and wafts
Both pity in and envy: both
The terror and the nothing loath.

This weakness, the uncertain eyes,
The back that will not rest and rise,
The fingers—they are strange as fear,
Though he has practiced it all year;

And would have faltered at the heart
Had he but known the helpless part;
Had he but mastered how the breath
Refuses what it can to death.

The wonder bends him to a cheek;
To the seen bone, and to the bleak
Burned-over forehead. Then the stare.
At which there have been days the air

Sorrowed with him, and the scent
Of older weeping came and went;
And he lay visible, as though
A current should forget to flow.

GARDEN GOD

He is the sun-white one that loves
High noon in the bean rows, or as you tie
Gourd tendrils fenceward comes like doves
And will not let your memory lie:

Pecks it till it lifts and wings
In bright near circles by him; floats
Like fire above your forehead; flings
Thought-atoms down, minute as motes,

In front of your eyes, that mingle green
With brown for study, and sift the clods
For such clear answers as are seen,
Not heard. So goes it with the gods.

So too with gardeners when the sun
Pours silence past them, and they hoe
Like men of old. Young though to one
Who still was older, and would know

Why all at once, nobody by,
They smiled and pulled it, or at the bend
Of some hot corn row looked on high
And frowned, reflecting; then the end.

COMPASS GOD

Which way this forest faces;
How sharp we angled there;
When the wind struck us, came it
Slantwise or square?

At home now is it certain—
The hay door—perfect west?
Our cousin in the spare room:
Will he rest?

He said he had it backwards:
Due south for simple north:
Turned full around, no matter
How he went forth.

There is a tall one watches
And pities our poor eyes:
Except that some are knowing;
Are needle-wise;

Were eastward set when Phosphor
Whitened the oldest dawn;
And are the eyes he blesses,
In babe or fawn.

CROWD GOD

He is untouchable, or he would cry
In the close press of bodies; he would tower,
Knee-tortured, numb, until his wrath must try
Some awfulness against our herded power.

He is invulnerable, and so he moves,
Unfeeling and unfelt, through what of space
Our lungs and elbows leave him; whence he proves
How alien is the day, how rank the race.

Time was when two or three upon a hill
Came tall together if he framed it so.
He was the lord of meetings, and his will
Was merely that they happen wise and slow.

And still they happen nightly; still at noon
Four walkers in a high wind hold apart.
And still he listens; haunted by the tune
Of half a million others heart to heart.

HORSE GOD

They are new comers too, the bent-necked
Pullers, the head-high starers, the stampers
Of flies: new legs, new tails in the hay.
So he picks a red foal as it scampers,

Breasting the flowers, and all a wet summer
Follows its misty feet; till cold days
Flatten the grass once more; till frost
Barrens the world; till bones of the old days

Show in the sod, and a wind reminds him
Of animals lost and gone. Yet ruffles
The coat of his rusty yearling; blows
All morning between the two, and muffles

The whinny that was a meadow's music;
Mingles the fencewire's hum with a neighing
Shriller and farther away. So he blinks
And follows the hoof-thuds closer, staying

Warm by a flank, wind-tossed at a foretop;
Turns, and approves the eyes. Then wanders,
Free of his charge, all day. But whirls
At sunset to that sound again, and ponders.

BIRD GOD

His study is the way we stand and peer,
Foot-lifted, toward a thicket where the shade,
Sewn suddenly with needle notes, declares
The wing most wild, the feathers most afraid.

Or openly at evening when the swifts
Cut the same blue as ever, when the crows
Rip the last hour of silence and subside;
He watches how we listen, and he slows

To a last clumsy pity; leans and waits;
Leans closer still. But still our birds are strange.
Still are we distant from them, and no arm
Of any wishful man can wave exchange.

He walked among them, numbering their beaks,
When the first forest shed them to the sky;
When the first eagle spiralled, and the owl's
Aimed silence wrapped a midnight mouse's cry.

Finches from his wrist looked down for seed,
And dropping to the grass heads picked and ate.
As long ago as ravens—but he pauses,
And pities once again our after date.

POSY GOD

Wherever a still apron,
Free of the stove awhile,
Descends among the rising
Sweet Williams, and a smile

Inhabits all the sunstrip
Betwixt woodshed and wall;
And then the rapid fingers;
And then the beetle's fall;

Wherever posy fringes
Keep time and darkness back:
Beyond the pump, the smokehouse,
Hotel or railroad track;

Wherever white and purple
Bring a brown hand to swing,
There is a hooded watcher,
Higher than hawk's wing,

Who folds his arms and listens,
Shady in morning shine,
To what he can remember
Of hum and bee whine

When flowery land was larger:
The center brilliant too;
All daisied, and all buzzing
Betwixt sun-up and dew.

HISTORY GOD

The young eyes leave the volume and stray out,
Weeping for greatness gone, but half in pride
That they have been the witness; they alone
May estimate the blank since wisdom died.

They wind among the water towers and pierce
The many moonwhite roofs, like gravestones laid
On courage; one far sepulchre of souls.
The city is long silent; not a maid

Expects upon her window any more
The tap of steel, the leather-handed love.
She has gone in forever; nor do clouds
Burst into fiery grief and clash above.

The eyes return, and words march on again
With the proud tramp of yesterday's green earth.
Brown are the branches now, and spent the sap
Of the well mind that guessed the body's worth.

So one across the room, observing, smiles.
And sleeps; for this is how the creatures grow:
Dim months of pain from out their little past;
Then lighted strength; and then the letting go.

BLACK NIGHT GOD

No further doubt now. He is near.
When your throat filled he was the fear.
When though you screamed you made no sound,
He answered, binding you around
With bull-voice echoes. Still they roar,
And when they weaken he has more.
Yet he may pull the quiet in:
The utter quiet, like the skin
Of bat wings beating; or may pause
While you imagine bludgeons, claws,
Snake-bellies, tushes, whetted teeth,
Dew-lapping dogs, and venom sheath.
It is the time he wakes and plays.
His nights, he says, are to your days
As man to son: earth-wiser, older;
And not to be afraid is bolder.
But have no horror now, no doubt.
Keep walking, slow; and when you shout,
Take comfort in his thunder crack.
It is an ancient talking back:
A god that gambols, never knowing
How on your head the fears are snowing.

TALL TALE GOD

If there were sound, the slapping
Of his reminded thigh,
The chuckle in the treetops—
As old, as high—
Would publish the true ages
Of our best brag and lie.

The colt that jumped North Mountain,
The macaroni dance;
The time we heard the breathing
Of boulders in a trance;
Midnight's lost meridians
Wheeling home from France;

The names we roared to rascals
Met on the back-hill road;
The insult at the picnic,
And how the children glowed;
The mica tree; the minted
Dollars in the lode—

He, long ago delighted,
Laughs now a double laugh:
At these, and at the wing-strength
Of so much dust and chaff;
The truth, he says, flew farther,
But not so high by half.

ANGER GOD

Report of thunder words arrives
Full minutes later than the flash
Of powder touched along a vein,
Of muscles whitening to ash.

Inside their clothes he scents the wrath
Like hackles risen; feels the flood
Move like a wall to where the heart
Will not acknowledge it for blood.

It is their hatred holds him close
And sweetens afternoons with gall:
He may not be transformed so soon;
He cannot be wrath-changed at all.

His judgment lighting on a fool,
His heart exiling drone and knave,
His glance corrective to a leap:
No one of these is half so brave.

Nor half so transient; that he knows,
And can predict the clasp of hands;
But sighs a little for the bruise
Of anger tightening its bands.

HAUNTED GOD

There is a kind of man can bring
Bystanders round him, one by one
Slow-risen in the dropping dark:
Litter of dead day, husks of the sun.

Bystanders merely, there they shade
Cold eyes with evening; lift no foot,
Advance no heel, as if the night
Broke into stems at its toughest root.

Expecting nothing, there they hang
Long arms like leaves to the finger pods;
As if the twilight were a plant
To step and pluck, and these the gods.

But these are growth of none but man,
Who reaping so, sees not the vast
Mild-shuttered lids of one that must
Himself be harvester at last.

However lone his greatness here,
He too will turn; is turning now;
Is motionless: his tallness ringed
By sudden others come to bow.

WHEEL GOD

Amazement never leaves him,
If gods can be surprised:
The ponderous swift stillness;
Center realized;

The whirling yet the slumber;
Circumference in act.
It is the only plaything
Primeval meadows lacked.

The sun and moon for circles,
A turning arm for spoke;
And lily leaves; but never
This lightness at a stroke:

This over, round, and over,
This oneness till it stops;
Then hub and ray and felloe,
Distinct—whereat he drops,

Distracted, by the mover,
The man with patient hands;
And begs another going,
And barters forty lands.

SCHOOLROOM GOD

Knowledge here will overgrow
Desk, aisle, and door, and tendril-running,
Climb the haystalks, loop the streets,
And cast an ocean round with cunning.

Knowledge here has outmost leaves,
And cannot live unless they flourish.
Far or near it is the same:
The end must the beginning nourish.

367

Except, he says, there is no end.
Nothing here but news of going.
Nor does green come round again
As comes the circle of his knowing.

Nor if it came would it be his,
That never starting, never finished:
Earth encompassed all at once,
When growth was not; nor since diminished.

Nor since made greater, for its arc
Lives at the limit, past all reaching:
Past all green; past thinnest blue;
Past even white, that time is bleaching.

BURIAL GOD

He is in love with patient death
That comes up here so slow and often,
Belling the mourners past the pine
Whose boughs are music to a coffin.

Set it down now, here is the place,
And let a man's words bury man.
But there are two, kind death and he,
Can say what sound nor silence can.

Among the many they declare
How none so upright but will come
The slow way also, through the gate
And underneath the needles' hum;

Up in sunshine, then the halt,
And then these two that no one hears:
Man is everlasting grass
Whose every fall renews its spears;

In this box a single blade
Descends to darkness, nor will rise;
And wind is rippling through the rest;
And day is on them shadow-wise.

MUSIC GOD

He does not hear the struck string,
The stretched voice, the blown brass.
The sudden start, the sweet run
Of notes are not for him; alas.

Then what the measure, what the pitch,
Whereof he is acknowledged lord?
What the laws for less than sound,
And whose the silence whence a chord?

He will not answer save with eyes
That feed on distance all the while;
With more of pleasure here than there,
But most at some remembered mile

Too far for count, or so we say
Who cannot number save with ears;
Who cannot stand with him and see
Triangles perfect after years:

From grove to grove the singing base,
Then on to where two rivers cry;
Or so we say of three clear tones
That in eternal quiet lie.

INDEX OF TITLES

371

372

INDEX OF FIRST LINES

377